MW01169826

Comparing Cultures

A new and important contribution to the reemergent field of comparative anthropology, this book argues that comparative ethnographic methods are essential for more contextually sophisticated accounts of a number of pressing human concerns today. The book includes expert accounts from an international team of scholars, showing how these methods can be used to illuminate important theoretical and practical projects. Illustrated with examples of successful interdisciplinary projects, it highlights the challenges, benefits, and innovative strategies involved in working collaboratively across disciplines. Through its focus on practical methodological and logistical accounts, it will be of value to both seasoned researchers who seek practical models for conducting their own cutting-edge comparative research and for teachers and students who are looking for first-person accounts of comparative ethnographic research.

MICHAEL SCHNEGG is Professor of Anthropology at Universität Hamburg.

EDWARD D. LOWE is Professor of Anthropology at Soka University of America.

Comparing Cultures

Innovations in Comparative Ethnography

Edited by

Michael Schnegg

Universität Hamburg

Edward D. Lowe

Soka University of America

CAMBRIDGE
UNIVERSITY PRESS

University Printing House, Cambridge CB2 8BS, United Kingdom

One Liberty Plaza, 20th Floor, New York, NY 10006, USA

477 Williamstown Road, Port Melbourne, VIC 3207, Australia

314–321, 3rd Floor, Plot 3, Splendor Forum, Jasola District Centre, New Delhi – 110025, India

79 Anson Road, #06-04/06, Singapore 079906

Cambridge University Press is part of the University of Cambridge.

It furthers the University's mission by disseminating knowledge in the pursuit of education, learning, and research at the highest international levels of excellence.

www.cambridge.org
Information on this title: www.cambridge.org/9781108487283
DOI: 10.1017/9781108766388

First published 2020

Printed in the United Kingdom by TJ International Ltd, Padstow Cornwall

A catalogue record for this publication is available from the British Library.

ISBN 978-1-108-48728-3 Hardback
ISBN 978-1-108-72001-4 Paperback

Contents

Figures

Tables

Contributors

NIKO BESNIER University of Amsterdam

CAROLINE B. BRETTELL Southern Methodist University

ANDRE GINGRICH Austrian Academy of Sciences

DANIEL GUINNESS University of Amsterdam

RICHARD HANDLER University of Virginia

JENNIFER S. HIRSCH Columbia University

EDWARD D. LOWE Soka University of America

CONSTANCE A. NATHANSON Columbia University

SHANTI PARIKH Washington University

HARRIET PHINNEY Seattle University

BIRGITT RÖTTGER-RÖSSLER Free University of Berlin

MICHAEL SCHNEGG Universität Hamburg

DANIEL JORDAN SMITH Brown University

GUIDO SPRENGER Heidelberg University

HOLLY WARDLOW University of Toronto St. George

Introduction

Comparative Ethnography: Its Promise, Process, and Successful Implementations

Edward D. Lowe and Michael Schnegg

Two decades into the twenty-first century, anthropology is considering anew its comparative foundations, moving away from the methodological and epistemological crises that shook the discipline at the end of the twentieth century. As Matei Candea (2019, 1) writes, "[C]omparison is back in the limelight and it is the 'crisis of representation' itself which is beginning to feel thoroughly *passé*. A new wind of epistemological confidence is blowing through the discipline, and comparison is explicitly reclaimed and brandished as a distinctive anthropological method." No longer yoked to an explicitly positivist project, and generally more careful about anthropology's past connections with colonial and imperialist projects, comparison in anthropology today makes use of a variety of heuristics and methodological strategies to make important contributions to the understanding of the human condition past and present. Yet, one legacy of the disciplinary critique at the end of the last century is that *explicit* considerations of why and how the varieties of comparative praxis might be successfully used in anthropology are rare. Leaving such considerations implicit prevents ongoing innovations in using comparative strategies and heuristics to produce valuable anthropological insights into complex and pressing human concerns. If the new enthusiasm for comparison is going to make a larger impact, it is essential to consider the methodological and epistemological promise and perils of working comparatively.

This book contributes to the aim of giving explicit attention to comparative praxis in contemporary anthropological research. The chapters are authored by an international panel of seasoned ethnographic researchers who have all conducted comparative projects or who have written about comparison since the reengagement with comparative approaches in anthropology at the end of

The essays collected in the volume were presented at a workshop organized in Hamburg, Germany, in May 2016. We thank all participants for the stimulating and productive discussions during those days. The Universität Hamburg and Deutsche Forschungsgemeinschaft (German Research Foundation) supported the conference financially. In addition to our funding agencies, the authors would like to thank Julia Pauli, the late Thomas Schweizer, the chapter authors, and two anonymous reviewers for the many insightful discussions and comments leading to the final production of this volume.

the 1990s and into the early 2000s. In convening the authors at a conference in Hamburg, Germany, in May 2016, we asked the participants not to write about comparison as a long-standing, if often "troubled" (Brettell 2009) or even "impossible" (Candea 2019), methodological and epistemological standpoint in anthropology and related fields. Several books and articles already provide excellent overviews (Candea 2019; Felski and Friedman 2013; Gingrich and Fox 2002; Holy 1987; Ingold 2011; Lazar 2012; Lewis 1999; Yengoyan 2006). Rather, we asked the chapter authors to write about how they conducted successful comparative ethnographic projects and about the challenges and benefits of having done so.

We do not intend to develop a consensual methodology for ethnographic comparison, particularly given the methodological ambivalence regarding the use of scientific "styles of reasoning" (Hacking 1992) in anthropology and the well-established plurality of comparative ethnographic strategies (Candea 2019; Fox and Gingrich 2002; Gingrich 2012, 2015). Instead, we explore the varieties of comparative practices that are represented in the works of the chapter authors. We believe that the resulting chapters provide an invaluable resource for researchers who might be interested in conducting comparative ethnographic research and who are looking for frank discussions about the different strategies available for doing so.

In this introduction, we present a synthesis of the central themes that emerge in the chapters of this volume. We begin by providing an overview of why ethnographic comparison is essential in anthropology while also considering the challenges that are presented by its main critics. We then provide a general overview of how comparative ethnographic research is generally conducted in anthropology today. Our focus is on the process involved in the kind of ethnographic comparison that is the main focus of the chapters in this book, contrasting small-*N* qualitative comparison with large-*N* quantitative and typological approaches (Ragin 2014; Ragin and Amoroso 2019). Finally, we provide a brief overview of how the contents of this book contribute to our understanding of the varieties of effective comparative ethnographic practice today. The main finding from reading across all the chapters is how the construction of *contextualized configurations* is an important methodological heuristic for developing successful ethnographic comparisons. The configurational comparisons we see as a common thread in all the chapters are positioned between particularistic and generalizing approaches. These configurational strategies depart from variable-based logic that emphasizes the covariation of phenomena. Instead, they highlight how configurations of social and cultural phenomena combine to pattern the particular way a phenomenon manifests within each case under study. These configurational comparisons better explain the diversity of social and cultural worlds that result from very different configurational logics in each case.

The Promise of Comparative Ethnography

Why should we compare? Of course, anthropology has always included comparison of various kinds as a major means of advancing theory in the discipline (Ember et al. 2014; Fox and Gingrich 2002; Handler 2009; Ingold 2011; Johnson and Hrushka 2015; Ragin and Amoroso 2019). But as an explicit research strategy, comparison has often existed in tension with either more particularistic approaches or more generalizing strategies. Here, as an example, we touch on a long-standing tension in discussions of anthropological practice between what Radcliffe-Brown (1952; as cited in Ingold 2011) described as ideographic and nomothetic forms of anthropological inquiry, where the aims of the former involved documenting "the particular facts of past and present lives" through ethnography, while the aim of the latter was "to arrive at general propositions or theoretical statements" through comparative ethnology (Ingold 2011, 229).

Many would agree that the aim of comparative research should not be to use comparison to arrive at generalizations, universal theoretical statements, or teleological metanarratives (Gingrich and Fox 2002; Hirsch et al. 2009; Ingold 2011). Most would also agree that we should not accept the imposition of an ideographic disciplinary straitjacket that relies exclusively on various strategies for writing "ethnographies of the particular" (Abu-Lughod 1991) or multisited ethnography of the unfolding of processes of globalization (Marcus 1995). Some balance between the two is needed if anthropology is to retain and enhance its standing among other disciplines. As Gingrich (2015) has observed, an academic field cannot "sufficiently address any larger issues nor sustain any credibility and legitimacy if [its claims are] based on nothing else but particularities" (412). Indeed, it is through what Laura Nader (1994) has called a "comparative consciousness" that anthropologists are best able to contribute new knowledge to our understanding of the processes that characterize the modern era of globalization. To paraphrase and quote Nader, an intellectually broad and methodologically diverse comparative consciousness can better illuminate the connections that anthropologists study, "between local and global, between past and present, between anthropologists and those they study, between uses of comparison and implications of its uses" (Nader 1994, 88; as cited in Brettell 2009, 656). Ethnographic comparison can do this because its focus is on highlighting not only the differences but also the similarities in the ways human beings inhabit and understand the world we share (Ingold 2011). It is in the tension between these two that ethnographic comparisons are better able to contribute to public understanding of pressing issues of the day.

All the chapter authors address the question of why explicit forms of comparison are essential to anthropological practice in one way or another. For example, Caroline B. Brettell (Chapter 1) argues that an explicit comparative framework of two or more cases has three benefits. First, it helps us to understand better the particularities of one case by revealing that case's internal structures and dynamics when juxtaposed against those of another, such as in the production of ethnic identity in upland Southeast Asia (Sprenger, Chapter 4), highland architecture in Arabia (Gingrich, Chapter 5), and the differential ontogeny of emotion across different social and cultural contexts (Röttger-Rössler, Chapter 8). Second, comparison also allows us to assess how and why different cases might be doing better or worse in terms of some particular outcome of interest such as the integration of migrants (Brettell, Chapter 1), the felt authenticity of cultural performance (Handler, Chapter 2), or vulnerability to suicide (Lowe, Chapter 3). Third, comparison can be used to explore "best practices" regarding public or institutional policies such as those aimed at HIV prevention for married couples (Hirsch et al., Chapter 7) or the management of collective natural resources (Schnegg, Chapter 6).

Explicit strategies of ethnographic comparison are important when studying phenomena at multiple scales, particularly those associated with processes of globalization, such as international trade and migration, or global-scale processes that can have diverse local impacts, such as climate change. As Besnier and Guinness argue in their chapter (Chapter 9, 207), the study of large-scale events or processes requires that we understand them "in all [their] manifestations and ramifications for different regions of the world, in different configurations, and over a significant period of time." An explicitly comparative ethnographic approach is well suited to successfully study such diverse global-local dynamics.

The Challenges for Comparative Ethnography

As advocates have written about the need to retain a comparative tradition in anthropology, we are struck by the regularity with which these authors include a discussion of comparison's "problematic" or "troubled" history in the discipline (Brettell 2009; Chapter 1; Hirsch et al. 2009; Schnegg 2014). These anxieties about the place of comparison in anthropology seem to have always been part of competing disciplinary currents (Brettell 2009; Fox and Gingrich 2002; Handler 2009; Ingold 2011).

The challenges of different comparative strategies have to do with the ontological and epistemological assumptions on which they are based (Brettell 2009; Handler 2009; Ingold 2011). Before we describe configurational comparisons as a heuristic for comparative ethnography that we find to be common to all the chapters in this volume, we must first review the tension between the different comparative approaches in anthropology historically. A fundamental tension has to do with the positivist or historical/interpretive ontological standpoints assumed by the researcher. Following Richard Handler (2009, 628), human societies or cultures are often imagined from a positivist standpoint to be spatiotemporally distinct and bounded units that comprise particular, causally independent social and cultural traits. These societal units are understood to vary regarding which of a universally identifiable collection of social and cultural traits are present and which are absent in a given societal unit, rendering the traits themselves social and cultural variables. The analysis of the distribution of these traits through comparison either to derive taxonomies, *à la* Radcliffe-Brown or Lévi-Strauss, or to use statistical procedures of correlation or covariation, *à la* George Peter Murdock's Ethnographic Atlas and the hologeistic method (Fox and Gingrich 2002), became the means through which fields like anthropology were thought to be a positive science that produces its own generalizations and master narratives of human culture and society and their evolution over time. This is not to say that there were not significant disagreements within the positivist tradition. These two styles of reasoning, the taxonomic and the statistical, exist in a tension of their own, as exemplified by Edmund Leach's (1961, 2–3) famous reduction of the taxonomic approach of Radcliffe-Brown and Lévi-Strauss as nothing more than "butterfly collecting." As Ingold (2011, 234) notes, Leach preferred generalizations that "would take the form not of a typological specification that would enable us to distinguish societies of one kind from those of another, but of a statement of the relationships between variables that may operate in societies of any kind."

While positivists understand discrete social and cultural phenomena to be objective facts to be identified, described, counted, and compared or correlated with one another, the historical/interpretive standpoint sees these as phenomena whose meaning and value derive from its historically contingent relationships to other phenomena in an "ever widening context within the phenomenal cosmos" (Kroeber 1952, 123; as cited in Ingold 2011, 231). From the interpretive standpoint, both human societies and the phenomena found within them cannot be placed on an etic universal scale of description and measurement because, as Ruth Benedict argued, human societies "are traveling along different roads in pursuit of different ends, and these ends and these means in one society cannot be judged in terms of those of another society, because essentially they are incommensurable" (1934, 46; as cited in Handler 2009, 634). But Benedict *did* believe that societies were comparable. As Handler (2009, 634) notes, "[S]he was able to show her readers that cultural comparison required sophisticated translation practices that went far beyond the naïve idea that each term, trait, or unit in one culture could be matched to a corresponding term, trait, or unit in another." Benedict employed a reflexive hermeneutic analysis, working back and forth among the materials for each case and her own understanding, until the pattern that characterized each case emerged that would also illuminate more clearly the terms of comparison itself.

If the comparative approach advocated by Benedict (1934, 1946) and later by Geertz (1973) allowed us to more carefully place our own and other societies' social and cultural patterns on a more equal, if incommensurate, footing, it still tended to reify cultural boundaries. Assuming the boundedness of culture tends to support a further problematic assumption that human cultural groups are maximally different from one another, rendering them as truly "Other" from the perspective of the anthropologist-observer (Ingold 2018). The criticism holds that human worlds only become interesting to anthropologists when they are assumed to be places of bounded, radical alterity, resulting in the muting or silencing of the human commonalities that exist among human societies in anthropological studies. Such a view also tends to "incarcerate" people in time and place, "denying them the capacity for movement, travel, and interaction that Westerners take for granted" in the modern and global era (Abu-Lughod 1991, 146; Appadurai 1996). The view of cases to be compared as bounded cultures also tends to promote an overemphasis on the internal coherence of the cases compared, as opposed to their being shot through with contradiction and conflict (Abu-Lughod 1991).

The boundary problem also points to the problem of scale. The unfolding historical processes in which the cases of comparison are embedded operate at different temporal and geographic scales, from the microscopic to the cosmic, from the immediate to the macroevolutionary. Understanding how phenomena that one might observe through ethnographic fieldwork within particular field sites might be embedded in larger regional and global processes has been particularly relevant in comparative anthropology of the globalizing political-economic system of capitalism (e.g. Mintz 1985; Wolf 1982; West 2012; Besnier and Guinness, Chapter 9). In addition, the comparison of cases that might be part of regional histories of emergence and transaction has a well-established history in anthropology (Gluckman 1960; Eggan 1953; Gingrich 2012, 2015).

One way to address the problem of scale is to use multisited ethnography. Marcus (1995) describes these studies as those that move "out from single sites and local situations of conventional ethnographic research designs to examine the circulation of cultural meanings, objects, and identities in diffuse time-space" (96). It would seem, however, that multisited ethnography addresses the problems of boundedness and scale by moving up in scale, from the local to the multisited as phenomena are configured when they move through the channels and pathways that are created by the systems of global capitalism and governance. It leaves for a comparative ethnography the problem of working between scales, such as the global, the local, and the temporally and spatially "disjunctive" (Appadurai 1996; Lazar 2012; Besnier and Guinness, Chapter 9; Brettell, Chapter 1; Lowe, Chapter 2; Schnegg, Chapter 6).

Another problem regarding temporal scales concerns those of a *longue durée* for a given historical period and even extending to the kinds of timescales that allow us to consider evolutionarily durable processes that operate at the epigenetic level. The latter have been of concern for social scientists interested in such topics as the nature of human sociality (e.g. Henrich et al. 2004) and the comparative study of emotion (Röttger-Rössler et al. 2015). However, unlike studies of processes embedded within global capitalism, comparative ethnographic studies working on an evolutionary scale tend to emphasize scale from the level of the shared human biological inheritance and its epigenetic ontogeny to the specific communities or sites that have been studied ethnographically and comparatively.

Finally, when conducting comparative ethnographic work, there is the problem of the reliability of what Handler (2009) calls the "person–people report" or the reliability and validity of the claims made about people's lives in each ethnographic document. When the comparative ethnographic study uses reports made by others, there is no way of assessing the validity and reliability of those sources. As Brettell (Chapter 1) and Gingrich (Chapter 5) each argue, this is a particularly difficult issue in comparative ethnographic studies of a historical nature.

The Processes and Kinds of Comparative Ethnography

Having addressed the question of why anthropologists should compare, and some of the main challenges of doing so, the next question we ask is: How do we do comparative ethnography? Again, a great variety of comparative approaches in anthropology has emerged from its origins as a discipline in the nineteenth century until the middle of the twentieth century (Candea 2019; Fox and Gingrich 2002). These different approaches were often associated with specific national anthropological communities and in the service of different theoretical projects (Gingrich 2012). These early comparative approaches in anthropology include German diffusionism, the British American cross-cultural or hologeistic method as instituted in the Human Relations Area Files, Boasian historical particularism, Kroeber's comparative studies of Californian indigenous societies, Julian Steward's studies of cultural ecology, the holistic comparisons of Ruth Benedict and Louis Dumont, the functionalist-typological method of Radcliffe-Brown, the regional comparisons of Lévi-Strauss and the Manchester School as advocated by Max Gluckman, and, finally, the controlled comparisons as advocated by Fred Eggan.

Many of these approaches to comparison aimed at providing empirical evidence to support grand explanatory narratives about universal laws of society and culture and the culture history of large regions. Such grand theoretical projects fell out of favor in the last decades of the twentieth century. But comparative projects in anthropology have continued to the present (see Fox and

Gingrich 2002; Gingrich 2012, 2015; Lazar 2012; Schnegg 2014 for reviews). The theoretical projects of these recent comparative studies tend to be in the service of what Fred Eggan (1954) called the "middle-range theory development," after Robert Merton (1949), meaning theoretical projects limited to understanding or explaining phenomena within more specific social and cultural domains.

Despite this great diversity of comparative traditions, methodological discussions rarely consider comparison explicitly except for those that reflect quantitative or large-*N*, variable-based social research strategies. For example, in the most recent edition of *The Handbook of Methods in Cultural Anthropology* (Bernard and Gravlee 2015), Johnson and Hrushka (2015) present experimental or quasi-experimental designs as the model research strategy for answering explicitly comparative questions in cultural anthropology. In the same volume, Ember et al. (2015) present only the cross-cultural, hologeistic method as a means of addressing anthropology's comparative agendas. Fox and Gingrich (2002) noticed this tendency in their earlier advocacy of giving greater explicit attention to the importance of what Fox and Gingrich label "subaltern" strategies, meaning those that are not the same as the mainstream hologeistic comparative approaches in anthropology but that are, nevertheless, critical for the production of anthropological knowledge. Indeed, Ragin and Amoroso's (2019) *Constructing Social Research* is one of the few social science textbooks that include specific treatment of, on the one hand, small-*N*, qualitative comparison as a strategy that is distinct from the qualitative case study and, on the other hand, the quantitative, variable-based strategies.

The restrictive association of quantitative research strategies with comparative research agendas is a problem because it is both unreflective of the plurality of comparative approaches in the social sciences and out of step with the broader methodological literature (Fox and Gingrich 2002; Ragin and Amoroso 2019). For example, Ragin and Amoroso (2019) argue that quantitative research strategies are specific to the study of the covariation among variables in order to meet specific quantitative research goals. These goals include describing general patterns of covariation among variables, testing theoretically derived hypotheses about the covariation among variables, and making theoretically informed predictions about how variables might covary in the future given the present-day events. All of these goals assume the collection of empirical indicators for the variables from a large, probabilistically representative sample of cases (i.e. hundreds to thousands).

Of course, many questions social researchers seek to answer do involve the goal of understanding covariation. But this is not often the case among those who work comparatively with ethnographic data. Much more typically, these researchers seek to describe and understand (or explain) the patterns or *configurations* of similarities and differences of a common set of attributes found among a small number of carefully selected cases (Handler 2009). In other words, comparative ethnographic strategies aim to document, understand, and explain *diversity* across a sample of cases, not covariation (Ragin and Amoroso 2019). In general, Ragin and Amoroso (2019) argue that the goals of small-*N* comparative research include exploring the diversity of patterned similarities and differences among the cases, interpreting the cultural and historical significance of diverse configurations, and advancing theory. Advancing theory in comparative research includes being open to the need to revise the theoretical frames with which the project began and exploring causal complexity or the different combinations or configurations of factors that can bring about the outcome of interest to the researcher (see Ragin 2014).

The Process of Comparative Research

We find that there is a consensus – at least implicitly – on the process of conducting comparative ethnographic research (Ragin and Amoroso 2019; Gingrich 2012; Schnegg 2014). Researchers typically begin by selecting some theoretically or societally significant category of phenomena that they seek to understand by using a comparative framework and by posing research questions that suggest that a comparative approach would be appropriate. Researchers then carefully select, often using a theoretical sampling approach (Glaser and Strauss 1967), a small number of comparable cases (typically between two and about twenty), ensuring that the cases belong to the same meaningful and empirically defined category (e.g. nations; communities; fields of practice; specific institutional settings such as schools, households, and hospitals; and mythological tales). Researchers then develop an analytic frame that provides the analytic categories that will be of interest in the study of each case. The researcher often also develops specific empirical criteria for the study of the cases. Both the analytic framework and empirical criteria may be developed prior to ethnographic data collection and analysis or as the study unfolds. Finally, the comparative researcher works with the empirical data, often iteratively, to identify the configurations or patterns of similarities and differences that characterize the diversity present among the cases. The researcher may also be simultaneously considering causal or explanatory accounts for the configurations so identified (Ragin and Amoroso 2019).

Social scientists who conduct comparative ethnographic projects often rely on a combination of historical documents and ethnographic texts as their empirical corpus (Gingrich 2012, 2015). There is a recognized issue of the priority of the design of ethnographic fieldwork and the comparative dimension of a research project relative to when ethnographic data are collected

(Gingrich 2012). In a priori comparative ethnographic research, the design of ethnographic fieldwork, often multisited, and the comparative design are developed prior to the collection of ethnographic data. More typically, the comparative ethnographic design is developed after ethnographic or historical documents have been produced. These use an a posteriori approach.

An Archetype for Comparative Ethnographic Research

While the process for comparative research summarized previously does fit well into those described in the chapters of this volume, it is important to keep in mind that the great variety of comparative approaches in anthropology likely exceeds the descriptive range of the process described here. In light of this variety of approaches, Matei Candea (2019) presents what he calls an "archetype" for comparison in anthropology. By "archetype" Candea (2019, 15) means "not a blueprint or single set of methodological injunctions for how to compare. Rather it maps … the different ends to which it can be put, and the common ground of methodological techniques and fixes commonly used to purse these divergent purposes." In this archetype, Candea (2019, 15) first distinguishes two forms: "frontal comparisons," where the "ethnographic 'other' is contrasted with the presumed 'us,'" and "lateral comparisons," where cases are "laid side by side, from which the analyst is absent." Most of the chapters in this volume represent Candea's lateral forms, but Richard Handler (Chapter 2) provides a compelling example of a frontal comparison. In addition, Candea (2019, 16) describes three other contrasts: between "the elucidation of sameness and the pursuit of difference, between pinpointing things and tracing relations, and between pursuit of objectivity and reflexivity." Each of these contrasts is also part and parcel of the comparative ethnographic projects described in this book. We find that these emerge not as "either/or" propositions but more as sites of tension in the design and conduct of the contemporary comparative ethnographic studies.

A Typology of Comparative Ethnographic Research

After reviewing the variety of approaches to ethnographic comparison, Gingrich (2012, 2015) has suggested a loose typology of five approaches. These are labeled as binary, regional, distant, fluid, and temporal comparisons. We briefly describe the characteristics of each.

Binary Comparison

This type involves the comparative study of some phenomenon in two cases. Binary comparisons are primarily aimed at exploring in depth how the phenomenon is configured differently in each case. While most ethnographic work is at least implicitly comparative in a binary sense, intentional binary comparisons make the terms of comparison explicit, employing equally rigorous scrutiny of each case (Handler, Chapter 2). Binary comparisons have a rich history in the ethnological sciences (e.g. Benedict 1946; Dumont 1994; Lock 1995). Binary comparisons are also often used as a form of cultural critique (Gingrich 2015; Handler, Chapter 2) where phenomena in a distant case and in one's own cultural community are given the same rigorous, side-by-side analysis with the aim of revealing more clearly and explicitly the social and cultural significance of the phenomena in one's own society.

Regional Comparison

This involves the comparison of a targeted phenomenon across three or more cases in the same geographical region during the same time period (Gingrich 2015). Regional comparisons have a long, rich history (e.g. Fortes and Evans-Pritchard 1940; Lévi-Strauss 1969; Strathern 1988). They have been productive when considering how the shared histories, emergent social networks, and positions within higher-scale social, political, and economic processes in the region might shape the diverse configurations of the phenomenon studied (Schnegg 2014). Regional comparisons have been quite effective when the goal of the study is to better understand the historical and cultural significance associated with the observed diversity of the phenomenon studied, as these are often better documented for regions than for other geographical dimensions.

Distant Comparison

These projects involve the comparison of three or more cases that are widely separated in terms of time and/or space. While true historical, social relational, or institutional independence is difficult to achieve, particularly in the context of processes of globalization (Schnegg 2014), the aim in these studies is to carefully select cases that are as independent from each other as possible. Distant comparisons typically aim at advancing theory of some general phenomenon. A classic exemplar of distant comparisons is Beatrice and John Whiting's *Children of Six Cultures* study (Whiting and Whiting 1975). More recent examples of the distant comparison are that of Hirsch et al. (2009, Chapter 7) in their study of marital infidelity in five countries and Birgitt Röttger-Rössler and colleagues' study of emotional development in three societies (Röttger-Rössler et al. 2015; Röttger-Rössler, Chapter 8).

Fluid Comparisons

These projects aim to understand and theorize "the flows of phenomena thought time as space," often by tracking a phenomenon across several cases that are embedded within the same macrostructural processes (Gingrich 2015, 413). Typically, these are flows associated with globalization, as well as the increased mobility of people, ideas, and objects, as a result of revolutions in global communication and transportation technologies and infrastructures. Well-known examples include Sydney Mintz's (1985) study of the global sugar industry and Eric Wolf's (1982) comparative study of the transmutations of capitalism in different social and cultural contexts. Niko Besnier and his colleagues' (Chapter 9) GLOBALSPORT study of mobility and aspirations among athletes in several countries of the Global South is another contemporary example.

Temporal Comparisons

These studies track the shifting configuration of a phenomenon across a temporal line of development while holding geographical locations constant (Gingrich 2015). The primary aims are to understand the phenomenon given historical and social-cultural context and to contribute to theoretical models that explain the reasons for change and stasis in phenomena over time. Temporal comparisons have long been a mainstay in history, sociology, and archaeology. Anthropologists often must rely on the work of historians or archaeologists for documentary evidence in their own temporal comparisons. However, in some cases, a rich corpus of ethnographic observations is available that allows temporal comparison that primarily uses available ethnographic data. An example of this sort of comparison is Edward D. Lowe's (2018) recent study of funerary rituals in the Micronesian islands of Chuuk, from the late nineteenth to early twenty-first centuries.

The Contributions in This Volume

The contributions in this volume represent the diversity of approaches to conducting ethnographic comparisons today. Taken together, these chapters address the importance of comparative ethnography as a means of understanding how and why context matters and, often, how to destabilize more universalizing approaches to the phenomena that the projects described in each chapter take as their main foci. They show the limitations of an overreliance on single-case ethnography, whether it is conducted in a single site or across multiple sites. These studies show that much greater theoretical insight and reflexive self-awareness are possible in the explicit comparison of the similarities *and* differences that obtain across multiple cases. Also, since all the studies described in these chapters represent ethnographic comparisons, they also show how both theoretical understanding and reflexive self-awareness are enhanced through the documentation of the ways in which context, or the unique configurations of phenomena that characterize each case, matters for any particular outcome of interest.

The chapters in this volume are presented in terms of four major kinds of ethnographic comparison. The first three chapters by Caroline B. Brettell

(Chapter 1), Richard Handler (Chapter 2), and Edward D. Lowe (Chapter 3) all represent binary comparison as the primary approach. The chapters by Guido Sprenger (Chapter 4), Andre Gingrich (Chapter 5), and Michael Schnegg (Chapter 6) represent forms of regional comparison. The chapters by Jennifer S. Hirsch and her colleagues (Chapter 7), Birgitt Röttger-Rössler (Chapter 8), and Niko Besnier and Daniel Guinness (Chapter 9) represent approaches to making distant comparisons. But Besnier and Guinness also describe the dimensions of fluid comparison that emerged late in their project.

The chapters by Brettell, Handler, and Lowe highlight how making explicit comparisons between only two cases can be a useful way of thinking (Brettell, Chapter 1) by giving explicit attention to both the similarities and differences between the cases and how the back-and-forth movement between these can illuminate the importance of context across multiple scales, thicken our theoretical understandings of important social and cultural phenomena, and enable more effective forms of reflexivity and cultural critique.

Caroline B. Brettell (Chapter 1) shows in her chapter how three different comparative studies that she has conducted over the course of her career have been important means of better understanding how different configurations of and values for a common set of variables can lead to diverse outcomes for communities where in- or out-migration is common or for communities of migrants themselves. In her work, ethnographic comparison has been a critical strategy for developing contextually rich theories of migration and migrant experiences.

Richard Handler (Chapter 2) explores how ethnographic comparison can be used less to highlight the configuration of difference across contexts and cases and more to explore better and worse examples of what should be the same thing. Handler, of course, notes that such evaluative comparisons are generally inappropriate when studying cultures and societies other than one's own. But these comparisons are essential when conducted effectively in the service of reflexive cultural critique. To support his case, Handler revisits the work of Dorothy Lee and her criticism of what she found to be versions of authentic and inauthentic forms of individualism for Native peoples as compared with the dominant, middle-class Euro-American culture in the United States.

Edward D. Lowe (Chapter 3) presents a critical comparative ethnographic study (Hirsch et al. 2009) of two well-documented suicide epidemics in the Pacific Islands of Samoa and Chuuk that took place in the 1970s and 1980s. Lowe's critical aim is to destabilize well-worn modernization theories about suicide epidemics such as those found in these Pacific Islands by highlighting the unique configurations of contributing factors in each case. Lowe develops a comparative lens to destabilize these dominant explanations by examining a combination of the ethnopsychologies associated with episodes of suicide, the patterns in the social organization of local political economy associated with differential vulnerabilities to suicide for different groups, and the particular flows of globalizing political-economic processes that contribute to very different epidemic profiles in each case. In doing so, Lowe addresses the issue of scale and the permeability of local human worlds to larger, regional, and global flows and processes.

The chapters that present forms of regional comparison by Sprenger, Gingrich, and Schnegg highlight ways that ethnographic comparison can be a means of avoiding the techniques that emphasize the identification of similarities across sites in the service of theorizing context-free universals but strategies for "systematizing differences" in the service of better theorizing diverse configurations of social and cultural processes documented on a regional scale (Sprenger, Chapter 4). An important part of the regional comparisons in these three chapters is the analysis of the flows, distribution, or transformations of social and cultural phenomena across sites within a region. All three studies find that regional comparisons alone are insufficient for the purposes of providing satisfying arguments in response to the research questions posed. Rather, other analytic frameworks and modes of analysis are brought in to complement the regional comparisons. In addition, both Sprenger and Gingrich give explicit attention to the problem of reifying regions and hardening regional boundaries, not only calling for caution when conducting regional analysis but also developing methodological tools for better understanding the boundary issue in specific contexts.

Guido Sprenger (Chapter 4) describes the distinct comparative strategies of Lévi-Strauss, Louis Dumont, and Niklas Luhman and how he has combined these distinct frameworks to study processes of ethnic differentiation and identity formation among different groups in upland Southeast Asia. The comparative strategies Sprenger reviews include the analysis of the transformations of cultural codes in a region as reflected in the work of Claude Lévi-Strauss, the study of value systems as part of larger social-cultural wholes in the work of Louis Dumont, and the question of cultural boundaries through processes of social-cultural autopoiesis as has been theorized by Niklas Luhman. Sprenger argues that by combining these three, he has been better able to account for processes of identity formation and cultural flows in upland Southeast Asia, given the context of intensified globalization.

Andre Gingrich (Chapter 5) argues that regional comparison remains a vital strategy for historical anthropology and summarizes three studies that he has been involved in to underscore his point. These studies include a comparison of rock art in West and Southwest Arabia, the study of harbor pilots in the heavily cosmopolitan region of the Indian Ocean during the tenth and eleventh centuries, and the study of multistory domestic architecture in Southwest Saudi Arabia. Gingrich finds that the success of these studies depended less on having conducted a comparative analysis *per se* than on how comparison was productively combined with other methodological procedures (e.g. insight from archaeology, other historical analyses from the region, or social network analysis) to best answer the research questions asked in each study.

Michael Schnegg (Chapter 6) describes his multisited regional study of water-governance practices in rural Namibia. This chapter presents the method of "ethnographic upscaling" that combines in-depth ethnography with larger-*N* systematic regional comparisons to better understand the diversity of water-governance practices that have emerged since the implementation of community-based resource management policies at the national level in recent decades. Schnegg and his team have found that, although all communities are exposed to the same national blueprint for setting up local water-management organizations, a diversity of actual water-management practices has emerged that vary in terms of the rules chosen to distribute rights to shared water resources. Using ethnographic data as a resource for generating hypotheses that might explain this variation, Schnegg then scales these ethnographic findings up in the use of regional survey data to test whether these ethnographic insights explain the regional distribution of management rules adopted by different local water-management organizations.

The final three chapters by Jennifer S. Hirsch and her colleagues (Chapter 7), Birgitt Röttger-Rössler (Chapter 8), and Niko Besnier and Daniel Guinness (Chapter 9) reflect contemporary applications of distant and fluid comparisons. In addition, these chapters reflect large, well-funded, multisited, collaborative, a priori comparative designs that have become more common in anthropology since the start of the millennium (e.g. Hastrup and Hastrup 2016). Jennifer S. Hirsch and her colleagues, Holly Wardlow, Daniel Jordan Smith, Harriet Phinney, Shanti Parikh, and Constance A. Nathanson (Hirsch et al. 2009, Chapter 7), label these projects "comparative ethnography," where ethnographic "researchers approach multiple different sites with a shared analytical framework and then strive to distinguish between observations that are unique to a particular field site and those that have broader theoretical relevance" (257). By working collaboratively with a team of ethnographers who already have substantial experience in their field sites, the research team is able to develop a common set of research questions and shared methodological procedures that will ensure the comparability of materials collected in each site. As a result, comparative ethnographies better address the problems associated with the availability and reliability of data that researchers who rely on secondary sources to conduct a posteriori projects must confront. By using theoretical sampling procedures (Glaser and Strauss 1967; Ragin and Amoroso 2019), these comparative ethnographic projects can also ensure greater independence across the cases and that the cases chosen are able to speak more clearly to the development of more general theoretical insight than other comparative designs allow.

In Chapter 7, Hirsch and her colleagues provide a detailed account of the challenges and successes in developing, funding, executing, and disseminating the results of a large, comparative ethnographic project called Love, Marriage, and HIV (Hirsch et al. 2009). This collaborative project was funded by the US National Institutes of Health and aimed at understanding comparatively the processes that place married women at risk of HIV across field sites in five countries in the Global South (Papua New Guinea, Mexico, Vietnam, Nigeria, and Uganda). Birgitt Röttger-Rössler (Chapter 8) describes a bidisciplinary collaborative ethnographic project aimed at exploring how "culture-specific forms of emotion socialization shape and structure the ontogenetic development of emotions" (Chapter 8, 296) in three largely horticultural or agricultural communities – the Bara of Madagascar, the Minangkabau of West Sumatra, and the Tao of Lanyu Island, Taiwan. This project was a collaborative effort between the anthropologists on Röttger-Rössler's anthropological team and a developmental psychologist. Niko Besnier and Daniel Guiness (Chapter 9) describe the large, comparative ethnographic project titled Globalization, Sport, and the Precarity of Masculinity, which conducted research along migration routes among professional athletes in several sites including Tonga, Fiji, New Zealand, Cameroon, Senegal, Kenya, Venezuela, Poland, Trinidad and Tobago, India, and Japan. The global sports that were the focus of the study included rugby, soccer, cricket, marathon running, and wrestling. The main aim of this comparative ethnographic project was to explore the "changing fate of men's bodies as they circulated in search for employment" in five sports, four of which are major components of the global sport industries (Besnier and Guinness, Chapter 9, 205).

One of the important themes in all three of these final chapters is the great efforts made to address the tensions between the comparative (nomothetic) and ethnographic (ideographic) dimensions of the collaborative projects (see also Brettell, Chapter 1). On the one hand, comparison called for the maintenance of a shared focus on a common set of research questions, conceptual frameworks, and methods of data collection that could contribute to the generation of theoretical insights from patterns observed across the different field sites. On the other hand, the particularities of each case and the unique ways in which the main phenomena of interest were locally configured both by the ethnographer and by his or her interlocutors and the life worlds they occupied often threatened to overwhelm the comparative aims of these projects. All three researchers describe how the research teams collaborated to counter these tensions, both in designing the projects during fieldwork and in collaborating actively during and after the periods of ethnographic fieldwork to ensure that the comparative aims of the projects remained on track.

A related theme in these studies was how the priorities of research-funding agencies, or collaboration partners from more positivistic disciplines, also added tension to the successful implementation of these projects. Hirsch and her colleagues (Chapter 7) and Besnier and Guinness (Chapter 9) describe the role that funding agencies and research review boards played in shaping their decision to design their studies in order to speak more clearly and explicitly to an audience that is interested in the use of methods that yield generalizable theoretical insights. This came at the cost of designing studies that would speak to a different audience that is instead interested in understanding how the phenomena studied is uniquely configured in each ethnographic case. Röttger-Rössler (Chapter 8) reports that their collaboration with a developmental psychologist forced much greater attention to the formal methods used despite the diverse and divergent realities each ethnographer faced in his or her field site. Similarly, Hirsch and colleagues (Chapter 7) also report that their desire to speak to a public health audience and to satisfy their funding agency helped to promote their giving greater weight to the general theoretical and policy-related aims of the project than the ethnographic. Interestingly, Besnier and Guinness (Chapter 9) report that their collaboration, comprised entirely of ethnographers, was initially grounded in first emphasizing the ethnographic particularities of each case and then adding a more explicitly comparative scalar and general theoretical dimension in the final year of the project. Their comparative ethnographic project was not aimed mainly at the generation of theory based on the comparison of configurations across distantly related cases. Rather, Besnier and Guinness describe a more fluid, "scalar comparison" aimed at understanding how the athletes from across the ethnographic sites were enmeshed in global-local processes specific to an era of neoliberalism.

Conclusion

The takeaway message from the chapters of *Comparing Cultures: Innovations in Comparative Ethnography* is that explicit comparative ethnographic strategies in anthropology and other social sciences are back as essential tools in our broader methodological toolkit. The chapters not only support the relevance of ethnographic comparison from a diversity of methodological, epistemological, and theoretical standpoints but also provide invaluable insight into how to conduct comparative ethnographic research that produces unique insights into some of the most pressing human issues. Researchers who spend time with the chapters of this volume will be enriched in terms of their understanding of different comparative ethnographic approaches as well as the practical means of successfully enacting different comparative projects using the accumulated wisdom of the experts who have contributed to this book.

The chapters help us to see the unique research findings that are provided through comparison: an understanding that helps to account for the diversity in human social and cultural worlds. This is a diversity that is constructed from the configurational logics that underlie most of the phenomena and the social and historical articulation of local, regional, and global processes that together produce the diversity of human lifeworlds that often become the focus of anthropological study. To read the chapters collected in this volume is to appreciate how comparative ethnography can be a productive middle path between ethnographies of the particular that do not generalize and universalizing quantitative studies that mask context-driven diversity. As such, the configurational comparisons the book further develops can serve as an invaluable resource in promoting the sort of successful comparative work that has long been among anthropology's most enduring contributions to the human sciences.

References

Abu-Lughod, Lila. 1991. "Writing against Culture." In *Recapturing Anthropology*, edited by Richard G. Fox, 137–62. Santa Fe, NM: School of American Research Press.

Appadurai, Arjun. 1996. *Modernity at Large: Cultural Dimensions of Globalization*. Minneapolis: University of Minnesota Press.

Benedict, Ruth. 1934. *Patterns of Culture*. New York: Houghton Mifflin Co.

Benedict, Ruth. 1946. *The Chrysanthemum and the Sword: Patterns of Japanese Culture*. Boston, MA: Houghton Mifflin Company.

Bernard, H. Russell, and Clarence C. Gravlee, eds. 2015. *Handbook of Methods in Cultural Anthropology*, 2nd ed. Lanham, MD: Rowman & Littlefield.

Brettell, Caroline B. 2009. "Anthropology, Migration, and Comparative Consciousness." *New Literary History* 40 (3): 649–71.

Candea, Matei. 2019. *Comparison in Anthropology: The Impossible Method*. Cambridge: Cambridge University Press.

Dumont, Louis. 1994. *German Ideology: From France to Germany and Back*. Chicago, IL: University of Chicago Press.

Eggan, Fred. 1954. "Social Anthropology and the Method of Controlled Comparison." *American Anthropologist* 56 (5): 743–63.

Ember, Carol R., Melvin Ember, and Peter N. Peregrine. 2015. "Cross-Cultural Research." In *Handbook of Methods in Cultural Anthropology*, 2nd ed., edited by H. Russell Bernard and Clarence C. Gravlee, 561–601. Lanham, MD: Rowman & Littlefield.

Felski, Rita, and Susan S. Friedman, eds. 2013. *Comparison: Theories, Approaches, Uses*. Baltimore, MD: The Johns Hopkins University Press.

Fortes, Meyer, and Edward Evans-Pritchard, eds. 1940. *African Political System*. London: Oxford University Press.

Fox, Richard G., and Andre Gingrich. 2002. "Introduction." In *Anthropology, by Comparison*, edited by Andre Gingrich and Richard G. Fox, 1–24. London: Routledge.

Geertz, Clifford. 1973. *The Interpretation of Cultures*. New York: Basic Books.

Gingrich, Andre. 2012. "Comparative Methods in Socio-Cultural Anthropology Today." In *The SAGE Handbook of Social Anthropology*, edited by Richard Fardon, Olivia Harris, Trevor H. J. Marchand, Mark Nuttall, Cris Shore, Veronica Strand and Richard A. Wilson, 211–22. Los Angeles, CA: Sage.

Gingrich, Andre. 2015. "Comparative Method in Anthropology." In *International Encyclopedia of the Social and Behavioral Sciences*, edited by James D. Wright, 411–14. Oxford: Elsevier.

Gingrich, Andre, and Richard G. Fox, eds. 2002. *Anthropology, by Comparison.* London: Routledge.

Glaser, Barney G., and Anselm L. Strauss. 1967. *The Discovery of Grounded Theory: Strategies for Qualitative Research.* London: Weidenfeld and Nicholson.

Gluckman, Max. 1960. "Tribalism in Modern British Central Africa." *Cahiers d'Etudes Africanes* 1 (1): 55–70.

Hacking, Ian. 1992. "'Style' for Historians and Philosophers." *Studies in History and Philosophy* 23 (1): 1–20.

Handler, Richard. 2009. "The Uses of Incommensurability in Anthropology." *New Literary History* 40 (3): 627–47.

Hastrup, Kirsten, and Frida Hastrup, eds. 2016. *Waterworlds: Anthropology in Fluid Environments.* New York: Berghahn.

Henrich, Joseph, Robert Boyd, Samuel Bowles, Colin Camerer, Ernst Fehr, and Herbert Gintis. 2004. *Foundations of Human Sociality: Economic Experiments and Ethnographic Evidence from Fifteen Small-Scale Societies.* Oxford: Oxford University Press.

Hirsch, Jennifer S., Holly Wardlow, Daniel Jordan Smith, Harriet Phinney, Shanti Parikh, and Constance A. Nathanson. 2009. *The Secret: Love, Marriage, and HIV.* Nashville, TN: Vanderbilt University Press.

Holy, Ladislav, ed. 1987. *Comparative Anthropology.* New York: Basil Blackwell.

Ingold, Tim. 2011. *Being Alive: Essays on Movement, Knowledge, and Description.* London: Routledge.

Ingold, Tim. 2018. *Anthropology and/as Education.* London: Routledge.

Johnson, Jeffrey C., and Daniel J. Hrushka. 2015. "Research Design and Research Strategies." In *Handbook of Methods in Cultural Anthropology*, 2nd ed., edited by H. Russell Bernard, and Clarence C. Gravlee, 97–131. Lanham, MD: Rowman & Littlefield.

Kroeber, Alfred L. 1952. *The Nature of Culture.* Chicago, IL: University of Chicago Press.

Lazar, Sian. 2012. "Disjunctive Comparison: Citizenship and Trade Unionism in Bolivia and Argentina." *Journal of the Royal Anthropological Institute* 18 (2): 349–68.

Leach, Edmund R. 1961. *Rethinking Anthropology.* London: Athlone Press.

Lévi-Strauss, Claude. 1969. *The Raw and the Cooked. Mythologies, Volume 1.* Translated by John Weightman and Doreen Weightman. Chicago, IL: University of Chicago Press. First published in 1964.

Lewis, Ioan M. 1999. "Arguments with Ethnography: Comparative Approaches to History, Politics, & Religion." *London School of Economics Monographs on Social Anthropology 68.* London: Berg Publishers.

Lock, Margaret. 1995. *Encounters with Aging: Mythologies of Menopause in Japan and North America.* Berkeley: University of California Press.

Lowe, Edward D. 2018. "Kinship, Funerals, and the Durability of Culture in Chuuk." In *Advances in Culture Theory from Psychological Anthropology*, edited by Naomi Quinn. Basingstoke: Palgrave Press.

Marcus, George E. 1995. "Ethnography in/of the World System: The Emergence of Multi-sited Ethnography." *Annual Review of Anthropology* 24 (1): 95–117.

Merton, Robert K. 1949. *Social Theory and Social Structure: Toward the Codification of Theory and Research*. Glencoe, IL: The Free Press.

Mintz, Sidney W. 1985. *Sweetness and Power: The Place of Sugar in Modern History*. New York: Penguin Books.

Nader, Laura. 1994. "Comparative Consciousness." *In Assessing Cultural Anthropology*, edited by Robert Borofsky, 84–96. New York: McGraw-Hill.

Radcliffe-Brown, Alfred R. 1952. *Structure and Function in Primitive Society*. London: Cohen and West.

Ragin, Charles C. 2014. *The Comparative Method: Moving beyond Qualitative and Quantitative Strategies*. Berkeley: University of California Press.

Ragin, Charles C., and Lisa M. Amoroso. 2019. *Constructing Social Research*, 3rd ed. Los Angeles, CA: Sage.

Röttger-Rössler, Birgitt, Gabriel Scheidecker, Lebrecht Funk, and Manfred Holodynsky. 2015. "Learning Feeling: A Cross-Cultural Comparison of the Socialization and Development of Emotions." *Ethos* 43 (2): 187–220.

Schnegg, Michael. 2014. "Anthropology and Comparison: Methodological Challenges and Tentative Solutions." *Zeitschrift für Ethnologie* 139: 55–72.

Strathern, Marilyn. 1988. *The Gender of the Gift: Problems with Women and Problems with Society in Melanesia*. Berkeley: University of California Press.

West, Paige. 2012. *From Modern Production to Imagined Primitive: The Social World of Coffee from Papua New Guinea*. Durham, NC: Duke University Press.

Whiting, Beatrice B., and John W. M. Whiting. 1975. *Children of Six Cultures: A Psycho-cultural Analysis*. Cambridge, MA: Harvard University Press.

Wolf, Eric R. 1982. *Europe and the People without History*. Berkeley: University of California Press.

Yengoyan, Aram A., ed. 2006. *Modes of Comparison: Theory and Practice*. Ann Arbor: The University of Michigan Press.

Part I

Binary Comparisons

1 Thinking with Comparison in the Anthropology/Historical Anthropology of Migration

Caroline B. Brettell

In a foundational article on urban anthropology published in the *American Anthropologist* in 1962, Philip Mayer engages in a comparison of two destinations for African migrants: the Copperbelt towns of Rhodesia, where he draws on the work of fellow anthropologists of the period Max Gluckman (1960) and J. Clyde Mitchell (1960), and East London, South Africa, where he conducted his own research. Mayer's central argument is that "very different pictures ... emerge ... between different modern towns in Africa, not only in the balance between extra-town and within-town ties, but also in the very nature and quality of the ties within each category" (p. 581). In the Copperbelt towns, the trade unions carried a good deal of weight, in part in response to the context of mining compounds. In East London, by contrast, there were neither trade unions nor other large-scale associations "of or for Africans, except, on a smaller scale, churches and sports clubs" (p. 582). Mayer went on to observe that there was no opposition between different tribal groups in East London where, at the time of his research, 96 percent of the entire African population in the city were Xhosa speakers with Xhosa loyalties. He argues that in the South African context of this era, all associations "were repressed or discouraged" (p. 582). This was in direct contrast to the encouragement (since the 1940s) of African trade unionism in the Copperbelt. Mayer comes to the conclusion that it is inappropriate to "apply to any South African town the forecast (rightly made by Gluckman in the Rhodesian context) that 'as soon as Africans assemble in towns they will try to combine to better their conditions in trade unions and so forth' (Gluckman 1960, 57)" (Mayer 1962, 582). Instead he emphasizes the "atomistic" structure of East London, arguing that rather than "a single 'unitary' structure (the mining company) controlling employment, accommodation, and almost all aspects of the employees' lives, there is a multitude of different employers. The East London locations – entirely municipal – illustrate this atomism in extreme form, for they are largely made up of private, not municipal housing" (p. 583). In this article, by means of a comparative approach, Mayer was drawing important differences between two urban receiving contexts for African migrants that impacted the social relations that they forged.[1]

More than fifty years later, in an article in the *International Migration Review*, sociologist Richard Alba, and his anthropologically trained sociologist and coauthor Nancy Foner (Alba and Foner 2014), engaged in a different scalar comparison regarding the success or failure of immigrant integration in North America and Western Europe.[2] Using four European countries (Britain, France, Germany, and the Netherlands) and two North American ones (the United States and Canada), these authors focus on five "grand narratives" and what these can tell us about similarities and differences in integration processes. These five grand narratives are national philosophies or models of immigrant integration (for example, Canadian multiculturalism or French republicanism); the nature of the political economy (for example, the social welfare state or the liberal market economy); the uniqueness of settler or historical immigration societies (Canada and the United States as opposed to European countries); US exceptionalism (that includes the US racial landscape emerging as a historical legacy of slavery and segregation); and the process of convergence whereby countries on both sides of the Atlantic are becoming more similar in policies related to immigration (for example, recent changes in German citizenship laws).

A brief summary cannot do justice to Alba and Foner's discussion, but it is important to emphasize the arguments that these authors make about the value of comparison. They write,

> Admittedly, comparative analysis cannot... isolate a small number of factors, whether demographic, economic, or institutional, that vary across societies and account for differences in integration; there are **too many degrees of freedom**, in other words. Yet there is still **great value in intelligent comparison**... Comparison offers a yardstick by which a society can evaluate how well it is doing in the domain of integration. Further, **a comparative approach can shed light on the "invisible"** – the systematic features of each society that, because they are national "constants" are often overlooked or taken for granted in single-country analyses. Comparison also lends itself to ideas about borrowings, that is, features of institutions in one or more societies that appear worthy of emulation for another. (Alba and Foner 2014, 265–66; emphases added by this author)

From the perspectives of these authors, then, a comparative framework helps us to (1) better understand a particular case that we are examining by revealing internal dynamics or characteristics that only become apparent when juxtaposed against one or more other cases; (2) better assess where different cases or units of comparison (cities, nations, regions, groups of different ethnic or national backgrounds) are situated along some dimension of interest (in Alba and Foner's discussion, levels of immigrant integration); and (3) explore "best practices" or a flow of comparable features among and between the units of comparison.

Inspired by these calls, half a century apart, to think with comparison, in this chapter I discuss comparative approaches, at various scales of research and analysis, in the anthropology and historical anthropology of migration. I begin with a **brief** review (in broad brushstrokes) of the rise and fall and – now, perhaps – reascent of comparison in anthropology. I then turn to three cases from my own ethnographic and historical research over several decades that illustrate the effectiveness and insights that comparative praxis yields by (to borrow again from Nancy Foner [2015]) making visible processes and structures in one context or case by highlighting differences from and similarities to another.[3] Along the way I also touch on some of the methodological challenges of engaging in such comparisons, and in the conclusion I summarize the particular contributions of a comparative approach to the study of migration and offer some suggestions regarding how the challenges of comparison can be met.

Anthropology and Comparison: Love It or Hate It

Several years ago, in an essay prepared for the journal *New Literary History* (Brettell 2009), I began to explore how comparison is understood in the anthropological study of migration. At the request of the editors, I spent several pages in that essay reviewing the history of the comparative method in anthropology. I do not need to repeat that discussion here, but I do want to highlight briefly anthropology's apparent love-hate relationship with cross-cultural comparison (what I labeled in the 2009 essay its "troubled history"). In my view, this relationship is about the tension between "particularizers" and "generalizers," and perhaps by extension between those who fall toward the more humanistic or interpretive end of the anthropological continuum and those who fall toward the more scientific or objectivist end. There are a host of anthropologists who argue that comparison is fundamental to anthropology – indeed, that it defines the discipline. Thus, Cora DuBois (1980, 8), in an article reflecting on her career in anthropology, discusses cultural anthropology as a residual category in relation to the subfields and suggests that the growth of "specialized disciplines and theories in adjacent disciplines such as economics, political science, and psychology increasingly affected cultural anthropology, which became in time a collection of specialized topics whose only claim to the designation 'anthropology' lay in its introduction of cross-cultural comparisons." These comparisons "added to our more detailed knowledge of population aggregates; [and] served to caution against overgeneralization of our culture-bound world view." Almost two decades later, Rena Lederman (1998, 433), in an essay on the future of culture areas in anthropological research, writes that rarely has anthropological area expertise "not been motivated by comparativist projects of one sort or another: whether positivist projects of typologizing for functional and developmental analysis (emphasizing cross-cultural similarities) or interpretive projects, reflexive or otherwise (emphasizing differences)." And five years later, Elizabeth Colson (2003, 3), writing about research on forced migration, observed that "anthropology as a discipline relies upon a back and forth process. We move from careful ethnography that deals with the particular in all its uniqueness to a comparison that provides a deeper understanding of the human condition."[4]

These three examples of claims to the fundamental centrality of comparison to anthropology can be juxtaposed with a trend that began to emerge in the 1980s in association with the "postmodern turn." This trend, labeled by Roy Ellen (2010, 389) as the "retreat into ethnography" and by Lila Abu-Lughod (1991) as the "ethnography of the particular," was characterized by an anti-comparativist, anti-"culture," antitheoretical generalization, and perhaps even an antiscience anthropological stance. This stance is perhaps most strongly represented in George Marcus's (2008, 200) challenge to comparison, which he identifies as one of "three dimensions that have defined the character and possibility of anthropology in diverse national settings." Marcus not only asks whether anthropologies have fulfilled the comparative goals but also queries "the extent to which comparison has been at the service of, and a supplement to, the nation-defining project – that is, the extent to which comparisons are produced on a universalizing canvas, or are at the service of a narrowly nationalist project of sorting out diversity within a particular historic project of nation-building." Embedded in his comment is certainly a critique of a scientific approach because undergirding that approach are issues of power and Western hegemony. Thus, in their own consideration of comparative approaches within anthropology, Richard Fox and Andre Gingrich (2002, 2) have suggested that it was concerns about the complicity with European imperialism, as well as greater awareness of the shortcomings of assumptions about self-contained, stable, and integrated cultures in the face of a capitalist world system of great historical depth, that resulted in a turn away from the comparative method that had characterized early- and mid-twentieth-century anthropology.

The postmodern, anticomparativist, antigeneralization stance was not without its critics. For example, writing in the early years of the twenty-first century, and in an effort to recapture comparison in anthropology, Thomas Gregor and Donald Tuzin (2001, 5) made the following ironic observation: "If cultures are islands unto themselves or texts composed in the imaginations of pseudo-observers, if all classification and generalization are nothing but the exercise of Western hegemony and arrogance, if, in short, all is vanity, then comparison would be at best impossible and at worst immoral." Clearly, the tension is real in the language of Gregor and Tuzin's comments, but it is not insurmountable. Indeed, as these debates within anthropology ensued over the course of the final decades of the twentieth century and into the early twenty-first century, many of us just went about our work, and we often found that some dimension of comparison was "good to think with." While mindful of the reflexivity that the critics of comparison brought into the debate, we proceeded on the assumption that one can in fact work simultaneously with the particularities of one case as well as the generalizations that a comparative praxis across cases yields. These are not the generalizations that an earlier generation of anthropologists sought – those of universal laws or grand theory. Rather they are the middle-range generalizations that serve to highlight differences as they highlight similarities, that are "variation-finding" (to borrow a term from Glick Schiller and Çağlar [2011]), and that in fact help to illuminate the significance of context or how a broader social process (in my case, migration) plays out in a particular place, at a particular time, or among a particular group of people.

I turn to three of my own projects to illustrate these dimensions of comparative framing. Two are projects in historical anthropology where comparative framing was invoked primarily during analysis (a posteriori), while the third is an ethnographic project where comparison was part of the original and collaborative research design and hence a priori.[5] It is worth noting that my engagement with historical cases was entirely purposive in the trajectory of my career as a scholar of migration who is interested in understanding a lived social process in all its dimensions and variations. History offers anthropologists the opportunity to extend the number of cases that we study (across time rather than across space) as well as the ability to capture change. Historical anthropologists tend to address big problems in local places. Thus, two of the best anthropologists working in this field, Jane and Peter Schneider (1996, 30), open their historical-anthropological study of fertility decline and the ideology of class in Sicily in the following way: "[T]he drama, and the trauma, of world population history since the mid-eighteenth century, and the ways people interpret it, are the broadest concerns of this study. The expansion and contraction of the population of one Sicilian community between, roughly, 1860 and 1980, are its narrowest concerns." These authors capture, in other words, both the general and the particular. While the work is not explicitly comparative, they are implicitly thinking about comparison as they consider "world population history."

Three Comparisons, *Molto Breve*

Nations and National Historical Contexts: Illegitimacy in Portugal and Ireland

I spent much of my early career working in northern Portugal both as an anthropologist and as a historical demographer.[6] In my book *Men Who Migrate, Women Who Wait: Population and History in a Portuguese Parish* (Brettell 1986), I addressed the impact of two and a half centuries of emigration, mostly of men from a northern Portuguese village, on marriage and fertility patterns as well as on changing household composition over time. It was useful to draw comparisons between what I was finding in Portugal and the data emerging from other historical demographic findings across Western Europe regarding household composition, age at marriage, rates of fertility, and so forth (Laslett 1965; Laslett and Wall 1972; Kertzer 1984; Knodel 1974). However, one comparison (between Portugal and Ireland) became most meaningful in helping me to understand and explain the patterns of out-of-wedlock births that my research had revealed. The rates of illegitimacy in the village where I was working were very high during the late nineteenth and early twentieth centuries.[7] This surprised me because I went into the field with the theoretical and conceptual frameworks that were prevalent at the time for the so-called anthropology of the Mediterranean – specifically ideas about honor and shame and about the "vigilance of virgins," to quote from the title of a very important article by Jane Schneider (1971). Supposedly, the chastity and modesty of unmarried women were of supreme importance in the countries of Mediterranean Europe – out-of-wedlock births should not exist![8] But Portugal, while part of southern Europe, was not really Mediterranean. If one were to draw comparisons with regard to illegitimate births, should they be better drawn elsewhere? I turned to Ireland, where rates of out-of-wedlock births were low for the same period, for what I thought might be a more apt comparison to consider. Indeed, I was inspired to pursue this comparison through my reading of Sundbärg's (1908) *Aperçus Statistique Internationaux*, where he noted the differences in rates of illegitimacy between Portugal and Ireland as early as the 1870s, noting that this was despite the fact that in both countries, age at marriage was late and the proportion of lifelong celibates was high. That is, the countries were similar regarding some purely demographic variables.

Geographically, both of these countries, Portugal and Ireland, are located at the margins of Europe, looking out toward the Americas. They are both part of what Conrad Arensberg (1963) and Michael Kenny (1963) labeled "The Atlantic Fringe" in an early attempt to delineate culture areas within Europe.[9] The regions of the Atlantic Fringe shared a Celtic past and were unified by the sea; they were, to borrow from Kenny (1963, 107), "land sedentary and sea migratory." Both of these countries have deep histories of emigration, but the flows expanded significantly in the latter part of the nineteenth century, albeit for different reasons. In both of these countries, during this period and well into the twentieth century, the Catholic Church was very powerful. But there are some salient differences, and I asked myself if some of these differences might be brought to bear to help me explain (or at least understand) the high illegitimacy rates in Portugal.

I homed in on a number of variables, not all of which I can discuss in the limited space here.[10] One was the contrast between partible inheritance practices in northern Portugal and impartible inheritance practices in Ireland (which were set in place in the nineteenth century in the aftermath of the Irish famine).[11] Women had rights to property in northern Portugal and could hence support themselves and a child born out of wedlock. They could pass this property on to an illegitimate son or daughter. As French sociologist Paul Descamps (1935, 72) observed in the 1930s, in northern Portugal, and the province of Minho in particular, "an illegitimate child belongs to the mother, or better still to her family who do not deny her legal right to inherit because of her sin." Very often, in fact, it was daughters who received the third share (the *terço*) of their parents' property and hence the family home, often as part of a premortem declaration that required them, in turn, to take care of their parents in old age. Young, unmarried Portuguese girls from villages in the northern sector of the country did migrate to work in domestic service in provincial towns or Lisbon, but their mobility was nothing in comparison with the mobility of Portuguese men, married and unmarried, to Brazil during the late nineteenth and early twentieth centuries. Some returned; many did not. The result was that single women were often left out of the marriage market or experienced marriage at a late age (the mean age at marriage was also rising during the latter part of the nineteenth century), and many married women became "*viuvas de vivos*" (widows of the living). It is in this demographic context that out-of-wedlock births occurred.

In Ireland during this same time period, one son inherited the property, if there was property to inherit, and often did so late in life. Other children had to move on. For many women in Ireland, this meant emigrating themselves, whether to England or to the United States. Only a third of Irish emigrants in the period between 1815 and 1844 were women, but in the aftermath of the Great Famine (1845–51), women left in numbers equal to those of men. As historian Deirde Mageean (1997, 96) has observed, "[F]amine created an environment that marginalized women economically and reduced their status in society. The virtual ending of partible inheritance, the eradication of the poorer classes among whom female labor was particularly important, the spread of arranged marriages and the dowry system, and the reduced opportunities for female wage earning combined to spur emigration." By the end the nineteenth century, women made up more than half of all Irish emigrants. Between 1885 and 1920, close to 700,000 young and mostly unmarried Irish women left their homeland (Nolan 1989). "They were the only significant group of foreign-born women who outnumbered men; they were the only significant group of women who chose to migrate primarily in female cliques. They also accepted jobs that most other women turned down" (Diner 1983, xiv). Women came to represent 52.9 percent of the Irish immigrant population in America.

Thus, unmarried women with no prospects in Ireland left the country. Demographically, this had an impact on birth rates, including the potential for out-of-wedlock births. If young women were pregnant, they might have left Ireland, thereby lowering the recorded numbers of illegitimate births within the country. Their departure to give birth elsewhere leads me to another dimension of this comparison that is useful to consider – the nature of Roman Catholicism in Ireland in contrast with Portugal, and, by extension, predominant codes of morality. Ireland was characterized by a much more puritanical Catholicism, which some scholars have described as Jansenist, although this is debated. The morally rigorous Catholicism of Ireland (including sanctions against premarital sex and illegitimacy) expanded during the second half of the nineteenth century under the influential archbishop of Dublin, Paul Cullen (1803–78). Ireland experienced a devotional revolution (Larkin 1972) at the time that strengthened the role of the Irish Roman Catholic Church in the lives of local populations of Ireland. Further, Irish Catholicism was deeply rooted in an Irish national identity formed under the rule of the British, and that eventually became the basis for the familiar internal religious conflicts of the twentieth century that ultimately resulted in independence.

By contrast, observers of nineteenth-century Portugal have described a more relaxed moral code. One British traveler to the country wrote in 1845,

> The female peasantry who depart from the paths of strict morality are not treated by their parents and acquaintances with the same rigor as in the more righteous England. They are compassionated for their misfortune more than punished for their fault and it is only when they obstinately persist in an evil course of life that they are turned away from their paternal homes. (Kingston 1845, 304)

By comparison with Ireland, the Portuguese Roman Catholic Church, at the time, had much less authority over its people. Church and state in nineteenth-century Portugal were often at loggerheads, and at certain periods, anticlericalism was rampant. Further, the Portuguese Catholic Church was never the champion of nationalist causes, whereas this was of prime significance to the Irish Catholic Church. It was only under the Estado Novo (launched in 1932) and the dictatorship of António Salazar that the Portuguese Catholic Church regained and solidified its hold on the countryside. Interestingly, in the village where I carried out my research, it was precisely at this time that rates of out-of-wedlock births declined significantly. But, then, so too did emigration itself, at least for a few decades.[12]

What was the fruit of this comparison? Viewing Portugal in relation to Ireland helped me to explore multiple avenues of explanation for the high rates of illegitimacy that my research had revealed. It led me to contextual dimensions that I might not otherwise have considered and to variations that I might otherwise not have identified. But this comparison also had, and continues to have, its challenges. My knowledge of Portugal is deep; of Ireland, less so. Was I drawing on the right sources, and did I fully understand all the nuances of the dimensions according to which I structured my comparison? Was I, for example, overessentializing the religious contexts, especially in the place where I had no firsthand historical and ethnographic experience? How does one evaluate these strengths and weaknesses? In my view, if the comparison yields a greater understanding of the case one is trying to explain, then the gains outweigh the limitations. My second example illustrates this further for a different scale of analysis in a different national context.

Regional Historical Contexts: French Canadian Immigrants in New England and the Midwest

The variation-finding aspect of comparative praxis that illuminated my work on Portugal has also characterized one of my more recent projects, another effort to marry anthropology and history. This project has documented the experiences of a group of French Canadians who migrated, during the middle of the nineteenth century, to central Illinois (Brettell 2015b). They were led to the Midwest by a charismatic French Canadian priest named Father Charles Chiniquy. Chiniquy immediately came into conflict with the Irish Catholic hierarchy in the state and eventually became schismatic, abandoning the Roman Catholic Church and becoming a Presbyterian minister. A large number of the immigrants who had followed him to Illinois converted with him. One of the central problems in this study was to explore the impact of the schism and the conversion on the lives of these immigrants.

In order to address this question, I found it useful to consider what I was discovering about the unstudied French Canadian immigrants in Illinois in comparison with the much better-known (at least in the history of migrations to the United States) French Canadians who moved to another region of the United States during the latter part of the nineteenth century – the factory towns of New England. This comparative thinking led to a host of intriguing research questions. For example, did the fact that one population remained propertyless industrial workers for two to three generations while the other quickly became property owners on the prairies affect local processes of incorporation and belonging? Did it matter that the Midwest population was rent asunder by a religious schism that created differences of faith in their community of settlement, while the Roman Catholic Church remained in powerful control among the French Canadians who had settled in myriad industrial towns across New England? How could the study of a population that settled in the Midwest nuance and enrich the way that we understand, represent, and yes, even generalize about French Canadians in the United States?

This last question is particularly important. French Canadians in the United States have been subjected to a particular characterization embodied in the phrase "The Chinese of the Eastern States." The appellation, used by

Carroll D. Wright in an 1881 report to the Bureau of Statistics of Labor, summed up a late-nineteenth-century assessment of this immigrant population as having no interest in the civil and political institutions of the United States, or in their educational system. He wrote,

> They do not come to make a home among us, to dwell with us as citizens and so become a part of us; but their purpose is merely to sojourn a few years as aliens… They are a horde of industrial invaders, not a stream of stable settlers. Voting, with all that it implies, they care nothing about. Rarely does one of them become naturalized. They will not send their children to school if they can help it. (Wright 1881, 469)

This description, which certainly should resonate with some readers in relation to attitudes about more recent immigrant populations (particularly those from Mexico), was much debated and later clarified and modified by Wright himself. However, Franco-Americans in New England lived for decades with the legacy of a stereotype that became more racist and nativist as it was rewritten by those who quoted Wright out of context. And in the 1920s, the Ku Klux Klan moved into the northeastern United States and made the Franco-American Catholics in the state of Maine an object of their derision. As historian Mark Paul Richard (2009, 287) observes, "[T]he French language, the Roman Catholic faith, and the formation of ethnic enclaves distinguished French-Canadian descendants in protestant Yankee New England and the Ku Klux Klan took notice." In short, the image that emerged of New England French Canadians was of an inward-looking population dominated by priests, with little interest in education and better housing, a low degree of both geographical and social mobility, minimal expectations, an unwillingness to get involved in strikes and other union activities, and low rates of naturalization and who generally were resistant to assimilation. All these attributes were supposedly inherently "French Canadian." They derived in part from early studies of French Canadians in Quebec that also emphasized the absence of any goal of social mobility as a central value in traditional French Canadian culture rather than a more appropriate approach, which might emphasize a set of responses to particular social, economic, and political contexts.[13]

In addition, this migrant population was portrayed as temporary and with a long-range plan to return to their country of origin and reinvest in family farms in Quebec (Louder and Waddell 1983). Roby and Frenette (2012) use the phrase "birds of passage" to describe them, while Sorrell (1981), comparing the French Canadians of the late nineteenth and early twentieth centuries with Mexican and Puerto Rican migrants of more recent periods, refers to "commuting immigrants." These ties to Quebec were fostered by the powerful priests who lived among them and preached about being Canadian and being Catholic, both of which were part of a nationalist ideology in Quebec. French Canadians were "duty bound to preserve their cultural identity" and were expected to "fulfill a sacred mission, namely to preserve Catholicism in America" (Brault 1986, 7). The French Canadian parish, in one writer's view, "offered to the Canadians the most favorable conditions within which to maintain for a long time their religion and their national language. They are truly at home. They live together, marry one another, become neighbors and property owners. They have their Church and their convent, what else do they need to form Canadian villages in the very heart of the United States?" (Hamon 1891).

The question for me was whether any of these descriptions of French Canadians in New England applied to those who settled in the Midwest. Did the process by which they became part of the American fabric happen at the same time or earlier? Did it look the same? Clearly, the context was fundamentally different. These immigrants encountered a frontier rather than a Yankee stronghold. They participated in the formation of a culture rather than struggling against absorption by one that was already formed. Their populations were not constantly renewed, as were those in New England. Jean Lamarre (2003, 20) has noted that while some young men went to Michigan and Wisconsin prior to 1860 to take temporary employment in the logging industry, "the migratory movement to the West before the Civil War was of a permanent and familial nature, centered around the acquisition of land with the intention of maintaining an agricultural way of life." This is a very important difference with the New England migrations. A second difference is that after the Civil War, these migrations to the American Midwest declined, not only, as Lamarre suggests, because it was no longer an agricultural frontier but also because agriculture in Quebec had itself recovered and new farming opportunities opened up in the Canadian west.

As with the New England migrations, the French-Catholic clergy was extensively involved in the settlements in Michigan, Wisconsin, and Illinois. In these concentrated rural communities, in areas where "society was still in the process of formation," there would be, they thought, an even greater opportunity to preserve religion, language, and nationality than in the cities and factory towns of New England (Wade 1950, 8). On the Michigan frontier, the French Canadian migrants "enjoyed considerable latitude or autonomy – their young communities could develop in continuity with their traditional values, without being obliged to integrate into a dominant culture. This situation contributed to the maintenance of their French-speaking, Catholic cultural identity, allowing the French Canadians to put off until later the task of defining themselves in terms of their new social and cultural environment" (Lamarre 2003, 80).

But what about the settlements in north-central Illinois that were the focus of my research? There the power of the Catholic Church was eroded from within soon after the arrival of the first generation of immigrants. What did this mean for their migration experience and for the way in which they formed their communities on the frontier? What did the schism mean for the relationships that they drew between a religious identity and an ethnic identity? How important was religion to preserving an ancestral heritage, as has been argued for the New England Franco-American communities? These were the questions, emerging out of an analytical comparison of two different regions of settlement, which guided my research. But, of course, the "bigger" question was about the supposedly "inherent" characteristics of French Canadian immigrants in the United States: Was this really about social, economic, and religious contexts?

The comparison revealed both similarities and differences. The French Canadian migrants in Illinois were not vilified to the same extent as their compatriots in the states of the East Coast. In addition, not only had they migrated to relatively unsettled territory, rather than moving into well-established bastions of Protestantism, but also a significant number of them abandoned their Catholic faith and converted to Protestantism. Their schism attracted national attention during a period when anti-Catholic sentiment in the United States was widespread and was supported by a broader national Protestant community. However, both migrant populations were characterized by kin-based links and family ties that persisted across generations, even when children and grandchildren of the Illinois settlers departed for other parts of the United States. Community endogamy endured into the 1880s, and early on, practices common in Quebec such as the *frérot* (marrying the widow of a deceased brother) could be found in the settler population. As in New England, use of the French language endured in the Illinois settlements into the second generation, as did ties with Quebec, although those who migrated to Illinois probably traveled back much less frequently than did the French Canadians who settled in New England.

But many differences were also revealed by the comparison. First, several French Canadian immigrant communities on the East Coast engaged in conflicts with the Irish Catholic hierarchy, but rarely did these conflicts lead to schism and conversion as they did in north-central Illinois. The religious change caused by this schism had an important, if sometimes subtle, impact on family and community life and undoubtedly laid the foundation for a more outward-looking community by comparison with many of the settlements in New England. Clearly, Charles Chiniquy had a good deal of influence over his converts, at least in the early years, but having quickly severed his connections with the Catholic religious elite, he instigated a different kind of religious institutional climate from that in New England where populations were very closely bound to the church, considered it essential for their survival, and did not openly question its leadership.

A second important difference is that those who settled in Illinois were able to continue their agricultural way of life, and some successfully built up substantial holdings of land. They were able to pass on real and moveable property to their children when they died. Here they have more in common with immigrant populations of other national backgrounds (comparisons I draw in my book) and with those French Canadian communities that were established in other parts of the Midwest than with the French Canadians who settled in mill towns of the eastern United States. While the first generation of French Canadians in Illinois generally intermarried with other French Canadians, these patterns were weakened by the second generation, and religious endogamy came to prevail, with Catholics marrying Catholics and Protestants marrying Protestants, often outside the ethnic group. Certainly, the size of families was already decreasing by the second generation, again with some differences between Catholic and Protestant populations. Although there were religious schools in the communities of settlement in the Midwest that persisted into the early twentieth century, these schools never had such tight control over the local populations as those in the more closely knit communities in New England.

So, did emigration to a rural area matter? Did the possibility of acquiring land matter? And did the schism matter in terms of pulling numerous families away from the Catholic Church and into mainstream Protestantism? Clearly, the answer to all these questions is yes, and in posing them within a comparative analytical framework, I came to understand them better and to nuance the broader story of the French Canadian immigrant experience in the United States. As in the previous case discussed, here too it was the comparisons that made visible a range of variables that needed to be considered in order to understand dimensions of settlement and integration in two different contexts. In short, comparison helped me not only to highlight these dimensions and differences but also to advance theoretical arguments and debates regarding processes of immigrant incorporation and changing identity. The challenge to this comparison was again the reliance on secondary sources and sources that did not necessarily engage in the same kind of detailed historical demography that was at the foundation of my own project. Nevertheless, the comparative frame enhanced my understanding of the particular case with which I was dealing and enriched my analysis of it.

A Comparison of Two Immigrant Groups in Dallas–Fort Worth

So far, I have been talking about an engagement with comparison that comes at the point of analysis (a posteriori) and that draws largely on secondary literature rather than being methodologically inherent (a priori) to a research project and hence part of initial data collection. The final project I wish to describe was structured from the outset as a comparison and involved collaboration. In 2005, with funding from the Russell Sage Foundation, anthropologist Deborah Reed-Danahay and I launched a comparative study of civic engagement among two very different Asian immigrant populations: Indians and Vietnamese (Brettell and Reed-Danahay 2012). At the time these were the two largest Asian immigrant populations in Texas. They ranked third and fourth, respectively, in the Dallas–Fort Worth (DFW) metropolitan area. Each population had grown since the 1990s. Clearly, these two populations are distinct from one another in any number of ways – in cultural and historical backgrounds, in their auspices of migration (education and economic migrants, on the one hand, and refugees, on the other hand), in English-language skills, and in socioeconomic status both before emigration and in the immigrant context. However, what we discovered as we proceeded with our research was a good deal of common ground, as well as some significant differences in the ways in which these groups were practicing forms of informal civic engagement and learning to "become" American as they were simultaneously working to reinforce their own ethnic identities. The comparison was essential to illuminate both the variations and similarities in how members of these two immigrant populations became civically engaged.

It is impossible to summarize here all the insights that this comparison revealed, but among them were the common ways in which members of these two populations entered the civic or public sphere through their religious institutions and ethnic organizations. Both communities also constructed similar cultural landscapes within the DFW metropolitan area as mechanisms for claiming space and establishing political presence. These landscapes included commercial centers, public festivals and banquets, and the ethnic media. When we engaged members of these two populations (both first and second generations) in discussions of identity and the meaning of citizenship, again we found much common ground, including ambivalence toward "Asian" and "Asian-American" and, in the case of Indians, "South Asian" categories, but we also found some important and sometimes subtle variations. For example, for both groups, whiteness figured prominently in the understanding of what it means to be an American. But first-generation Indians are guided here by their class status and hence tend to place less emphasis on their "brownness" than do their children. By contrast, both generations of Vietnamese emphasize their "yellowness" (sometimes using a banana metaphor) as a barrier to full-fledged American identity.

Within both populations there are high rates of naturalization. Individuals in both groups recognize the benefits of US citizenship, but the Vietnamese placed somewhat more emphasis on rights and on "democracy as freedom" than did Indians. This difference relates directly to the prior experiences of members of these two groups: Indians moved from what they always referred to as the "biggest" democracy, while the Vietnamese fled a homeland ruled by a communist regime in the aftermath of the fall of Saigon.

When we explored the social responsibility dimensions of citizenship, we were able to represent the activities of members of these two populations in relation to emic religious concepts of *seva* (for Hindu Indians) and *trach nhiem* for the Vietnamese, the former referring to selfless service to the poor and suffering and the latter to a sense of responsibility to do good that is linked to Buddhist beliefs in karma and loving kindness. Indians spoke about "giving back" to the community, using a common idiom in US society, while the Vietnamese who were interviewed did not use or recognize this idiom, something we attribute to less familiarity with the English language. The children of Vietnamese immigrants were more apt to articulate the obligation of "giving back."

One interesting difference between these two groups was the way in which religious organizations provided resources for political mobilization. This was quite common in Vietnamese churches and temples. Deborah found in her research that the commemoration of Vietnamese culture heroes that occurred at the Catholic Church, and the invitation of elected officials to a forum to protest the persecution of a Buddhist monk in Vietnam, illustrated well the intertwining of politics with religious expression. Such mobilization was less common in Indian religious institutions, although after 9/11, local mosques did organize their members to respond to public relations crises that faced Muslims in America. But there were also major differences in relation to homeland politics. What is politicized for the Vietnamese is framed by the communist/anticommunist division in Vietnam. This conflict draws Catholics and Buddhists together. By contrast, homeland religious divisions are more polarizing in India, and hence, Indian immigrants frequently choose either not to bring the intensity of these divisions with them or to keep them as tightly controlled as possible. Even within more secular pan-Indian associations, efforts are made not to engage in any activities or make any position statements that might indicate support for either Hindu or Muslim causes in India.

In our research, we also found that the higher educational levels and better command of English-language skills facilitated Indians in their efforts to reach out and participate in organizations within mainstream American society – indeed, they talked about "the mainstream" and "mainstreaming" with frequency by comparison with the Vietnamese. This made it important for this population to present an image of harmony and working together. We identified more Indians who were moving into mainstream organizations than their first-generation counterparts among the Vietnamese. But that said, it was a member of the Texas Vietnamese community, a man from Houston, who had been elected to the state legislature.

We came to the conclusion through our comparative methodology that the work we carried out contributed to debates about the analytical utility of the category "refugee" as a "naturally self-delimiting domain of anthropological knowledge" (Malkki 1995, 496) but not in any obvious ways. For the Vietnamese, interactions with the state and experiences of sudden rupture and displacement have a significant impact on their subjective experience of being in America and provide a platform from which they engage the American public sphere. However, they manifest similar kinds of civic activities as the Indian economic migrants, despite the linguistic, educational, and economic advantages of members of the latter group. Thus, the category of refugee is important for some dimensions of analysis and has some subjective characteristics for those who have lived this experience, but being a refugee does not permanently differentiate some populations from others. All migrants, we concluded, experience a form of displacement, and all strive toward emplacement in the country to which they have moved.

It is also worth commenting on the challenges of this project in terms of a collaborative and "synchronized" methodology, something with which anthropologists are not always comfortable. We designed the research instruments for this project together – using the same interview schedules and short surveys. However, as all anthropologists know, fieldwork is unpredictable and can take you in directions that you would never have anticipated. Events happened in the Vietnamese community for which there were no counterparts in the Indian community and vice versa. When we came together, we had to spend a good deal of time talking about what we had found; sometimes this suggested new directions of inquiry for one of us in order to collect potentially comparable data; sometimes the absence of comparable data revealed a unique point of distinction for one of these populations and hence opened avenues of explanation. One of the greatest challenges was to write up this project with a single voice, the result being our book *Civic Engagements* (Brettell and Reed-Danahay 2012). Once we had decided on the broad parameters (chapter outlines), we had to see what we each had in our data that could be brought to bear on the central questions we were posing. This book took much longer to complete than any book that either of us has written on our own. And yet, the collaboration itself probably meant that we could be more thorough in our field research on each population because we were two ethnographers in the field, not one.

Conclusion

In her essay "Comparisons: Possible and Impossible," Sally Falk Moore (2005) observes that anthropologists have adopted many different approaches to comparison, each of which yields its own type of understanding. In this chapter I have offered three examples of different approaches to comparison in my own anthropological and historical anthropological projects. These comparisons have operated at different scales of analysis from national and regional contexts to two different immigrant populations in a single urban context. In two cases, the comparative framing was primarily invoked at the stage of analysis, while in the third it was built into a collaborative methodology from the beginning. The comparisons, in my view, have opened up possibilities for explanatory insights, but they also bring with them challenges because one often has to rely on the work of others drawn from contexts with which one is less familiar.[14] Sometimes it is necessary to sacrifice detail, and as a consequence one might be opening oneself up to criticism because we cannot always speak with the same degree of "ethnographic authority" about the two bodies of data that we might be juxtaposing for purposes of comparative insight. Perhaps one solution for anthropologists is to engage in more collaborative projects (such as the last one I described) involving parallel field research: projects where comparison is inherent in the methodology.

I have no crystal ball regarding the future of comparison in the anthropological enterprise. I can only observe that despite the challenges, and despite the anathema that comparison is to some members of the anthropological community, I believe it is a fundamental dimension of what we do and how we think and that as we move forward, we choose wisely regarding what we are comparing and why in relation to critical questions regarding the human experience, past, present, and future. In other words, there is much to be gained from careful and purposeful comparison. It helps to make similarities and differences more visible and hence deepens and extends our understanding of critical social and cultural processes; it highlights the significance of context in explanation; and it addresses (although it might not fully resolve) the tension between the general and the particular, a tension that has been fundamental to anthropology throughout its history.

Notes

1 More recently, a number of scholars, myself included (Brettell 1981, 2003, 2011), have focused on different urban contexts as these might impact the settlement and processes of inclusion/exclusion of migrants (Sanjek 1998; Mollenkopf 1999; Foner 2000; Stepick et al. 2003; Hanley et al. 2008; Price and Benton-Short 2008; Singer et al. 2008; Foner et al. 2014). In their edited volume *Locating Migration: Rescaling Cities and Migrants*, Çağlar and Glick Schiller (2011, 2–3) formulate a comparative theory of locality, arguing that "cities differ in how they participate in and are affected by… global trends [and hence] the impact of migration varies and must be assessed in relationship to specific localities. Consequently, to examine the relationship between migrants and cities is to think comparatively within the intersection of migration and urban studies." Glick Schiller and Çağlar describe their book as an effort at developing a comparative method (à la the historian Charles Tilly) that is "variation-finding" in "comparing big structures and large processes."

2 See their further discussion in Alba and Foner (2015).

3 Specifically, Foner (2015, 886) observes that comparison "can cast differences into sharper relief and put familiar issues in a new light," thereby increasing "the visibility of processes and structures in one society by highlighting differences and similarities with another."

4 As discussed by Richard Handler in this volume, this back and forth process was characteristic of the work of Dorothy Lee.

5 This distinction between a priori and a posteriori deployments of comparison is made by Gingrich (2012).

6 I pursued NIH-funded postdoctoral training in historical demography at the University of Texas at Austin. Prior to this study, I had worked on contemporary Portuguese immigrants in two different urban contexts: Toronto, Canada and Paris, France. I specifically chose to follow the research in Toronto with that in Paris because I hypothesized that, in the latter context, there might be more back and forth movement between Portugal and the city of destination. I published one essay that was a comparison of these two cities as receiving areas for immigrants (Brettell 1981).

7 The proportion of the total number of baptisms that involved illegitimate children rose from 6.5 percent in the 1840s to 11.3 percent in the 1860s to 15 percent in the 1870s; it dropped to 14 percent in the 1890s and to 13 percent in the 1900s. By the 1940s, it was down to 3.6 percent and by the 1960s down to 1.5 percent. For national-level discussion of these rates, see Livi Bacci (1971).

8 See Brettell (2015a) for a discussion of the honor and shame debate in the Mediterranean context.

9 Clearly, the issue of culture areas is equally controversial within anthropology. However, the association here is useful for broad-based thinking. See Brettell (2015a) for a discussion of culture areas within the broader framework of associations between anthropology and geography.

10 The argument in the chapter of my book on this topic is layered and complex. I am simplifying here in order to address one mode and scale of comparative consciousness in particular.

11 For another example of a comparison that focuses on the relationship between inheritance practices and rural out-migration, see William Douglass's (1971) classic article on two villages in Spain.

12 Recently, popular films such as *Philomena* have drawn attention to convent homes for unwed mothers and the international adoptions of illegitimate Irish children. In Portugal, as in other parts of Europe, there were foundling homes where children were abandoned (Brettell and Feijo 1989). Bringing these practices and institutions into comparative perspective might also be informative in relation to rates of out-of-wedlock births and differences in the way these children were treated within broader "moral contexts."

13 Even as late as 1964, sociologist and demographer Leon Bouvier (1964) described the low level of educational and occupational achievement of Franco-Americans living in the New England area.

14 Eric Wolf (1982, 13) points to the "limitations of time and energy in the field [that] dictate limitations in the number and locations of possible observations and interviews." Although he views these limitations as constraints on the development of explanatory theory, they can also be viewed as constraints on the formulation of comparisons that might reveal explanations.

References

Abu-Lughod, Lila. 1991. "Writing against Culture." In *Recapturing Anthropology: Working in the Present*, edited by Richard G. Fox, 137–54. Santa Fe, NM: School of American Research Press.

Alba, Richard, and Nancy Foner. 2014. "Comparing Immigrant Integration in North America and Western Europe: How Much Do Grand Narratives Tell Us?" *International Migration Review Supplement* 48: 263–91.

Alba, Richard, and Nancy Foner. 2015. *Strangers No More: Immigration and the Challenges of Integration in North America and Western Europe*. Princeton, NJ: Princeton University Press.

Arensberg, Conrad M. 1963. "The Old World Peoples: The Place of European Cultures in World Ethnography." *Anthropological Quarterly* 36 (3): 75–99.

Bouvier, Leon. 1964. "La Stratification Sociale du Groupe Ethique Canadien Français aux États Unis." *Recherches Sociologiques* 5 (3): 371–79.

Brault, Gérard. 1986. *The French Canadian Heritage in New England*. Hanover: University Press of New England.

Brettell, Caroline B. 1981. "Is the Ethnic Community Inevitable? A Comparison of the Settlement Patterns of Portuguese Immigrants in Toronto and Paris." *Journal of Ethnic Studies* 9 (3): 1–17 [reprinted in Brettell, Caroline B. 2003. *Anthropology and Migration: Essays on Transnationalism, Ethnicity, and Identity*. Walnut Creek, CA: Altamira Press].

Brettell, Caroline B. 1986. *Men Who Migrate, Women Who Wait: Population and History in a Portuguese Parish*. Princeton, NJ: Princeton University Press.

Brettell, Caroline B. 2003. "Bringing the City Back In: Cities as Contexts for Immigrant Incorporation." In *American Arrivals: Anthropology Engages the New Immigration*, edited by Nancy Foner, 163–95. Santa Fe, NM: School of American Research Press.

Brettell, Caroline. 2009. "Anthropology, Migration, and Comparative Consciousness." *New Literary History* 40 (3): 649–71 [reprinted in Felski, Rita, and Susan Stanford Friedman, eds. 2013. *Comparison: Theories, Approaches, Uses*. Baltimore, MD: Johns Hopkins University Press].

Brettell, Caroline B. 2011. "Scalar Positioning and Immigrant Organizations: Asian Indians and the Dynamics of Place." In *Locating Migration: Rescaling Cities and Migrants,* edited by Nina Glick Schiller and Ayşe Çağlar, 104–22. Ithaca, NY: Cornell University Press.

Brettell, Caroline B. 2015a. *Anthropological Conversations: Talking Culture Across Disciplines*. Lanham, MD: Rowman and Littlefield.

Brettell, Caroline B. 2015b. *Following Father Chiniquy: Immigration, Religious Schism, and Social Change in Nineteenth Century Illinois*. Carbondale, IL: Southern Illinois University Press.

Brettell, Caroline B., and Rui Feijo. 1989. "The Roda of Viana do Castelo in the 19th Century: Public Welfare and Family Strategies." *Cadernos Vianenses* 12: 217–69 [reprinted as "Foundlings in Nineteenth-Century Northwestern Portugal: Public Welfare and Family Strategies." In *Actes de Colloque International, "Enfance Abandonnée et Société en Europe, XIV–XX siècle"*, École Française de Rome, 1991, 273–300].

Brettell, Caroline B., and Deborah Reed-Danahay. 2012. *Civic Engagements: The Citizenship Practices of Indian and Vietnamese Immigrants*. Stanford, CA: Stanford University Press.

Çağlar, Ayşe, and Nina Glick Schiller. 2011. "Introduction: Migrants and Cities." In *Locating Migration: Rescaling Cities and Migrants*, edited by Nina Glick Schiller and Ayşe Çağlar, 1–19. Ithaca, NY: Cornell University Press.

Colson, Elizabeth. 2003. "Forced Migration and the Anthropological Response." *Journal of Refugee Studies* 16 (1): 1–18.

Descamps, Paul. 1935. *Portugal: La Vie Sociale Actuelle*. Paris: Firmin-Didot.

Diner, Hasia. 1983. *Erin's Daughters in America: Irish Women in the Nineteenth Century*. Baltimore, MD: Johns Hopkins University Press.

Douglass, William A. 1971. "Rural Exodus in Two Spanish Basque Villages: A Cultural Explanation." *American Anthropologist* 73 (5): 1100–14.

DuBois, Cora. 1980. "Some Anthropological Hindsights." *Annual Review of Anthropology* 9: 1–13.

Ellen, Roy. 2010. "Theories in Anthropology and 'Anthropological Theory'." *Journal of the Royal Anthropological Institute* 16 (2): 387–404.

Foner, Nancy. 1987. "Introduction: New Immigrants and Changing Patterns in New York City." In *New Immigrants in New York*, edited by Nancy Foner, 1–33. New York: Columbia University Press.

Foner, Nancy. 2000. *From Ellis Island to JFK: New York's Two Great Waves of Immigration*. New Haven, CT: Yale University Press.

Foner, Nancy. 2003. *American Arrivals: Anthropology Engages the New Immigration*. Santa Fe, NM: School of American Research Press.

Foner, Nancy. 2010. "How Exceptional is New York? Migration and Multiculturalism in the Empire City." In *Anthropology of Migration and Multiculturalism: New Directions*, edited by Steven Vertovec, 39–63. New York and London: Routledge.

Foner, Nancy. 2015. "Is Islam in Western Europe Like Race in the United States?" *Sociological Forum* 30 (4): 885–99.

Foner, Nancy, Jan Rath, Jan Willem Duyvendak, and Rogier van Reekum, eds. 2014. *New York and Amsterdam: Immigration and the New Urban Landscape*. New York: New York University Press.

Fox, Richard G., and Andre Gingrich. 2002. "Introduction." In *Anthropology, by Comparison*, edited by Andre Gingrich and Richard G. Fox, 1–24. London and New York: Routledge.

Gingrich, Andre. 2012. "Comparative Methods in Social Anthropology Today." In *The Sage Handbook of Social Anthropology*, edited by Richard Fardon et al., 211–22. London: Sage.

Glick Schiller, Nina, and Ayşe Çağlar, eds. 2011. *Locating Migration: Rescaling Cities and Migrants*. Ithaca, NY: Cornell University Press.

Gluckman, Max. 1960. "Tribalism in Modern British Central Africa." *Cahiers d'Etudes Africanes* 1 (1): 55–70.

Gregor, Thomas A., and Donald Tuzin. 2001. "Comparing Gender in Amazonia and Melanesia: A Theoretical Orientation." In *Gender in Amazonia and Melanesia: An Exploration of the Comparative Method*, edited by Thomas A. Gregor and Donald Tuzin, 1–16. Berkeley: University of California Press.

Hamon, Edmond. 1891. *Les Canadiens-Français de la Nouvelle-Angleterre*. Québec: Hardy.

Hanley, Lisa M., Blair A. Ruble, and Allison M. Garland, eds. 2008. *Immigration and Integration in Urban Communities: Renegotiating the City.* Washington, DC and Baltimore, MD: Woodrow Wilson Center Press and The Johns Hopkins University Press.

Kenny, Michael. 1963. "Europe: The Atlantic Fringe." *Anthropological Quarterly* 36 (3): 100–19.

Kertzer, David I. 1984. *Family Life in Central Italy, 1880–1910.* New Brunswick, NJ: Rutgers University Press.

Kingston, William. 1845. *Lusitanian Sketches of the Pen and Pencil.* London: John W. Parker, West Strand.

Knodel, John. 1974. *The Decline of Fertility in Germany, 1871–1939.* Princeton, NJ: Princeton University Press.

Lamarre, Jean. 2003. *The French Canadians of Michigan: Their Contribution to the Development of the Saginaw Valley and the Keweenam Peninsula, 1840–1914.* Detroit, MI: Wayne State University Press.

Larkin, Emmet. 1972. "The Devotional Revolution in Ireland, 1850–1875." *American Historical Review* 77 (3): 625–52.

Laslett, Peter. 1965. *The World We Have Lost.* London: Methuen.

Laslett, Peter, and Richard Wall, eds. 1972. *Household and Family in Past Time.* Cambridge: Cambridge University Press.

Lederman, Rena. 1998. "Globalization and the Future of Culture Areas: Melanesianist Anthropology in Transition." *Annual Review of Anthropology* 27: 427–49.

Livi Bacci, Massimo. 1971. *A Century of Portuguese Fertility.* Princeton, NJ: Princeton University Press.

Louder, Dean R., and Eric Waddell, eds. 1983. *Du Continent Perdue à l'Archipel Retrouvé: Le Québec et l'Amérique Français.* Québec: Presses de l'Université Laval.

Mageean, Deirdre. 1997. "To Be Matched or to Move: Irish Women's Prospects in Munster." In *Peasant Maids, City Women: From the European Countryside to Urban America*, edited by Christiane Harzig, 57–98. Ithaca, NY: Cornell University Press.

Malkki, Liisa. 1995. "Refugees and Exile: From 'Refugee Studies' to the National Order of Things." *Annual Review of Anthropology* 24: 495–523.

Marcus, George. 2008. "Postscript: Developments in US Anthropology since the 1980s, a Supplement." *In Other People's Anthropologies: Ethnographic Practice on the Margins*, edited by Aleksandar Boskovic, 199–214. Oxford: Bergahn Books Inc.

Mayer, Philip. 1962. "Migrancy and the Study of Africans in Towns." *American Anthropologist* 64 (3): 576–92.

Mitchell, J. Clyde. 1960. "The Anthropological Study of Urban Communities." *African Studies* 19 (3): 169–72.

Mollenkopf, John H. 1999. "Urban Political Conflicts and Alliances: New York and Los Angeles Compared." In *The Handbook of International Migration: The American Experience*, edited by Charles Hirschman, Philip Kasinitz, and Josh DeWind, 412–22. New York: Russell Sage Foundation.

Moore, Sally Falk. 2005. "Comparisons: Possible and Impossible." *Annual Review of Anthropology* 34: 1–11.

Nolan, Janet A. 1989. *Ourselves Alone: Women's Emigration from Ireland, 1885–1920.* Lexington: University of Kentucky Press.

Price, Mari, and Lisa Benton-Short, eds. 2008. *Migrants to the Metropolis: The Rise of Immigrant Gateways*. Syracuse, NY: Syracuse University Press.

Richard, Mark Paul. 2009. "'This Is Not a Catholic Nation': The Ku Klux Klan Confronts Franco-Americans in Maine." *The New England Quarterly* 82 (2): 285–303.

Roby, Yves, and Yves Frenette. 2012. "L'Émigration Canadienne-Française vers la Nouvelle-Angleterre, 1840–1930." In *La Francophonie Nord-américaine*, edited by Yves Frenette, Étienne Rivard, and Marc St.-Hilaire, 123–32. Québec: Presses de l'Université Laval.

Sanjek, Roger. 1998. *The Future of Us All: Race and Neighborhood Politics in New York City*. Ithaca, NY: Cornell University Press.

Schneider, Jane. 1971. "Of Vigilance of Virgins: Honor, Shame, and Access to Resources in Mediterranean Societies." *Ethnology* 10 (1): 1–24.

Schneider, Jane C., and Peter T. Schneider. 1996. *Festival of the Poor: Fertility Decline and the Ideology of Class in Sicily, 1860–1980*. Tucson: University of Arizona Press.

Singer, Audrey, Susan Hardwick, and Caroline Brettell, eds. 2008. *Twenty-First Century Gateways: Immigrant Incorporation in Suburbia*. Washington, DC: The Brookings Institution Press.

Sorrell, Richard. 1981. "The Survivance of French Canadians in New England 1865–1930: History, Geography and Demography as Destiny." *Ethnic and Racial Studies* 4 (1): 91–109.

Stepick, Alex, Guillermo Grenier, Max Castro, and Marvin Dunn. 2003. *This Land Is Our Land: Immigrants and Power in Miami*. Berkeley: University of California Press.

Sundbärg, Gustav. 1908. *Aperçus Statistiques Internationaux*. Stockholm: Imprimerie Royale.

Wade, Mason. 1950. "The French Parish and Survivance in Nineteenth-Century New England." *Catholic Historical Review* 36 (2): 136–89.

Wolf, Eric. 1964. *Anthropology*. Englewood Cliffs, NJ: Prentice Hall.

Wright, Carroll D. 1881. *12th Annual Report of the Bureau of Statistics of Labor*. Boston, MA: Rand Avery.

2 Comparing Tangerines

Dorothy Lee and the Search for an Authentic Individualism

Richard Handler

One Friday evening in February 2015, I found myself in the bar of a hotel in Williamsburg, Virginia, where the scholarly meeting I was attending was being held. A jazz quartet was playing in one corner of the very large, open room where perhaps a hundred people clustered in small groups, chatting and mostly not listening to the music. The music was surprisingly good. The band's gig was a long-standing one, and every Friday night, some version of the group was put together, I learned, based on the availability of local musicians.

That night, the quartet was made up of an alto saxophonist, a guitarist, a bassist, and a drummer. That combination of instruments and musicians – suitably amplified acoustic guitar and double bass and an extremely skillful drummer who knew how to swing quietly – made for an open, airy sound, a sound aided by the acoustics of the room and not overwhelmed by an audience that, while inattentive, was not loud. And the alto saxophonist, who, in that combination of instruments, was responsible for playing all the melodies, had both a light tone and the skill to improvise long lines supplely and fleetly.

There was a pillar directly in front of the band's space in the corner of the room, and I took up a station there, leaning against it (as if it could hide me). I listened carefully to the band for about an hour, talking occasionally to the saxophonist, who saw that I understood what they were doing. They often took several minutes to negotiate among themselves to choose their next song, and so at last I asked them if I could make a request, for "Tangerine."[1] They talked for a moment and agreed and then conferred about the proper tempo. I told the saxophonist, who was calling up the tune from the "fake book" on his electronic reader, that the great alto player Paul Desmond had recorded a wonderful version of "Tangerine." He was only vaguely familiar with the tune, but as he scanned the chart, he told me that he'd give it "the old college try."

Thanks are due to Daniel Segal, Susan Seymour, and Pauline Turner Strong, who provided extensive comments on the first draft of this chapter; the editors of this volume, Edward Lowe and Michael Schnegg, who helped me improve the chapter at each stage of its development; and the participants at the original conference, all of whom together created thoughtful discussions of each chapter and of the overall project.

Alas, the old college try did not produce good jazz. These were skilled artists capable of making excellent jazz, but despite their professional confidence in being able to use the skeletal "charts" provided in their fake books to play anything, they apparently didn't have enough experience with "Tangerine" to understand its subtleties. Trying to improvise over its tricky chord changes, they got lost. Their jazz didn't cohere.[2]

To my surprise, however, I found that as I listened to, and later thought about, their failed attempt, I learned quite a bit – about both the structure of "Tangerine" and the brilliance of Desmond's version of it. The unsuccessful attempt turned out to be instructive comparatively. Moreover, it was instructive not only musically but also anthropologically, for it led me to consider the question of explicit value judgments in cross-cultural comparisons.

What Is a Bad Version?

Anthropologists' famed, or notorious, tolerance for cultural diversity and for the related concept of cultural relativism has always made it difficult for us to criticize a cultural performance, interpretation, or pattern as "bad" – whatever that might mean. To pronounce something bad is, of course, to make a value judgment, and anthropologists think of themselves as scientific or objective or neutral students of human values, not as judges of them.[3]

We of course recognize that cultural insiders make value judgments all the time (Lambek 2015, 7–10); indeed, if cultures are patterns of values, and if insiders live those values intuitively, then living itself must mean implementing those values and responding to others' attempts to implement them – attempts that will and must be recognized, by insiders, as more or less successful. Perhaps insiders don't respond to all, or even most, bad instantiations of a "point in the pattern" of a value system (Sapir 1925, 46). They tolerate all sorts of mistakes. But those that people consider important can trigger protest, correction, scorn, or even violence.

These everyday value judgments are always comparative: they depend on measuring particular acts and performances against the insider's intuitive understanding of what is good, true, or correct. And as Durkheim pointed out long ago, negative value judgments reinforce the social order. In Durkheimian social theory, shared values (whatever their content) constitute a social order, since people who uphold them act in unison or in an "integrated" fashion. When people's actions violate norms, society's sanctions not only serve to bring them back in line but also highlight, and thereby reinforce, the ideal (Durkheim 1933[1893], 80–82).

Anthropological theories that privilege social or cultural integration have fallen out of fashion in the past three decades. In the contemporary world, clear boundaries separating nation-states, cultures, or communities seem increasingly difficult to find, as does cultural integration based on consensus. With respect to the present issue of negative value judgments, people have pointed out that there are always competing versions of the valued, the good, in any social group and that one person's "bad" might be another's acceptable alternative or preferred certainty. Whatever it is, beyond naked force and bureaucratic routine, that holds people together in a group with some self-consciousness of being a group, absolute consensus in making value judgments is not, apparently, the primary factor.

If we anthropologists have changed our tune about the nature of the relationship between values and sociality, we have also, to some extent, changed our tune about value judgments as part of anthropological work. George Marcus and Michael Fisher's *Anthropology as Cultural Critique* was a key document in the fin-de-siècle shift from an "objective" to a "critical" anthropology. Taking the pulse of the discipline in 1986, they thought that insecurity concerning the veracity of ethnographic representation, coupled with political doubts engendered by postwar postcolonialism, was making anthropologists more willing to use their work in explicitly critical ways. The object of anthropological critique was more often "us" than "them," but Marcus and Fisher wanted to reform the critical impulse to make it less romanticized, less dualistic, and more contextualized in terms of an interconnected global world in which "we" are not disconnected from "them," nor "they" from "us."

They acknowledged and drew upon the long tradition of cultural critique within Boasian anthropology, taking Margaret Mead as the prototypical figure. But they pointed out that in this tradition, people such as Mead, Ruth Benedict, and Edward Sapir used cultural juxtaposition, contrast, or comparison grounded in deep study of other places to make critical (often satirical) jabs at features of American life that they knew intuitively, not on the basis of ethnographic study. In other words, these comparisons were methodologically unbalanced, since the two sides of the comparison were unequally and differently known. This sometimes led, in their estimation, to "simplistic better-worse judgments about two cultural situations being juxtaposed" (Marcus and Fisher 1986, 139; see also Starr 2016).

And yet, without denying the relevance of the larger argument of Marcus and Fisher, it is just such better-worse judgments that interest me here. People compare tangerines all the time. They make value judgments. Those judgments are informed by cultural knowledge that can be intuitive and embodied (like a musician's expertise) or verbally explicit (like the rules of an etiquette manual), or both together, as people draw on such knowledge, often without realizing it, to make sense, comparatively, of experiences and objects in daily life. In the remainder of this chapter, I want to examine the work of a forgotten Boasian, Dorothy Lee, née Dorothy Demetracopoulos, who wrote a number of essays in which she compared tangerines – which is to say, two instantiations of the same species, individualism – to pass judgment on her own world.

Dorothy Demetracopoulos Lee

Dorothy Demetracopoulos was born in Constantinople in 1905; her father was a pastor there in a Greek Evangelical church. Educated in an American school run by missionaries, she won a scholarship to Vassar College and from there went on to the University of California at Berkeley, where she earned her PhD in anthropology in 1931 (Ehrenreich 1976). She did fieldwork among Wintu people in California and published a number of technical articles on Wintu grammar, language, and culture.

Her marriage to Otis Lee in 1933 led to her return to Vassar, when Otis was appointed a professor of philosophy there in 1938. Dorothy became a lecturer of anthropology at Vassar in 1939, but Otis died suddenly in 1948, and she decided to leave Vassar in 1953 to teach at the Merrill-Palmer School in Detroit. The move, which one of her daughters attributed to her need to find a more lucrative position than the one she held at Vassar (Seymour 2015, 96), "was apparently encouraged and supported by her friend Margaret Mead, although many of her other colleagues were appalled" (Ehrenreich 1976, ix). Lee had worked with Mead on a postwar UNESCO project, writing "a large part of the '*Manual of Technological Change in Mental Health: Cultural Patterns and Technical Change*', edited by Margaret Mead."[4] And one can imagine that Mead's war work and her interest in applied anthropology led her to encourage Lee to take up the Detroit position, where she was "increasingly more oriented toward practical problems and the home economics movement" (Ehrenreich 1976, ix).

In 1959, Lee went to Harvard at the invitation of the sociologist David Riesman to participate in the freshman seminar program. But two years later, she left to work with Edmund Carpenter at San Fernando State College. The rest of her career, Ehrenreich notes, "was spent on the periphery of mainstream anthropology. She moved about the country as a lecturer, consultant, workshop teacher and visiting scholar at such places as Iowa State, Oklahoma State, Duquesne, and Immaculate Heart College in Los Angeles. Her affiliations were ... with departments of home economics and not anthropology" (1976, ix–x).

As Ehrenreich suggests, Lee's peripatetic career can be explained in part by her own account of her dismay at the success of her first book, *Freedom and Culture* (1959), which went through six printings in seven years. In the four-page introduction to her second book, *Valuing the Self*, published in 1976, the year after her death, she described the "horror and guilt" she experienced when she learned that her essays, in use in "undergraduate courses," were taken by students as "*the* truth":

> I was the author, I gave the authoritative statement. I could not even argue with them because they answered me back from the authority of my book. I felt that I had dumped a load of gravel on new, thin, weak, gloriously alive grass.... I had killed. I vowed that I would never publish a collection of papers again. (Lee 1976, 2)

Lee went on to describe her subsequent refusal to write and then her refusal to give lectures. "I was trying," she explained, "to reach the point where I could help people whose thinking and sensing had not been honored and had been substituted [for] by the 'correct' ideas and perceptions of their teachers and textbooks" (1976, 2). She eventually found what she was looking for in seminars with "young adults and middle-aged students" who were "full of their own responses." Those seminars made her realize that as a teacher, she was "opening alternatives, not laying down dogma." And finally, she "decided to publish [a] small selection" of essays on the topic of "community and autonomy" (1976, 3).

Searching for a Satisfactory Individualism

Ehrenreich, who talked to some of Lee's family and friends, concluded that Lee "loved anthropology with a passion, but she thought of herself first as a mother, family member and friend" (1976, xi). Indeed, in an essay on "Personal Significance and Group Structure," she implied that her decision to leave Vassar for the Merrill-Palmer School was motivated in part by her worries about raising her children after the death of her husband. Otis and Dorothy "shared" a belief "that the self should never be conceived as an isolate, nor as the focus of the universe, but rather that it should be defined as a social self. We valued society." And apparently they succeeded in creating a family life based on that principle, as their children, according to Dorothy, "were completely involved" in family life and moved outward from it to make individual friendships. But these children rejected the organized groups, like "the Scouts," that are so central to US social organization, and "this reluctance to see meaning in organized groups ... seemed completely un-American" to her (1957, 16).

While her husband, who "came from generations of Americans," was alive, Lee wrote, she "did not worry about this."[5] But after his death, she feared that her children would be caught between the "family-centered" Greek culture that was congenial to her and a wider US culture that she could not help them grow into. It is almost as if the culture that was intuitive for her, and which she could convey unselfconsciously to her children, was (in her conscious estimation) useless to her children, while she felt herself incapable of teaching them the culture they needed to know, since she herself knew it only imperfectly – by the book, as it were, like the musicians who could read the chart for "Tangerine" but couldn't play it fluently. "I was afraid," she wrote, "that, falling between two stools, my children would grow into isolated individuals, cut off from all social nourishment." And so, she moved the family to Detroit, "where group awareness and participation was being implemented at all levels in the schools" (Lee 1957, 16).

In Detroit, however, the Lee family did not find what it was looking for. Her children were "unhappy at school," but not until she attended a parents' open night did Lee come to understand why. Visiting two of her children's rooms, the fourth and seventh grades, she found group art projects on display in which each child's individual work had been sacrificed for the sake of a standardized product. In a war scene from ancient Egypt, she could not recognize the horses her son, she was told, had drawn. The horses he drew on his own were "full of straining movement and savage life," but the school horses were "placid" and "lifeless." The teacher explained to her that her "son had not been allowed to paint his own unique horses; they were too different. Since this was a group project, [the teacher explained], uniformity was essential" (Lee 1957, 17). Lee found a similar pattern in the projects of her other children.

The social pattern is, of course, conformity, and in the 1950s, this was a major concern of US social scientists, not least of whom was Riesman, the author of one of the most celebrated books on the topic, *The Lonely Crowd* (1950). Riesman's analysis of the demise of an "inner-directed" national character in the United States and the rise of "other-directedness," that is, conformity, set the tone of debates about freedom and authority during the Cold War. And if Riesman valued, above all, "a commitment to pursue one's own way" (Gitlin 2002), the rising virulence of anticommunism in US politics, epitomized in the House Un-American Activities Committee, demonstrated that the forces backing conformity were powerful, to say the least. It is thus understandable that Lee worried that she would produce un-American children.

As it was explicated in books such as *The Lonely Crowd*, the contrast between autonomous motivation and conformity was drawn from a perspective situated within the cultural pattern of US individualism. At issue is a comparison between a good individualism and a bad one. As we shall see, like Riesman and his crowd, Lee drew on this US model to some extent. But because she had immersed herself in the anthropological study of many Native American cultures, her work took her well beyond the confines of US individualism. Studying, comparatively, the Wintu, Dakota, Hopi, Navaho, and other peoples – through fieldwork, grammatical analysis, and extensive reading – Lee found the authentic individualism she was seeking, cultural patterns in which the self was strengthened and liberated not in opposition to, but through its connection with, a vital social order.

The urtext for the analysis of modern individualism is Alexis de Tocqueville's *Democracy in America* (1835–40). Unlike most subsequent analyses of individualism and US culture, Tocqueville compared not good and bad individualisms – autonomy and conformity – but individualism and hierarchy. Writing just after the French Revolution, and schooled in the aristocratic and hierarchical ways of the old order (as Lee had been in traditional Greek ways), Tocqueville could stand apart from the emergent individualistic social order of American democracy and compare it to what he called "aristocracy," that is, to a way of life that did not enshrine the individual person as a primary source of value. While this is not the place for a more complete discussion of Tocqueville's comparative project (see Handler 2005c), two of his most celebrated observations will be useful for us now.

First is Tocqueville's understanding of conformity as a structural entailment of individualism – which is to say, modern individualism as a structure of values and as a social structure gives rise to conformity, which is, thus, central to the system and not, as the 1950s social critics thought, a social pathology. As Tocqueville explained, while individualism celebrates each person as free and equal, it also celebrates each as the equivalent of all the others. Moreover, despite each individual's belief in the primacy of selfhood, each also knows that all other individuals are similarly empowered – knowledge that leads, paradoxically, to the recognition of one's own insignificance. And feelings of insignificance lead, in turn, to conformity as a kind of natural social form of individualism – for, as Tocqueville put it, "at periods of equality men have no faith in one another, by reason of their common resemblance; but this very resemblance gives them almost unbounded confidence in the judgment of the public; for it would seem probable that, as they are all endowed with equal means of judging, the greater truth should go with the greater number" (1840, 11). Conformity to "public opinion" therefore took on an outsized role in the organization of the democratic societies Tocqueville observed in North America to a degree that his counterparts in aristocratic France could not have imagined.

Thus, Tocqueville shows us that conformity and individualism, at least as he observed them in North America, are inseparable, although it takes a comparison to a social formation beyond individualism (like medieval European hierarchy) to comprehend that. And whereas critics inside modern societies dislike conformity, they are happy to celebrate another feature of these societies that Tocqueville stressed: the proliferation of voluntary associations or interest groups. Again, Tocqueville understood the significance of these groups comparatively, starting from their absence from aristocratic societies. In an aristocracy, there was little of what we call social mobility; rather, people were bound together in permanent groups, in ascribed roles that subordinated them to the lord of the manor, the aristocracy, the church hierarchy, and the monarch. There were thus individuals in positions of authority who could command their subordinates to participate in necessary social projects. "Every wealthy and powerful citizen," Tocqueville wrote, "constitutes the head of a permanent and compulsory association, composed of all those who are dependent upon him or whom he makes subservient to the execution of his designs" (1840, 115).

By contrast, in modern mass societies, individuals are disassociated, as it were, and weak – "independent and feeble," in Tocqueville's words. But they "learn voluntarily to help one another" (1840, 115). To accomplish a specific task or reach a common goal, they band together. We call such associations interest groups because individuals aggregate themselves into groups based on consciously chosen purposes or interests: citizens sign a petition to block the construction of a highway, or they join a temperance association to refrain from drinking alcoholic beverages. Tocqueville was at first mystified by US temperance groups, wondering why a person who objected to "spirituous liquors" could not be contented with "drinking water by their own firesides" (1840, 118). But he at last understood, he tells us, that to join an association was a structural imperative of individualism: sociality itself was organized in this way.

Lee apparently tried to appreciate voluntary associations as important sites for her children's training for US citizenship, but she was put off by the conformity that she found they required. A voluntary association in the form of an interest group is composed of individuals who have joined it freely to pursue what they understand as their specific interests. But the groups Lee's children experienced – age-graded classrooms and extracurricular clubs – were organized by bureaucratic authorities to engage all participants in the same tasks, tasks chosen by others and not by the children. Worse, in such groups, children's success in accomplishing the set tasks was evaluated by others, according to standards imposed on, not developed by, the participants.

Lee gave her fullest critique of such classrooms in an essay on "autonomous motivation," describing her son's ninth-grade experience:

> He went to his school with a passion for mathematics. He was filled with an urgent inquiry into logic and values and metaphysics.... But the school could not recognize his urgency, and felt responsible to protect him against the enormity of his own appetite for knowledge and exploration.... So they stopped his immoderate appetite by feeding him what was moderate and good for him, what was appropriate for a boy of his age. (1961, 19–20)

The school, in short, stifled the boy's vigorous quest for knowledge and experience, just as Lee felt she did, years later, by publishing a book her student readers took as authoritative. And although none of her published essays dwell on US conformity and the social institutions that enforce it, those phenomena constituted the comparative starting point, the bad example, in her search for an authentic individualism.

Wintu Ontology

Lee wrote an account of Greek culture for Mead's UNESCO volume on cultural patterns and technical change. The focus was on what we would today call "development": how could people conditioned by traditional Greek culture be encouraged to participate in the postwar modern world economy? Lee began with Greek *philotimo*, which she translated as self-esteem and which she discovered in embodied practices, folk aphorisms, and the rationalizations individuals used to explain their behavior. But *philotimo* is not congruent with the US variety of individualism (with its equal, isolated units), since, as Lee went on to show, it is connected through the person's body to the person's family. Ultimately, she wrote, personal responsibility is "family responsibility" (in Mead 1953, 149), and Greek people's fierce independence, as individuals and as a nation, could not be easily adapted for impersonal, bureaucratic forms of economic and political organization. Modern social forms require conceptually isolated individuals, and Greek sociality did not value individuals abstracted from particular social (local and familial) contexts.

Greek individualism, as described by Lee, met the standard she and her husband set for their family life, according to which the social was to be valued as much as the individual. But her analysis of Greek individualism was formulated long after her professional formation in Boasian anthropology and linguistics at Berkeley. And her writings on Wintu, and later on other Indian peoples, have a much greater comparative "punch" than the piece on Greek culture. The Wintu seem to have stimulated her analysis of individualism far beyond what her Greek experience taught her. Indeed, we could say that her work with Native American cultures entailed a properly anthropological approach to comparison, a self-consciously *disciplined* confrontation, through various forms of study, with cultures beyond those that the anthropologist intuitively understood.

In the introduction to her first book, Lee described her interpretive method. An anthropologist's "most difficult work," she wrote, "is to make his way into another codification of reality." Despite the brevity of the "cultural descriptions" conveyed by her essays, each, she asserted, "represents the work of years." To carry out each study – both those based on her own fieldwork and those based on the published reports of other experts – she "paid attention even to apparently irrelevant detail." "Noticing the obscure or seemingly trite or obvious," she went "back and forth" in her reading "until nothing remained queer anymore" (Lee 1959, 3).

Lee's description of her methodology is strikingly similar to that of Ruth Benedict, a colleague Lee greatly admired (see Lee 1949). In the introduction to *The Chrysanthemum and the Sword*, her study of Japanese culture, Benedict had described anthropology's "techniques" for the comparative study of difference, particularly the apparently trivial differences of "commonplace" customary behavior in different societies. The more "bizarre" a commonplace "act or ... opinion" appeared to her, she wrote, "the more I therefore assumed that there existed somewhere in Japanese life some ordinary conditioning of such strangeness" (1946, 11).

These back-and-forth interpretive techniques were (and are) profoundly comparative, since that which sticks out as bizarre to the anthropologist is bizarre first of all in contrast to her own culture. And, starting from that initial moment of contrast, the anthropologist reads back and forth *within* the culture under study to contextualize details vis-à-vis one another until their patterning becomes apparent to the analyst. And seeing a pattern, it then becomes possible for the anthropologist to interpret significance or meaning. As Benedict put it, "I started from the premise that the most isolated bits of behavior have some systematic relation to each other. I took seriously the way hundreds of details fall into over-all patterns" (1946, 11–12).

Another model available for Lee, whose most technically detailed cultural interpretations were grounded in grammatical analyses, was Benjamin Lee Whorf. In his classic analysis of Hopi and Western conceptions of time and space, Whorf explained that "the seemingly endless task" of describing the morphology of the Hopi language was only preliminary: "I knew for example the morphological formation of plurals, but not how to use plurals." Because "plural in Hopi was not the same thing as in English," it took Whorf "nearly two more years" to translate (as it were) Hopi grammatical categories into English terms – or, rather, to show, comparatively, how the two organizations of thought differed (Whorf 1941, 77).

Lee's essays on the Wintu worldview are, precisely in this sense, Whorfian. They work outward from grammatical analysis of the Wintu language toward an interpretation of Wintu thought. And they work comparatively constantly. Indeed, in her struggles to understand Wintu language and thought, Lee states repeatedly that for long periods of time, she assumed a particular interpretation, based on English grammatical categories that she had been unable to call into question, only at last to be "overpowered" by evidence that required her to posit a completely different form and meaning. And yet, in several examples she discusses, she could never finally be sure of her interpretation: "I cannot tell," she confesses, even after years of work, whether her understandings of a particular grammatical formation "are present for the Wintu" (1950, 136).

In an essay titled "Linguistic Reflection of Wintu Thought," Lee starts from the contrast between the English and Wintu grammatical treatment of the particular in relation to the generic, and the singular in relation to the plural, to build an interpretation of an attitude toward lived experience that is very different from that of her own society. "Implicit in the nominal categories" of Indo-European languages, and hence in what Sapir might have called the intuitive ontology of the speakers of those languages, are the convictions that (1) the "given" world is "a series of particulars, to be classed into universals" and (2) "the plural is derived from the singular" (1944b, 122; see also Lee 1938, 1944a). In other words, Lee's cultural compatriots, whether English or Greek speakers, imagine that the world consists of discrete objects (things and events) and that the mind learns to group or count those objects – more and more correctly with respect to their nature or ultimate reality over developmental time.

For the Wintu also, according to Lee (1944b, 121), there is a "reality," an "ultimate truth," that "exists irrespective of man." It is "unbounded, undifferentiated, timeless." The Wintu believe in its existence but do not ever (in contrast to us) claim to know it. Instead, a Wintu person acts, freely, in such a way as to actualize temporary instances of ultimate reality:

> Within his experience, the reality assumes temporality and limits. As it impinges upon his consciousness he imposes temporary shape upon it. Out of the undifferentiated qualities and essences of the given reality, he individuates and particularizes, impressing himself diffidently and transiently, performing acts of will with circumspection. (1944b, 121)

Lee's adverb, "diffidently," is crucial, for it marks the contrast she wants to draw between the Indo-European or, more particularly, the mid-twentieth-century US orientation to reality and that of the Wintu. The Wintu person would seem to be, in her reading, more active and more individualistic than a self-consciously individualistic American, and yet less aggressive and assertive than the ideal US person. The Wintu person brings the world into being, into human experience, by particularizing the generic. In the timeless world beyond humanity, deer, for example, exists as "deerness." When a hunter kills a deer, the act is constructed, grammatically, by means of "derivative suffixes," such that the Wintu speaker's intuitive understanding of the act implies delimitation. As Lee puts it, "[H]e delimits a part of the mass": "The deer stands out as an individual only at the moment of man's speech; as soon as he ceases speaking, the deer merges into deerness" (1944b, 123). And deerness is not something Wintu "desire to control and exploit." Rather, "the Wintu relationship with nature is one of intimacy and mutual courtesy" (1944b, 129).

While it is impossible to know (and Lee admits as much) whether hers is a good or useful reading, from grammatical categories to worldview, Lee seems to have found, in Wintu ontology as she understood it, an orientation to reality that she finds to be superior to that of her own society. The Wintu value what in today's jargon we call "agency" – the agency of the individual person – but they also subordinate their agency to a greater reality, one that transcends (as they see it) their individual experience.

This Wintu ontology of the generic and the particular – "the premise of primacy of the whole" (1944b, 124) – structures Wintu conceptions of personhood. Lee reports that she could not get her Wintu consultants to articulate a mind-body distinction as we routinely do. As she explained in an essay on the Wintu conception of the self:

> When I asked... Sadie Marsh what the word for *body* was, she said *kot wintu*, the whole person. To the Wintu a person is holistic; he is psychosomatic, but without the suggestion of synthesis which this term holds. They have no word for body or corpse, and the so-called parts of the body are [grammatically] aspects or locations. Neither do they have a word for the self. (1950, 134)

Thus, Wintu do not say, as we do, "my head aches," but "I ache head" (Lee 1944b, 124).

The Wintu "premise of the primacy of the whole" is crucial, according to Lee, for understanding their conceptions of sociality. The Wintu person blends into other persons, into the social group. "When speaking about Wintu culture," she tells us, "we cannot speak of the self *and* society, but rather of the self *in* society" (Lee 1950, 132). Lee illustrates this with examples of "the grammatical expression of identity, relationship and otherness." For example, the Wintu phrase "he and his sister" becomes, in her charming literal translation, "the two who sibling-together." There is, in such phrases, she claims, both togetherness (implying two individuals) and "one point of view," that of the merged individuals (Lee 1950, 134). It is this merging of the individual in the group, in a culture that also valued individual agency, which Lee found to be so comparatively attractive while she wrestled, both as an anthropologist and as a mother, with American individualism and conformity.

Dakota Education

Dorothy Lee's analysis of Wintu ontology is foundational to a series of less technical essays she wrote on the topics of "freedom and culture" and "valuing the self," to use the titles of her two published collections of essays.[6] We have seen that she was troubled by her son's teacher who would not accept his drawings of horses, full of "movement" and "life," requiring instead pictures that were "placid" and "lifeless." It may take an imaginative leap to see Lee seeing, in the child's drawings, a bringing into being akin to her understanding of Wintu agency. And yet, consider her description of newborn humans:

> I saw them seeking to exercise their muscles without limit; sucking with all their strength, expressing limitless outrage with all the force of kicking legs, plunging arms, straining muscles, while roaring with all the capacity of lungs and vocal chords. I saw them pursuing their curiosity with all their senses, enduring discomfort, exerting. (Lee 1965, 31)

She saw them, in sum, enter into the world "with the urge to exert their own selves," with the potential to develop the personal "autonomy" she so valued (1965, 31). Such children would have to be taught, against their natural inclinations, to create "lifeless" pictures.

Lee's interest in children's autonomy was developing at the moment when she articulated a trenchant critique of the concept of basic human needs.[7] In a brief essay titled "Are Basic Needs Ultimate?" she argued that the model of culture prevailing at midcentury, in which culture was understood to develop in response to basic human needs, was misguided. For one thing, the "list" or "inventory" of basic needs expanded or contracted depending on the theoretical bent of those who propounded it (Lee 1948, 70). Upon inspection, those basic needs seemed little more than rationalizations of theorists' cultural presuppositions – a point that Clifford Geertz (1966, 41–42) made two decades later when he pointed out that there was no way to test claims that such and such cultural institution was a response to such and such psychological or biological need.

But Lee's more basic critique of the idea of basic human needs was that it derived from a "stimulus-response" model of human behavior that was grounded in "a negative conception of the good as amelioration or the correction of an undesirable state" (Lee 1948, 70, 72). Such a negative view "perhaps" was "natural" to "a culture which also holds that man was born in sin, whether in Biblical or psychoanalytic terms" (1948, 72). But it would not do to account for cultural values in general. Indeed, for Lee, culture was about values and not needs. And values entailed the bringing into being of the good and not the suppression of the bad. Human "striving" sought, and created, the good, guided by cultural values (1948, 73). To define culture as an organization of norms to control individuals, to stop them from exerting themselves, was upside-down theory for Lee. Such a theoretical orientation perhaps made sense in Cold War America, but it was not a theory that made sense of the way the other cultures Lee studied approached life.

Take, for example, the Dakota. In her essays on the Wintu worldview, Lee had worked outward from grammatical categories, using data from "biographical texts and recorded mythical material," while lamenting that "I have no other record of actual behavior" from that "dead and remembered culture" (1950, 131).[8] Her later, less technical essays on individualism, autonomy, freedom, and culture were grounded not in grammatical analysis but in detailed accounts of living cultures written by members of those cultures: texts such as Black Elk's *Black Elk Speaks* (1932), Ohiyesa's *Indian Boyhood* (1902), and Luther Standing Bear's *My People the Sioux* (1928).

Lee's 1965 essay on "Autonomy and Community" draws heavily from Ohiyesa's superb *Indian Boyhood*. She begins by noting that in the US culture of her time, autonomy and community were assumed to be opposites. In US folk sociology (and, of course, in most of its professional sociology as well), the two terms referred to "non-interfering orbits." Self and society were "separate units," and "when there is infringement, there is trouble." Either the individual is "violated, encroached upon" or a rebellious individual "may work havoc upon the community." The central cultural "principle of non-interference" led at one end of the spectrum to "permissiveness" and at the other end to "armed hostility, the strategy of the cold war" (1965, 29); Lee was unhappy with either outcome.

In Ohiyesa's account of his Indian boyhood, Lee found an educational model in which community, in the person of a child's elders, at once instructed young people, and trusted and expected them to go out, independently, to discover the world for themselves. Lee recounts how the five- or six-year-old Ohiyesa was free to roam the woods, going where he wished, returning at his own pace. The only instruction his elders gave him was "[l]ook closely to everything you see." But when he returned, those same elders questioned him closely:

> The boy describes the birds he has seen, their color, the shape of their bills… He ventures a name; but it is only a guess. It is not for him to name; this depends on the language of the community. So the uncle corrects him and gives him the "proper" name. The whole process is autonomous—but what would it have been without the involvement of the uncle? (Lee 1965, 35–36)

Lee notes that the uncle was "a busy man, a famous hunter, a great warrior." But such a man "had time for the little boy" (1965, 35); in this way, the collective resources of the community were made readily available for each child's education.

The climax of Lee's essay recounts Ohiyesa's account of his first sacrifice. He is eight, and his grandmother (who has taken the place of his deceased mother) informs him that now is the time for him to make his first sacrifice to "the Great Mystery," to "the Mystery of Mysteries, who controls all things" (Ohiyesa 1902, 102–05). The boy, who is eager to become a hunter and a warrior – or, as Lee glosses it, to "grow into… a true Dakota, effective in the hunt, in war, in his relation to his community and to the universe" (Lee 1965, 40) – tells his grandmother that he will give up anything she deems worthy. He offers his bow and arrows, his paints, and his necklace, but she "is not satisfied with any of these." He repeats his offer to sacrifice anything, until "she points to the one possibility he has not thought of, because it is not a possibility for him: his dog" (1965, 40). Eventually he agrees, but, as Lee puts it, "the pain of the loss is piercing."

The story continues, in both Ohiyesa's and Lee's accounts. The boy retires to his teepee to prepare his dog for death. He also paints his face for mourning. But when he emerges, his grandmother "will not allow him this small comfort, this small evasion." A sacrifice must be given freely and without regret; a person cannot at once make a sacrifice and mourn its loss. "The boy has to go through the unbearable experience, without padding." This experience, "in all its pain and unrelieved sharpness," is thus "his own" experience. But he does not go through it alone. His grandmother guides him, and the boy knows that she is there (Lee 1965, 40–41).

Lee hews fairly closely to Ohiyesa's account. Her insistence on its importance seems fair. Ohiyesa himself recounted it in the third person, in a book that was otherwise written in the first person – as if it remained for him, throughout his life, too intense an experience to narrate in his own voice. But there are ways in which Lee's interpretation overwrites Ohiyesa's story. About the injunction to separate sacrifice and mourning, Ohiyesa writes only that his grandmother said, "No, my young brave, not so! You must not mourn for your first offering. Wash your face and then we will go" (1902, 109–10) – at which he "obeyed" and gave up his dog to the executioner "with a smile" (1902, 110). It is Lee who emphasizes both the intense pain of the experience and the fact that Dakota pedagogy requires children to own it completely, without subterfuge, on their own. This, for Lee, was a quintessential example of a pedagogical practice in which community and autonomy are inseparable – with no need to be linked, syntactically, by the word "and" (1965, 41).

Conclusion: The Moral Motivations of Anthropological Comparisons

Ohiyesa's biographer, Raymond Wilson, describes *Indian Boyhood* as a book "written mainly for children ... idealizing and romanticizing his [Ohiyesa's] past" (1983, 132). In contrast, historian Frederick Hoxie considers Eastman as one among a group of Indians of the Progressive Era who, in comparing Indian ways to those of the white society, were "talking back to civilization" (2001, 2). Young American readers of Ohiyesa's time, not to mention anthropologists then and now, might well be enchanted by the romance of an Indian boyhood, as he described it, but our romantic orientation to the life he describes is already comparative – a function of our own sense of the "disenchantment" (to use Max Weber's word) of our world.

Yet, "utopian" may be a better word than "romantic" for Lee's reading of Ohiyesa. Indeed, we can interpret the unconventional trajectory of her career as a function of her quest for an authentic pedagogy, one built from a combination (without the "and") of the community's accumulated wisdom and the student's right to autonomy. And utopian projects are explicitly comparative, working from a bad version of society to a good (or better) one.

Lee's essays on Wintu grammatical categories and Dakota autobiographies are founded on cultural comparisons, but while her comparisons entailed a critique of US culture, their focus is elsewhere, on the pedagogical models that other cultures might offer her and her contemporaries. Here, it will be useful to compare Lee's comparative focus to that of her Boasian peers to see a range of possibilities for structuring comparisons, depending on an author's motivation or purpose.

Benedict's book on Japan, *The Chrysanthemum and the Sword*, grew from her work for the US government during World War II, when among other projects, she was asked in 1944 to write a report on Japanese culture to help the US military understand the enemy's ways of thinking. The book based on that work was published after the war, and in the introduction, Benedict explained its wartime motivation: "The question was [to learn to understand] how the Japanese would behave, not how we would behave if we were in their place" (1946, 5).

In Benedict's hands, this "assignment" was inherently comparative. To explain the Japanese worldview, she had to explain how Americans were likely to misinterpret it. Explaining American misinterpretations of Japan revealed American cultural patterns – patterns that, once made explicit for the reader, could be used to provide openings for the explication of Japanese patterns. While most of the substantive analysis of the book concerned Japan, that analysis was always underpinned by a back-and-forth interpretive methodology. To give but one example, trying to explain Japanese fealty to the emperor, Benedict found it necessary to explain American attitudes concerning individual liberty and state control:

> The Japanese point of view is that obeying the law is repayment upon their highest indebtedness, their ko-on [debt to the Emperor]. The contrast with folkways in the United States could hardly be more marked. To Americans any new laws, from street stop-lights to income taxes, are resented all over the country as interferences with individual liberty in one's own affairs. (1946, 129–30)

And Benedict concludes the passage with a remarkable doubled comparison: "The Japanese judge therefore that we are a lawless people. We judge that they are a submissive people" (1946, 130). Each side misunderstands the other, but the anthropologist uses this example of mutual misunderstanding to reveal central cultural attitudes in each culture comparatively.

Mead's wartime book, *And Keep Your Powder Dry* (1942), was written not to reveal an enemy's cultural motivations but to help US policymakers understand the strengths and weaknesses of the American national character (1942, 164). Unlike *Chrysanthemum*, it was not explicitly comparative. Yet, as Mead wrote several years later, "[E]very single statement that an anthropologist makes is a comparative statement" (1955, 9) – which is to say, anthropologists' grounding in the discipline's literature, and their own fieldwork, means that their particular observations and interpretations are always contextualized (whether implicitly or explicitly) in relation to contrasting examples. Thus, while *Powder* does not systematically explicate another culture in relation to that of the United States, underpinning its main focus on such topics as American family structure and child-rearing practices are comparative insights gained from Mead's experiences among various New Guinea and Pacific peoples.

While *Powder* was ultimately celebratory of American democracy (Handler 2005a, 149–50), Jules Henry's 1963 monograph about US culture, *Culture against Man*, was satirical – both angry and funny. Here, as in Mead's book, the focus was on US culture, and the comparative underpinning was constructed as Mead's was, developed from Henry's extensive fieldwork in South America, beginning with his doctoral research (under Boas and Benedict) among the Kaingang (Henry 1941). Like Mead and Benedict, Henry contributed to the war effort, working for both the Mexican and the US governments (including a stint in postwar Japan). But Henry, who was deeply involved in the culture-and-personality movement during the 1930s at Columbia, began relatively early in his career to conduct fieldwork in the United States, observing hospitals and classrooms in several cities (Handler 2005b, 160, footnote 2).

Culture against Man and its sequel, *Pathways to Madness* (1971), are based on extensive fieldwork in multiple settings in the United States, research often carried out by students under Henry's direction. The key interpretations, nonetheless, are generated from the comparative perspective that Henry brought to the work. The first quarter of the book, for example, is a critique of the modern economy and its grounding in unlimited consumption. Henry introduced his argument with "some comparisons between the modern and primitive worlds" (1963, 8). The most important of these is one that Marshall Sahlins famously explicated a few years later in his essay on "the original affluent society" (1972): in the Native American societies Henry had studied, human needs and demands are culturally limited and thus even what we would see as their low productive capacity is sufficient to satisfy them. In modern America, by comparison, the assumption of infinite and insatiable human desires powered an economy that was required constantly to "grow." In one of the many humorous sallies through which Henry explicated this argument, he compared the training of children in hunter-gatherer societies to education in the United States:

> *Homo sapiens* trains his children for the roles they will fill as adults. This is as true of the Eskimo three-year-old who is encouraged to stick his little spear into a dead polar bear as it is of an American child of the same age who turns on TV to absorb commercials; the one will be a skilled hunter, the other a virtuoso consumer. (1963, 70)

Here Henry's voice is that of the scientist, the anthropologist, who controls a wealth of examples about people such as "the Eskimo" – an example for which no footnote is provided. None is needed: the primitive-modern comparison is part of a sustained critique of the United States, without an extended treatment of the other comparative pole.[9]

As a final example, consider again Whorf's essay on language and habitual behavior. While there has been considerable discussion of his claims about grammatical categories and human experience (see Lucy 1992a, 1992b) – a discussion that would also apply to Lee's essays on Wintu – my focus here is on the rhetorical strategy of Whorf's "Standard Average European"-Hopi comparison. As Tocqueville did in *Democracy in America*, Whorf devoted equal time to each linguistic-cultural pole of the comparison. His portraits of the structural features and ontological premises of each system emerge comparatively, as his analysis of each facilitates his analysis of the other. We might paraphrase T. S. Eliot to say: in Whorf's hands, grammatical analysis becomes a criticism of one language by another.[10]

And Whorf is indeed critical: he wanted to knock European languages (which he satirizes as dialects of Standard Average European or SAE) from the pedestal upon which Euro-American socio-evolutionary theory had placed them. He wanted to show that the grammatical categories of Native American languages were every bit as useful as tools of thought as SAE categories. There is thus a cutting edge to Whorf's comparison. For example, SAE languages (in Whorf's analysis) objectify aspects of reality, like time, that have no objective existence at all. Hopi doesn't commit such an imaginative error. Yet, despite such strictures, the overall structure of Whorf's essay is balanced – he devotes equal time to each language and uses each to reveal the secrets of the other.

These examples of comparative analysis differ in the relative attention they devote to the two poles of analysis: self and other. Yet each reveals the truth of Mead's assertion that comparison is built into anthropological thinking. Indeed, this comparative habit of thought might be said to define a professionally "disciplined" anthropologist, at least those who had been trained by Boas or by his first generation of students.

In the work of Lee, Benedict, Mead, Henry, and Whorf, the anthropologist's personal, experiential version of US culture lies, always, just beneath the surface of argument and analysis, "peep[ing] silently through," as Sapir once said of the regular poetic meter he thought underlay apparently "free" verse (1921, 217). But, of course, these analysts did not attempt to silence their own culture when it spoke to and through them. They brought it into the light that their study of another culture shed. Or better, through them, the comparative encounter created a new kind of light that allowed for new insights about the old, well-learned cultural patterns they carried with them.

Such insights could be built upon through sustained historical and anthropological analysis of the home culture – as in Whorf's dissection of SAE grammatical patterns and Henry's critical readings of midcentury US culture. By contrast, those works in which the central object was a different, distant culture – as in Benedict's study of Japan – required disciplined and deep readings of the other, by way of as many kinds of cultural documents as the anthropologist could muster. But in either case, the work of comparison displaced, as it were, the home culture within the anthropologist's vision and thinking, unsettling taken-for-granted assumptions and thereby creating possibilities for new interpretations of both self and other.

The creativity generated by these cross-cultural comparisons could lead to moral as well as intellectual insight. In Lee and her Boasian colleagues, the "shock of recognition" (Wilson 1943) they experienced, analyzed, and wrote about was usually self-critical: "[W]e in the U.S. do such-and-such, and now we see that this is hardly natural, necessary or useful." But at least for Lee, her utopian quest led beyond critique to a celebration of the other. And given her diffidence about several of her grammatical analyses (1950, 135–36), she might well have admitted that she occasionally read into the Native American materials the authentic individualism that she so wanted for her children (as in her reading of Ohiyesa's first sacrifice). For, in the final analysis, Dorothy Demetracopoulos Lee was interested in bringing to the attention of a wide range of students the real human possibilities that other cultures (often those deemed primitive) have to offer. She clearly says that these societies have better versions of individualism than we have. And she says this not only, perhaps not mainly, as an anthropologist but also as a teacher and a mother.

Appendix

Most "standard" tunes that jazz musicians play – that is, tunes not written by jazz musicians but by popular composers, often for Broadway shows – have the musical form A–A–B–A. There is primary melody and chord sequence (A), which is played and then repeated (AA). There is a "bridge" (B), a secondary melody and chord sequence that leads back to the final statement of the primary melody and chord sequence (A). Each of these sections is the same length, usually eight "bars," or 32 beats (in standard, 4/4 time). Played once, the entire song, A–A–B–A, thus has 32 bars and 128 beats.

The primary melody and chord sequence (A) works, simply enough, by asserting a dominant key and then moving melodically over or through a series of chords that first disrupt or move away from the dominant key and then return to it. The bridge (B) disrupts the dominant key without asserting it; the work of the bridge is to return to the beginning of the primary melody and chord sequence (A) via one or more modulations that are too complicated to have been included in the main sequence.

Much of the tension or movement in the playing of one of these standard tunes comes from the bridge or, more precisely, from the musicians' mastery of the bridge, which is at once a secondary strand of the song (often less well known than the primary strand, by both musicians and listeners – "I've forgotten the bridge") while also being crucial to its successful resolution, the return to the main melodic statement and the dominant key.

"Tangerine," while still considered a standard tune, is different. Its form is A–A–A–B. The A section is repeated three times, with slight variations, and then the final section of the song is a frenetic and harmonically complicated sequence that returns to the dominant key. Ending with a "bridge" (the B segment), "Tangerine" provides no final statement of the main segment (A).

The Williamsburg musicians got lost trying to improvise on the bridge (the B segment). While I didn't ask them about this, it seemed obvious to me that the unusual structure of the tune and its tricky chord changes proved too much for them to use as a basis for improvisation, without having rehearsed or studied the tune beforehand. And indeed, jazz musicians (myself included) have all experienced such difficulties. In jazz, which is not primarily a written music, the response to such difficulties is to study the tune aurally; to listen to, and break down, its melody and chord sequence until one can memorize and master them; and then to practice improvising on them.

Such study can include listening to great players' recorded versions of the difficult tune. As noted earlier, I was hearing the Williamsburg version with Paul Desmond's version of it in mind. Listening to the stumbles of the local musician gave me a new appreciation of Desmond's ability to float above the complicated melodic and harmonic sequences of the tune, especially its bridge, improvising apparently freely within the constraints provided by the structure of the tune, because he understood it (I infer) in a deep, "intuitive" way. And his mastery of the tune, compared to the local musicians' lack of mastery of it, provided me with a means to work up the self-conscious analysis of it that I have sketched earlier. The bad or failed version led me to a new understanding of the good or successful version comparatively.

Notes

1 "Tangerine" was published in 1941, with lyrics by Victor Schertzinger and music by Johnny Mercer; it was used in the 1942 Paramount Pictures movie, *The Fleet's In.*

2 For a musical analysis of the good and bad versions, see the Appendix.

3 An important exception is professional gatekeeping; anthropologists, like other academics, are perfectly willing to make value judgments about their peers' work in reviewing it for publication and in reviewing their peers for tenure and promotion.

4 Press release, Office of Public Relations, Vassar College, undated [summer 1953?]. The volume was published as *Cultural Patterns and Technical Change*, which was described on the title page as "A manual prepared by The World Federation for Mental Health and edited by Margaret Mead" (Mead 1953). The 348-page manual was written by an "editorial staff" of the following people: Lawrence Frank, Eliot Chapple, Claire Holt, Dorothy Lee, Margaret Mead, George Saslow, and John Useem. It was divided into topical chapters and sections, but it is difficult to tell which editor wrote which sections; an exception is the 37-page section on Greece, the first footnote of which states that "the writer" is "herself a Greek by birth and upbringing" (Mead 1953, 77). Lee published a shorter version of this paper with the title "Value of the Self in Greek Culture" in *Freedom and Culture* (Lee 1953).

5 Lee seems to have been sensitive to the idea that "old American" ancestry gave people a kind of cultural authority that she did not think she had. Speaking about a pending visit to Vassar of Ruth Benedict in 1944, Lee is reported to have explained that Benedict was "well suited by her background to dispel bigoted ideas about race, since she writes as an old American descended from a line of Revolutionary ancestors" (*Vassar Miscellany News*, May 10, 1944, http://newspaperarchives.vassar.edu/cgi-bin/vassar?a=d&d=miscellany19440510-01.2.4&srpos=58&e=-------en-20--41--txt-txIN-otis+lee------).

6 Pending further research, I have to assume that Lee was familiar with the work of John Dewey, in particular, his 1939 book, *Freedom and Culture*. Her husband, whose intellectual influence she credits in the preface to her own *Freedom and Culture*, earned his PhD at Harvard in 1930, where "he came under the influence of the pragmatism of C.I. Lewis and the metaphysics of A. N. Whitehead" ("Otis Lee," obituary notice written by his Vassar colleagues, biographical files at Vassar College). In *his* book of that title, Dewey had written, "[T]he idea of Culture, which has become a central idea of anthropology, has such a wide sociological application that it puts a new face upon the old, old problem of the relation of the individual and the social. The idea of culture outlaws the very terms in which the problem has been conceived … for most statements of the problem have been posed as if there were some inherent difference amounting to opposition between what is called the individual and the social" (1939, 27).

7 While writing this chapter, I sent Lee's paper on basic needs to my colleague Daniel Segal, who read it and wrote, "I think 'Are Basic Needs Ultimate?' is among a handful of the best things ever written in anthropology." He went on to note that he knew very little of Lee's work – which, I think, is true for most contemporary anthropologists, a fact that I hope this chapter can play some small role in changing!

8 Seymour's account of Cora Du Bois's and Dorothy Demetracopoulos's fieldwork in the summer of 1929 makes it clear that Wintu culture had not disappeared. These anthropology graduate students were working under Alfred Kroeber, whose orientation derived from Boasian salvage ethnography. They sought out informants to query them about the old ways, even while religious revivalism was happening all around them and even as Du Bois became intrigued by "Wintu shamans going into altered states of consciousness after frenetic dancing and singing" – hardly a scene of cultural disappearance (Seymour 2015, 79; Du Bois 1935, 88–119).

9 There are moments, however, when Henry's others are ones he knows through the personal experience of fieldwork. For example, writing about music classes and the production of conformity in US elementary schools, he gives the example of "our Pilagá Indian friends, all of them excellent musicians," who exactly copy the off-key singing that American missionaries learned in school (1963, 290).

10 Eliot defined translation as "a criticism of one language by another" (1916, 102).

References

Benedict, Ruth. 1946. *The Chrysanthemum and the Sword: Patterns of Japanese Culture*. Boston, MA: Houghton Mifflin Company.

Black Elk. 1932. *Black Elk Speaks, Being the Life History of a Holy Man of the Oglala Sioux*. New York: William Morrow.

Dewey, John. 1939. *Freedom and Culture*. New York: Putnam.

Du Bois, Cora. 1935. *Wintu Ethnography*. Berkeley: University of California Publications in *American Archaeology and Ethnology*, 36 (1): 1–148.

Durkheim, Emile. 1933. *The Division of Labor in Society*. Translated by George Simpson. Glencoe, IL: Free Press. First published 1893.

Ehrenreich, Jeffrey. 1976. "Prologue: Valuing Dorothy Lee." Foreword to Lee, Dorothy, *Valuing the Self: What We Can Learn from Other Cultures*, v–xii. Englewood Cliffs, NJ: Prentice-Hall.

Eliot, Thomas S. 1916. "Classics in English. Review of The Poets' Translation Series, I–IV." *Poetry* 9 (2): 101–04.

Geertz, Clifford. 1966. "The Impact of the Concept of Culture on the Concept of Man." In *The Interpretation of Cultures (1973)*, edited by Clifford Geertz, 33–54. New York: Basic Books.

Gitlin, Todd. 2002. "David Riesman, Thoughtful Pragmatist." *Chronicle of Higher Education*, May 24, p. B5.

Handler, Richard. 2005a. "American Culture in the World: Margaret Mead's And Keep Your Powder Dry." In *Critics against Culture: Anthropological Observers of Mass Society*, edited by Richard Handler, 141–53. Madison, WI: University of Wisconsin Press.

Handler, Richard. 2005b. "Critics against Culture: Jules Henry, Richard Hoggart, and the Tragicomedy of Mass Society." In *Critics against Culture: Anthropological Observers of Mass Society*, edited by Richard Handler, 154–85. Madison, WI: University of Wisconsin Press.

Handler, Richard. 2005c. "Individualism Inside Out: Tocqueville's Democracy in America." In *Critics against Culture: Anthropological Observers of Mass Society*, edited by Richard Handler, 22–48. Madison, WI: University of Wisconsin Press.

Henry, Jules. 1941. *Jungle People*. New York: J. J. Augustin.

Henry, Jules. 1963. *Culture against Man*. New York: Random House.

Henry, Jules. 1971. *Pathways to Madness*. New York: Random House.

Hoxie, Frederick E. 2001. "American Indian Activism in the Progressive Era." In *Talking Back to Civilization: Indian Voices from the Progressive Era*, edited by Frederick E. Hoxie, 1–28. Boston, MA: Bedford/St. Martin's.

Lambek, Michael. 2015. *The Ethical Condition: Essays on Action, Person, and Value*. Chicago, IL: University of Chicago Press.

Lee, Dorothy. 1938. "Conceptual Implications of an Indian Language." *Philosophy of Science* 5 (1): 89–102.

Lee, Dorothy. 1944a. "Categories of the Generic and the Particular in Wintu." *American Anthropologist* 46 (3): 362–69.

Lee, Dorothy. 1944b. "Linguistic Reflection of Wintu Thought." In *Freedom and Culture*, 121–30. Englewood Cliffs, NJ: Prentice-Hall.

Lee, Dorothy. 1948. "Are Basic Needs Ultimate?" In *Freedom and Culture*, 70–77. Englewood Cliffs, NJ: Prentice-Hall.

Lee, Dorothy. 1949. "Ruth Fulton Benedict (1887–1948)." *Journal of American Folklore* 62 (246): 345–47.

Lee, Dorothy. 1950. "The Conception of the Self among the Wintu Indians." In *Freedom and Culture*, 131–40. Englewood Cliffs, NJ: Prentice-Hall.

Lee, Dorothy. 1953. "View of the Self in Greek Culture." In *Freedom and Culture*, 141–53. Englewood Cliffs, NJ: Prentice-Hall.

Lee, Dorothy. 1957. "Personal Significance and Group Structure." In *Freedom and Culture*, 15–26. Englewood Cliffs, NJ: Prentice-Hall.

Lee, Dorothy. 1959. "Introduction." In *Freedom and Culture*, 1–4. Englewood Cliffs, NJ: Prentice-Hall.

Lee, Dorothy. 1961. "Autonomous Motivation." In *Valuing the Self: What We Can Learn from Other Cultures*, 15–27. Englewood Cliffs, NJ: Prentice-Hall.

Lee, Dorothy. 1965. "Autonomy and Community." In *Valuing the Self: What We Can Learn from Other Cultures*, 28–41. Englewood Cliffs, NJ: Prentice-Hall.

Lee, Dorothy. 1976. "Introduction." In *Valuing the Self: What We Can Learn from Other Cultures*, 1–4. Englewood Cliffs, NJ: Prentice-Hall.

Lucy, John. 1992a. *Grammatical Categories and Cognition: A Case Study of the Linguistic Relativity Hypothesis*. Cambridge: Cambridge University Press.

Lucy, John. 1992b. *Language Diversity and Thought: A Reformulation of the Linguistic Relativity Hypothesis*. Cambridge: Cambridge University Press.

Marcus, George, and Michael Fischer. 1986. *Anthropology as Cultural Critique*. Chicago, IL: University of Chicago Press.

Mead, Margaret. 1942. *And Keep Your Powder Dry: An Anthropologist Looks at America*. New York: William Morrow.

Mead, Margaret, ed. 1953. *Cultural Patterns and Technical Change*. Paris: UNESCO.

Mead, Margaret. 1955. "Theoretical Setting – 1954." In *Childhood in Contemporary Cultures*, edited by Margaret Mead and Martha Wolfenstein, 3–20. Chicago, IL: University of Chicago Press.

Ohiyesa [Charles Eastman]. 1902. *Indian Boyhood*. Boston, MA: Little, Brown and Company.

Riesman, David. 1950. *The Lonely Crowd: A Study of the Changing American Character*. New Haven, CT: Yale University Press.

Sahlins, Marshall. 1972. "The Original Affluent Society." In *Stone Age Economics*, 1–39. Chicago, IL: Aldine-Atherton.

Sapir, Edward. 1921. "The Musical Foundations of Verse." *Journal of English and Germanic Philology* 20 (2): 213–28.

Sapir, Edward. 1925. "Sound Patterns in Language." *Language* 1 (1): 37–51.

Seymour, Susan. 2015. *Cora Du Bois: Anthropologist, Diplomat, Agent*. Lincoln: University of Nebraska Press.

Standing Bear, Luther. 1928. *My People the Sioux*. Boston, MA: Houghton Mifflin.

Starr, Julie. 2016. "Bodily Selves, Beauty Ideals, and Nature: An Ethnographic Comparison of Cultural Difference in Shanghai, China." Unpublished doctoral dissertation, Department of Anthropology, University of Virginia.

Tocqueville, Alexis de. 1955. *Democracy in America*, vol. II. Translated by Henry Reeve. New York: Vintage Books. First published 1840.

Whorf, Benjamin L. 1941. "The Relation of Habitual Thought and Behavior to Language." In *Language, Culture, and Personality: Essays in Memory of Edward Sapir*, edited by Leslie Spier, 75–93. Menasha, WI: Sapir Memorial Publication Fund.

Wilson, Edmund. 1943. *The Shock of Recognition*. Garden City, NY: Doubleday.

Wilson, Raymond. 1983. *Ohiyesa: Charles Eastman, Santee Sioux*. Urbana: University of Illinois Press.

3 A Comparative Ethnographic Study of Suicide Epidemics in Two Pacific Island Societies

Edward D. Lowe

Building further on Caroline Brettell's discussion, in Chapter 1, of the value of comparative thinking in anthropology as being "good to think with," this chapter aims to show how explicit comparative methods can be an effective means of developing middle-range theories in anthropology that offer more historically and culturally contextualized accounts of the general phenomena we want to better understand (Fischer 2018; Gingrich and Fox 2002; Ragin 1987). As Andre Gingrich (2002, 244–45) has written, culturally and historically situated comparative case studies can help to better "identify and explain [the] dimensions of specific local-global processes and to situate local-global processes in wider contexts more effectively than 'thick' and 'finely-textured' descriptions and analyses alone were able to carry out." In addition, *critical* comparative work (Hirsch et al. 2009) uses ethnographic materials to productively destabilize existing middle-range concepts or theories that are taken by many social scientists to be well established and universally applicable, revealing instead how their meanings and articulations often vary across different social-cultural and historical contexts, including and in contradistinction to those assumptions that inform academic theory (see also Jackson 2013; Strathern 1988). Explicit critical comparisons can inform theory that is sensitive to the role that political-economic and social organizational processes play in structuring forms of difference that unevenly and unjustly distribute the vulnerabilities and resiliencies that accompany processes of globalization and economic development (Hirsch et al. 2009). Further, a middle-range theory that is sensitive to context is supported through critical comparative studies that consider how general trends are sensitive to changes in particular historical trajectories for the cases placed into a comparative juxtaposition. These disparities are often indicated by group-level or social-spatial variations in important measures of human health and well-being. Of these measures, variations in rates of suicide have long been recognized as indicators of vulnerability to worsened mental health in a population (Durkheim 1951).

As an example of the preceding discussion, this chapter presents a critical comparative analysis of well-documented, late-twentieth-century suicide epidemics in the Pacific Islands of Chuuk and Samoa with the aim of generating a more context-sensitive, middle-range theory of these historically well-documented cases than has been offered elsewhere (e.g. Booth 1999; Hezel 1976, 1984; Marsella et al. 2005; Macpherson and Macpherson 1987; Macpherson 2010; Matangi Tonga 2014; Rubinstein 1995). The ethnographic accounts of suicide in Chuuk and Samoa regularly report that suicide is commonly a culturally elaborated expression of anger stemming from conflicts involving close kin. So, to contextualize the experience-near dimensions of the phenomenon of suicide in these islands, the analysis begins with an incommensurate (Handler 2009; Lazar 2012) mode of comparison by examining the ethnopsychologies of emotion and the management of anger as these contrast with dominant understandings in Western academic "psy-disciplines" (Rose 1996). The second phase of the comparative analysis involves making critical-processual comparisons at two scalar levels. The approach here is similar to the "variation-finding" strategies described in Chapter 1 by Caroline B. Brettell. The first step of this scalar analysis involves "drilling down" from a discussion of variations in suicide rates for different age and gender groups in Chuuk and Samoa to compare how local processes of social organization can create disparities in terms of the distribution of vulnerability and resilience with regard to how self-harm emerges as a strategy when negotiating heated social conflicts within the family and close kin group. The second scalar variation-finding step involves "scaling up" and engaging in a case-oriented comparative study (Ragin 1987) of the particular historical intersections that contributed to the sharply increasing suicide rates in Chuuk and Samoa in the 1970s and 1980s. The sections that follow guide the reader through each of these comparative strategies.

Incommensurate Comparison of Emotion and Suicide in Chuuk and Samoa

The first phase of the approach I am advocating comparatively juxtaposes the similarities in ethnopsychological understandings of emotion and the management of anger in Chuuk and Samoa as these relate to suicidal behavior and their differences vis-à-vis those understandings that circulate widely among members of what Nikolas Rose (1996) has labeled the globalizing psy-disciplines. This phase of comparison is similar to Handler's (2009) "incommensurate" strategy. As Handler (2009, 627) argues, in order to compare similar phenomena, such as the management of emotion and interpersonal conflict, that are situated within two or more distinct "lifeworlds" (Jackson 2013), the comparison must be incommensurate. By "incommensurate" Handler means that phenomena from two distinct social-cultural lifeworlds cannot be easily placed into some a priori value scheme that allows for their measurement according to some universally applicable metric. The reason is that while elements of the phenomena to be compared do share some behavioral or material similarities, they are also enmeshed in distinct symbolic systems or forms of collective representation (i.e. "culture"). So, to render the phenomena in one cultural context meaningful in terms of another cultural context requires an act of translation that makes it difficult to claim that the translated phenomena can be easily rendered in the culturally defined values of the translator's system of symbolic representation from which he or she might derive an a priori metric for measurement. As Michael Jackson (2013, 25) argues, the point of such a comparison is less the generation of theories that might explain human "universals" or "laws" than the engagement in a comparison that "juxtaposes perspicacious examples ... to throw into relief certain 'family resemblances' among the ways human beings struggle for well-being."

As such, the sort of comparison I summarize in this section brings together relevant elements of three ethnopsychologies: one for Chuuk, one for Samoa, and one widespread within the psy-disciplines. By "ethnopsychology" I mean the "way in which people conceptualize, monitor, and discuss their own and others' mental processes, behavior, and relationships. [Moreover] they both construct and result from people's observation in consciousness, action, and relationships" (Lutz 1985, 35). Following Lutz, ethnopsychologies are not merely local abstractions but also are fundamental to local pragmatics and moralities as they inform the inferences people make about the intentions, goals, and abilities of social actors. They inform understandings of self as distinct from other persons and the meaningful material objects that are fundamental to the enactment of local lifeworlds (Hallowell 1955).

The way the psy-disciplines often conceptualize, monitor, and discuss mental processes, behavior, and relationships is considered as an ethnopsychology to be placed alongside those of other places (Lutz 1985). Anthropologists have generally been suspicious of the distinction between ethnopsychology and academic psychology, and with good reason, as evidence suggests that most psychological theories have been developed through the study of a very narrow set of research subjects, mainly college students in Western, educated, industrialized, rich, and democratic (i.e. WEIRD) societies (Henrich et al. 2010). Moreover, it would be a mistake to view ethnopsychologies in places like Chuuk and Samoa as internally coherent, bounded entities that are culturally and spatially distinct from those of the psy-disciplines. With the rise and globalization of psy-disciplines, Western (or WEIRD) academic and therapeutic understandings of human selves have become instituted in a wide variety of settings globally, particularly as these have become commingled with Western religious evangelism since the nineteenth century (Stromberg 2015). Given the way theories from the Western social sciences entered into the discourse expressing popular concern in the earliest media reports about the suicide problem in parts of Oceania (e.g. Hezel 1976), I suspect that both the public alarm over this problem and the ways of understanding and addressing it are partly a reflection of the spread of midcentury psy-disciplinary discourse in the region, just as it has been in other locations such as India and Sri Lanka (Chua 2012; Widger 2015).

One particularly resilient ethnopsychological trope that circulates through the globalizing professional and often elite psy-disciplines constructs suicide, particularly for adolescents and young adults in rapidly modernizing and globalizing societies, as a result of the loss of "traditional" socialization practices that promote the internalization of moral codes that had once effectively restrained the immature impulsivity that can lead to youth suicide attempts, particularly as a form of protest over what the victim perceives to be unfair, often premodern familial or societal demands (Chua 2012). This trope has circulated in mental health circles in Europe and North America since the late eighteenth century, when a public sensation emerged over the problem of youth suicide, which was believed to be caused by the impulsive emulation of the main character in Goethe's *Die Leiden des Jungen Werthers (The Sorrows of Young Werther)* (Bell 2011). This trope is fully articulated in Durkheim's (1951) theory of anomie and his characterization of "anomic" suicides. In its present form, this understanding can be found in reports of public alarm over the perceived rise in childhood and adolescent suicide in Kerala, India (Chua 2012), and in scholarly work on the late-twentieth-century rise of mental health problems such as substance abuse and suicide among youth in the Pacific Islands (Marsella et al. 2005).

How does the preceding discussion compare to the ethnopsychological understanding of emotion and suicide in Chuuk and Samoa? Suicide is rarely explained in terms of the loss of traditional values for young people. Instead, suicide is understood to emerge from the dilemmas that accompany the culturally defined management of emotion. The expected management of emotion in important social relationships in Samoa and Chuuk is connected to local moral understandings and behavioral enactments of personhood (Hollan 2001). As one matures and becomes more responsible for the management of their social conduct in public settings, being a "good person" includes managing emotional expression appropriately (Gerber 1985; Mead 1961; Rubinstein 1995).

In both Chuuk and Samoa, personhood and the management of emotion are enacted on an everyday level within the organization of kinship and the social organization of (re)production. Kin relations in both contexts are hierarchical, being primarily organized in terms of relative gender, sibling birth order, generation, lineage, and chiefly authority (Goodenough 1978; Lowe 2002, 2018; Tcherkezoff 2015). At the household level in Samoa and Chuuk, parents hold authority over their children's activities and labor and that of their spouses (Goodenough 1978; Lowe 2002, 2018; Mead 1961; Tcherkezoff 2015). In Chuuk, the oldest brother and the oldest sister of a sibling set hold authority over the labor of their junior siblings and their spouses, even those who reside in households other than the oldest siblings' households. Political authority and social status in Samoa are vested in a system of chiefly titles (*matai*), which are each ranked in terms of prestige and authority. The prestige of *matai* titles benefits and confers status not only upon the holder of the title but also upon his spouse, siblings, and members of his family. Chuuk does not have a system of chiefly titles. But chiefly authority within kin groups is vested in the oldest son of the most senior woman of a local matrilineage. This man holds the title of *samon* ("chief of the local lineage"). Matriclans in Chuuk are also ranked, and the *samon* of the most senior clan of a village is considered the high chief for that village (*soupwun* or "chief of the land").

In both Chuuk and Samoa, kinship relations are expected to be harmonious and enacted through regular exchanges that represent expressions of what correspond in English to terms such as "love/compassion" and "respect" (Gerber 1985; Lowe 2002; Mead 1961). For higher-status individuals, these are expressed through acts that are sensitive to the apparent needs of the more junior person, particularly by providing various kinds of nurturing support in the fulfillment of those needs. This might include giving permission to the junior person to do something important, giving requested material goods and items, providing access to land and other productive resources, and providing support when in conflict with others. In return, lower-status individuals enact sentiments of love and respect by submitting to the authority of the higher-status person, by doing as they are asked and through their proper management of their public comportment so as to protect the kin group's status and reputation. In these relationships, the direct, outward expression of anger and displeasure is the prerogative of the higher-status person. Lower-status persons' expressions of anger are expected to be controlled or redirected away from the higher-status person, so as not to openly challenge the latter's authority.

Suicide in Samoa and Chuuk is often understood as a crisis involving the management of acute feelings of anger or rage, typically aimed at close kin who occupy a higher-status position than the suicide victim (Gerber 1985; Hezel 1984; Lowe 2003; Macpherson and Macpherson 1987; Rubinstein 1995). In Chuuk, the target of one's anger is most often a parent or older sibling. In Samoa, it could not only be a parent but also a titled *matai* or a member of the village council of chiefs. It is important to note that suicidal acts are but one extreme of a range of options that lower-status persons use when managing anger that they feel toward higher-status persons. It is more common on an everyday level to express these as either *musu* in Samoa or *chipwang* in Chuuk. Both terms are phenomenologically similar in everyday experience and have been summarized by Macpherson and Macpherson (1987, 324) as follows:

> [T]hey become sullen and withdrawn; say very little to those around them; do no more than what they are told; and show little interest in social life. In most cases one who is *musu* will treat a particular person with special uninterest to underscore the supposed source of discontent. The Samoan concern with personal relationships leads those around the person involved to attend to the source of discontent and to restore the relationship (*teu le va*). Where the matter is soluble gentle pressure is applied to both parties to move towards a compromise.

If the aggravating issue for the lower-status person is much more serious, then he or she may run away from the family household, often to stay with relatives in another village or in another household nearby. The more intense the feelings of dissatisfaction, the further the offended party seeks to run away. In Chuuk, this behavior is called *amwunamwun* (Rubinstein 1995), which I have witnessed on several occasions. In one instance, an elderly man in his seventies felt so aggrieved that his children were not caring for him well enough and were not honoring his wishes at home that he was asking for help to secure an airfare to Japan, where he intended to live out the rest of his days if necessary. In another case, a young woman in her early twenties was angry with her father over his failing to support some request she had made of him; she left for several weeks to stay with her mother's oldest brother on their lineage land on another nearby island. In Chuuk, this more intense feeling of anger is called *song*, which is always associated with a perception of a moral breach in the relationship, particularly those involving the expectations of being good kin of a particular kind (cf. Lutz 1988).

In cases where someone feels aggrieved within a hierarchical relationship, even apparently trivial-seeming refusals or disagreements can explode into fits of rage-filled protests. It is during these moments that one's actions can take on a high degree of risk of harm both to others and to oneself. During these moments of conflict and protest, other family members often intervene, attempting to both soothe the pain and anger of the injured parties and encourage the junior party to apologize and the higher-status party to make appropriate gestures of generosity and concern. But if the person has already injured himself or herself critically, such interventions may come too late to save him or her.

So, while many in the psy-disciplines portray suicide epidemics in places like Samoa and Chuuk as the result of social and cultural changes that lead to a failure among young people to internalize available traditional moral codes that would have provided psychological restraint for earlier generations, the ethnopsychological understandings in Chuuk and Samoa frame suicide and other acts of self-harm within a larger framework of moral action involving the management of emotional expression and enactments of respect and caring concern as these relate to intimate, hierarchical relationships. As Doug Hollan (1990) has argued for suicide among the Toraja of Sulawesi, it is not the loss of local moral codes that generates suicide in these societies. Suicide is, rather, a reflection of the way ethnopsychological understandings and embodiments constrain the possibilities for emotional expression as they intersect with the enactment of moral ways of being within local lifeworlds.

Critical-Processual Comparisons: Drilling Down and Scaling Up

The incommensurate ethnopsychological comparison helped to situate suicidal behavior in Chuuk and Samoa within larger moral worlds and within the social projects of people who inhabit them. It alludes to the fact that most people in these islands, regardless of age or gender, can enact lethal acts of self-harm as a result of the attempt to manage either shame or anger within the hierarchical relationships that obtain both among intimate kin and in the wider community and to marshal support in defense of their cause. Given this, suicide is a practice that could involve just about anyone, as the epidemiological data for suicide in both Chuuk and Samoa during the height of the suicide epidemic in the mid-1980s show (see Tables 3.1 and 3.2).

But these same epidemiological data given in Tables 3.1 and 3.2 show that the burden of vulnerability for suicidal acts is not borne equally by all in either Chuuk or Samoa. In Chuuk, for example, while older adolescents in general were more vulnerable than other age groups, older boys and young men in the early to midtwenties were particularly vulnerable (Hezel 1984). In Samoa, older teens and young men throughout their twenties are particularly vulnerable, but, and in contrast to Chuuk, so were young women in their later teens and early to midtwenties (Macpherson and Macpherson 1987). Tables 3.1 and 3.2 summarize these patterns. Table 3.2 shows that while girls and women were much less vulnerable than boys and men, the vulnerability of young women between fifteen and twenty-nine was much greater in Samoa than in Chuuk, where girls' and women's vulnerabilities were more evenly distributed across age groups.

Of course, for members of the psy-disciplines, these vulnerabilities might simply reflect the Stürm und Drang of late adolescence and emerging adulthood that all youth must endure, an unfortunate consequence of finally leaving the carefree days of childhood behind and taking on the weightier responsibilities of adulthood. But, since Margaret Mead's (1961) original work, anthropologists have been critical of such universalizing accounts, shifting the focus instead to the way the everyday troubles of youth reflect the continuity or discontinuity of their experiences within larger social-institutional arrangements.

Table 3.1 *Suicide risk for males in Chuuk and Samoa during the peak years of the suicide epidemics*

	Chuuk (source: author's calculations)			Samoa (source: Bowles 1985)		
Age Group	Male Population 1980	Total # of Cases '80–82	Average Annual Rate (per 100,000)	Male Population 1981	Total # of Cases '81–83	Average Annual Rate (per 100,000)
10–14	2,622	3	38.1	10,950 (est.)	1	3.0
15–19	2,060	18	291.3	10,919	19	58.0
20–24	1,628	9	184.3	7,868	21	89.0
25–29	1,435	4	92.9	4,968	13	87.2
30–34	1,128	1	29.6	3,412	6	58.6
35–44	1,246	3	80.3	10,813	8	24.7
45+	2,572	4	51.8	10,813	5	15.4
Total 10+	12,691	42	110.3	48,793	73	49.9

Table 3.2 *Suicide risk for females in Chuuk and Samoa during the peak years of the suicide epidemics*

	Chuuk (source: author's calculations)			Samoa (source: Bowles 1985)		
Age Group	Female Population 1980	Total # of Cases '80–82	Average Annual Rate (per 100,000)	Female Population 1981	Total # of Cases '81–83	Average Annual Rate (per 100,000)
10–14	2,300	0	0.0	9,810 (est.)	2	6.8
15–19	1,978	2	33.7	9,977	8	26.7
20–24	1,657	0	0.0	7,132	13	60.8
25–29	1,419	1	23.5	4,705	3	21.3
30–34	1,075	0	0.0	3,450	2	19.3
35–44	1,305	1	25.5	6,136	2	10.9
45+	2,574	1	13.0	10,811	0	0.0
Total 10+	12,308	5	13.5	42,211	30	23.7

More contemporary work in anthropology is critical of the work of Mead's generation, for it often implied that the social conditions that generated different vulnerabilities in different societies reflected the local, bounded, and static organization of different societies. As Jennifer Hirsch and her colleagues have noted, contemporary work in anthropology now recognizes that disparities in outcomes such as these reflect nested local-global, social-structural processes as opposed to static cultural traits or configurations. This shift toward considering "processes implies attention to history, global-local connections, and the agency of local actors" (Hirsch et al. 2009, 81).

Another important dimension of contemporary work in anthropology that is important to consider when trying to explain disparate vulnerabilities and resiliencies is the recognition that culture is differentially shared and that people who occupy different social positions are both differentially enabled and constrained in terms of their possibilities of action and therefore can differentially experience and strategize around more general cultural processes (Hirsch et al. 2009). Working comparatively provides greater insight into how these local social-structural processes create sites of both risk and resiliency in comparable and contrasting ways across cases. It can also enable a view of how different historically contingent local-global intersections can further exacerbate or ameliorate the risks and resiliencies that accompany different social positionings and both the cultural repertoires and strategic actions available within them.

This critical-processual turn requires a two-stage, variation-finding approach. The first stage involves drilling down from a general ethnographic discussion of ethnopsychology to a comparison of the everyday organization of social and material reproduction in each site. This analysis can provide insight into the local articulation of political-economic processes that create the social positions of actors and the variation in levels of vulnerability and resiliency that might obtain within these social positions. The second stage involves scaling up and engaging in a case-oriented comparative study (Ragin 1987) of the particular historical intersections of the social, political, economic, and cultural at the interface of the global and the local that raise the local profile of differential vulnerability further. I now turn to a summary of the first of these comparative analytics, "drilling down."

Drilling Down: Social Organization and the Production of Disparities of Vulnerability and Resiliency

Why is the vulnerability to the kinds of acute shame or anger that can precede suicidal acts of self-harm so much greater for older teens and young adults in their twenties? Why is this vulnerability much greater for young men in Chuuk and Samoa? Why are young women in Samoa at greater risk while young women in Chuuk are not? Middle-range theoretical insights into the answers to these questions can emerge through a comparative study of the position of older teens and young adults within the wider organization of local political economies in these island groups. Again, such an analysis shifts from an emphasis on the incommensurate cultural aspects of each case to a variation-finding strategy that might explain differential patterns of vulnerability and resilience to suicide in Chuuk and Samoa.

In Chuuk and Samoa, there are three primary sites where social status and family prestige are produced and contested (Lowe 2003, 2018; O'Meara 1990; Tcherkezoff 2015). The first is at the level of kin-group relations beyond the level of households, extending out into the village and to much broader kinship networks at the island level and higher. A close second are the relationships one has within the church, particularly through participation in its meeting groups and ritual activities. Third, there is the level of participation in modern institutions of the state, including the school and various bureaucratic offices and agencies. Through vigorous participation in these sites, mature adult men and women are able to both display their status and compete for higher offices that might become available in any of these three domains.

As fully mature adult men and women, according to local life-course understandings (in their forties and fifties typically), pursue their political interests in kin groups, the church, and (to a lesser extent) the modern postcolonial state, their need for a reliable source of labor to help them fulfill their obligations in these offices and associated ritual activities intensifies. Labor is needed to produce both the food and the ritual valuables that serve as items of exchange and demonstrations of generosity that are the heart of the ritual events that drive political life. At the same time, labor is needed to sustain local households and their members. As young, unmarried men and women exit schooling and enter from the mid to late teens into their early twenties, they are expected to work on behalf of their parents and lineage or village elders both to take care of everyday tasks in support of households and in more occasional preparations in support of ritual events (Lowe 2003; O'Meara 1990; Tcherkezoff 2015). In both Chuuk and Samoa, younger men and women are expected to work in support of their parents' households until they marry and form households of their own, often moving to either the new husband's village in Samoa or the new wife's household or village in Chuuk. But service to the village council of chiefs (*matai*) in Samoa continues for men in Samoa so long as they remain untitled. For women in Samoa, the same is true of their service to the women's committees under the direction of the *matai*'s wives, who carry the ranking of their husbands' titles in the women's associations (O'Meara 1990; Tcherkezoff 2015). As noted, Chuuk does not have a system of chiefly titles beyond those based on lineage, village, or island-level leadership. Nevertheless, more junior men and women are expected to provide service to their villages and wider community associations under the direction of more senior men and women until they reach a sufficient age and maturity level to enter into offices of leadership of their own.

In Chuuk and Samoa, the division of labor in both everyday productive tasks and ritual activities is organized in terms of chiefly status, generation and age, and gender. Higher-status men, particularly of chiefly rank, plan and organize the activities for the tasks to be performed by their younger or lower-status subordinates. They then delegate authority to other men and senior women or issue directives for what needs to be done. More junior or lower-ranking men and women are expected to follow the commands and directives of higher-status men and women without question, as humble obedience and submission are understood as signs of love and respect shown to the more senior or higher-ranking person.

Unless they have a wage-paying or salaried job, which tends to be gender balanced, the productive tasks themselves are distributed differently among males and females. In Chuuk and Samoa (O'Meara 1990), men work on their farming plots or plantations to grow and harvest a range of foods and marketable commodities. Men also do most of the fishing, although women gather seafood from the beach and adjacent reefs. Men also build and maintain the family household structures and other locally produced productive tools. While agricultural work may be accomplished by individual men, particularly if they are caring for their own Taro patches and other small gardens, everyday productive labor in the gardens, harvesting tree crops, or fishing is typically shared with other men and older boys of similar age and rank. In Chuuk, small groups of older youths and young men also produce the cooked breadfruit pudding (*kkón*). Women, particularly younger women and older female youths, take on a range of tasks in support of the household itself. These may include cooking daily meals, cleaning houses and surrounding compounds, childcare, cleaning clothes, and so forth. In Samoa, older girls and young women also assist in certain labor-intensive tasks on their family plantations, such as collecting coconuts and cutting copra for sale in the market (O'Meara 1990). In Samoa, young women are also actively involved in weaving, particularly in production of fine mats (*'ie toga*) that are the central cultural artifacts used in ritual exchanges and status competitions in Samoa (O'Meara 1990; Tcherkezoff 2015). These objects are produced only by older girls and women, and a family's need of them is inexhaustible, so their production can occupy most of a girl's or young woman's free time (O'Meara 1990, 100).

In addition to providing productive service to their parents, older siblings, and high-ranking men and women of their villages, young, unmarried men and women are considerably interested in the social projects that are meaningful among their peers. One of the primary interests for young men and women from their late teens onward is their sexual exploits and romantic interests (Lowe 2003; O'Meara 1990). These are complicated pursuits because in both Chuuk and Samoa, sexual activities must remain completely out of the public eye and hidden from one's cross-sex siblings and, often, one's parents. To get around these constraints, young men engage in "night crawling" or "sleep crawling," where they enter a girl's house at night to try and court or seduce her. If a young man is caught in the house at night, he risks violent reprisals by the young woman's family, as it is deeply shameful for an affair to come out in the open in this way. Young men and women also arrange to meet in the bush away from the household. This strategy is not without risks. In Chuuk, a highly matricentric society, there is little concern over an older girl's or young woman's virginity, and she does not face many serious consequences should she become pregnant as a result of her affairs. There is concern that she should not flaunt her romantic interests in public, thereby angering her brothers, both real and classificatory. In Samoa, on the one hand, a family is very concerned to control a young woman's sexual activities and goes to great lengths to keep young, unmarried women in the house or to chaperone them whenever in public. On the other hand, should an unmarried young woman in Samoa become pregnant, her family is greatly shamed in the eyes of the broader public (O'Meara 1990; Tcherkezoff 2015).

A second concern for young men and women is that of their individual projects to build a reputation for themselves as capable and promising young men or women in the wider community. Part of establishing a reputation involves developing and demonstrating one's skills as a capable and productive worker. For those who have done well in school, this may include pursuing postsecondary education with the ambition of finding a good job in town or as a government worker locally. It might also include a plan to migrate to a regional metropole in Australia, New Zealand, Hawai'i, or the mainland United States for additional education or work. For many youths who will not pursue additional education, salaried work, or migration, establishing oneself as a capable and effective household worker is an important project. In Samoa, for example, a young man might establish his own plantation on the family land, in anticipation of establishing his own household in the future (O'Meara 1990).

Young men and women are also interested in establishing their reputations in their villages and in wider kin and community networks. They can do this in part by humbly and willingly providing service to the kin-based and community organizations that animate village life, particularly through participation in religious and kin-based ritual events, under the direction of their superiors. But equally important in the social worlds of young men and women in Chuuk and Samoa is the project of establishing themselves as strong, brave, and savvy operators within their peer networks and, as such, that they are not people to be trifled with too easily. These reputations are needed both to support their romantic pursuits and in their pursuit of being granted titles in Samoa or of occupying an office of high status in Chuuk later in adulthood. Many of these pursuits are risky, both personally and socially. For example, young men who accomplish great feats of strength, endurance, and bravery gain much esteem in the eyes of their peers. This can include not only successful athletic prowess but also dangerous feats such as swimming several kilometers across on open channel from one island to another at night. Even acts of "night crawling" are as much feats of bravery as they are outlets of erotic desire. In addition, young men and women can build their reputations by being prepared to defend their own or their family's reputations against the insults of others. This can be accomplished not only through verbal jousting but also through physical assaults – even lethal blows if the situation calls for it. Finally, for young men in particular, bravery and endurance can be demonstrated through participation in extensive bouts of competitive alcohol consumption with their peers, often to great excess (Marshall 1979; Lowe 2003).

One can see in the summary of political economy, the adult life course, and the social organization of labor given earlier how older youths and young men and women might become vulnerable to exploitation by their family and village superiors, who might take advantage of their labor in the pursuit of their own political projects rather than properly reciprocating through acts of care and generosity in return for humble service delivered. Within a social-structural position that carries such a potential for exploitation and strong cultural prohibitions against directing the outward expression of anger toward one's superiors, it is not surprising to see such a broad elaboration of angry affect in the ethnopsychological understandings of emotion in Chuuk and Samoa. From a political-economic vantage point, one can see the increased possibilities for young adults in Chuuk and Samoa to carry suppressed anger and for the associated attempts to deal with them through avoidance and withdrawal, occasionally escalating to moments of rage that can precede attempts of suicidal self-harm as described earlier.

But the explanation for the different risk profiles presented in Tables 3.1 and 3.2 would be incomplete if it focused exclusively on the potentialities of exploitation. A second concern is the possibility for disjuncture in the social projects of older youths and young adults as compared to their social projects regarding families, extended kin, and villages under the authority of parents, chiefs, and community leaders. As I have argued (Lowe 2003), many of the activities of unmarried older youths and young adults who have status-enhancing currency among their peers, such as "night crawling," binge drinking, and fighting, run the risk of bringing shame to their families if these activities lead to a serious moral breach in the eyes of the community. Young people risk the ire of their parents, chiefs, and community elders, who might also, in managing anger, show less concern and generosity to their children or subjects, leaving the younger person feeling neglected or unloved (Rubinstein 1995). In more extreme moments of rage, the senior person might lash out with a sharp, painful rebuke of the youth or young adult. On the one hand, if the rebuke is perceived to be justified, the younger person might experience acute feelings of shame. On the other hand, given that the same young adult may have been actively attending to the directives of the more senior person, and thereby realizing a positive sense of personhood in family and community, such an angry rebuke may be perceived as an unjust expression of anger, provoking a justified angry reaction by the young person in response.

With these two explanations in mind (exploitation and disjunctive social projects), we can consider comparatively the patterns of vulnerability in Table 3.1. It is interesting that in Samoa, on the one hand, the risk for suicide among males rises sharply in the later teen years and remains high through the late twenties and into the thirties. In Chuuk, on the other hand, the rate rises sharply in the late teen years and early twenties and then declines rapidly thereafter. While there is evidence that both disjunctive and exploitative processes are present for young men in particular in Samoa and Chuuk (as young men's socially risky status-enhancing activities are present in both locations), it is possible that young men in Samoa experience much greater perceptions of exploitation for longer into adulthood than those in Chuuk, as untitled Samoan men must provide service to the council of *matai* for their entire adult lives or until they receive a title of their own. No set community-service organizations exist in Chuuk. Experiences of disjuncture in the pursuit of meaningful social projects in Chuuk might be a more important explanatory process for young men's risk for suicide and other acts of self-harm. Older teens and young men in their twenties might be particularly vulnerable in the sense that their immaturity in pursuing socially risky but peer-status-enhancing activities might lead to moral breaches or neglect of their family responsibilities that lead to angry rebuke and rebuffed requests by their parents and older siblings.

In comparing the risk profiles for females in Chuuk and Samoa in Table 3.2, we can see that the relative vulnerability is relatively flat for girls and women of different ages in Chuuk, but in Samoa, it rises sharply for older teens and young women in their early twenties and then declines rapidly for older women. Other than the vigorous pursuit of secret romances in Chuuk, young women do not engage in the same kind of socially risky activities as young men, and there are few social consequences for pregnancy before marriage. Moreover, in a highly matrilineal and matrilocal society, young women have much stronger ties to family land and authority over their households than young men in Chuuk. I suspect that young women in Samoa also engage in fewer of the socially risky activities that young men engage in. But there is much greater concern with a young woman's sexual activities to the point of constant surveillance and control by all family members before she is formally engaged to be married. An unmarried young woman's apparent virginity is a key site of family-prestige pursuit in Samoa (O'Meara 1990; Tcherkezoff 2015). Young women's sexuality can also be a strategically important weapon used to punish their parents for unjustly angering them (O'Meara 1990). This, then, opens a site of disjuncture that may raise the risk profile for young, unmarried women in their late teens and early twenties, a risk that diminishes rapidly as young women become engaged and marry over the course of their twenties.

Scaling Up: Historical Factors That Contribute to Epidemic Suicide Rates in Chuuk and Samoa

The second variation-finding comparative strategy used to generate a middle-range theory of suicide in Chuuk and Samoa involves "scaling up" to a consideration of historical factors that might explain the epidemic rise in suicide rates in each case. This stage uses a case-oriented comparative strategy (Ragin 1987) to explore the particular historical intersections at the interface of the local and the global that raised the epidemic risk for general suicide rates. While the previous section has examined the differential vulnerability for suicide among people occupying different social-organizational positions in Chuuk and Samoa, this section is concerned with the different historically contingent factors that may have contributed to the sharp rise in suicide rates in Chuuk and Samoa, starting in the early 1970s and peaking in the early 1980s at rates well above global averages and declining to below world averages by the early 2000s (Lowe 2019). Figure 3.1 shows epidemic trajectories of suicide deaths in Chuuk State and Samoa from 1960 through 2005, based on data made available to the author by the Micronesian Seminar in 2008 and the Samoan Suicide Group and Samoan Ministry of Health (i.e. Bowles 1985; Bourke 2001; Lowe 2019).

Two conspicuously similar historical circumstances preceded the onset of the suicide epidemics in Chuuk and Samoa during this period. Both regions were transitioning from a period of outright colonial control as United Nations Trust Territories: Chuuk as part of the US Trust Territory of the Pacific Islands (USTTPI) and Samoa as part of a UN Trust under New Zealand. The United States was granted its trust from a League of Nations mandate to Japan in 1947. New Zealand had taken (formerly Western) Samoa from the German administration in 1917. Samoa gained formal independence from New Zealand in 1962. The Micronesian polities (Palau, Yap, Chuuk, Pohnpei, Kosrae, and the Marshall Islands) were transitioning from US Trusteeship, beginning with the election of the Congress of Micronesia in the late 1960s. In 1979, the first constitutional government of the Federated States of Micronesia (of which Chuuk is a part) was seated with others to follow for Palau and the Marshall Islands. The period from the mid-1960s through the early 1980s was also a period of rapidly increasing development assistance in the region.

These two historical precedents led many of the scholars and expatriates from community-based organizations and NGOs, who first took notice of the rising incidence of suicide in Chuuk and Samoa, to look to classic modernization theories of the late nineteenth century to explain these trends (see Lowe 2019 for review). The take-home message of most of these explanatory models was that these islands had become stuck between the "utopian" modern world of technological progress, liberal individualism, democratic family life, and full employment in capitalist enterprises and the romantic image of a locally

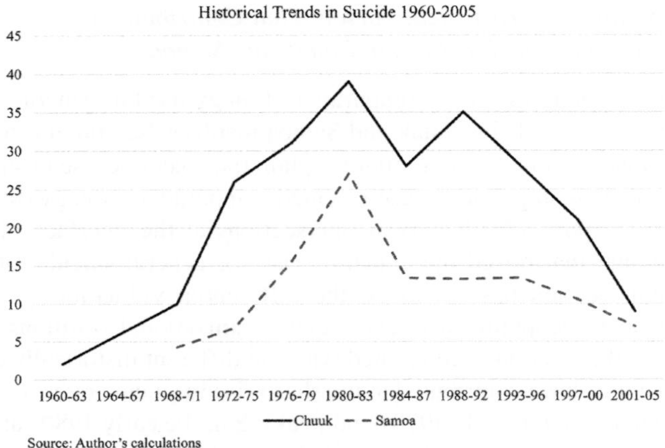

Figure 3.1 Historical trends in suicide for Chuuk and Samoa (1960–2005).

bounded, harmonious cultural world of eternal recurrence that had become perfectly adapted to its particular ecological niche some time in its mythical past. Presumed socialization and interpersonal imbalances in the family and kin group, lost cultural meaning systems that had once assuaged existential concerns, or a new anomic rage associated with having new modern aspirations thwarted by selfish, old-fashioned parents and community leaders were used to explain these trends in suicide in the region (e.g. Booth 1999; Salzman 2005; Hezel 1984; Macpherson and Macpherson 1987; Macpherson 2010).

But a more careful examination of the available historical evidence surrounding these cases suggests that explanations that try to place them into a universal grand historical narrative miss the mark (Lowe 2019). Instead, circumstances of a much more historically particular nature seemed to contribute to the sudden increases and decreases in suicide rates during this period. For example, the sudden increase and then equally dramatic decrease in suicide rates in Samoa by the mid-1980s correlate well with the initial introduction of paraquat into Samoa as part of the Samoan State's agricultural development policies of the 1970s when 70 percent of the population lived in rural villages, with its rapid adoption as a means of self-poisoning and then its regulation and control as part of an effort to address suicide after 1980 leading to a much lower subsequent availability (Bowles 1995). Bowles (1995) has shown convincingly that much of the increase in suicide death rates during the mid-1970s to the early 1980s can be attributed to paraquat poisonings. A secondary factor in the Samoan case may have been the increase in out-migration by working-aged young adults in the late 1960s and continuing into the 1980s, raising demographic dependency rates and possibly the strain on young adults in terms of the levels of service they were then required to provide their families and village leaders (Macpherson and Macpherson 1987; Macpherson 2010). This explanatory factor is particularly compelling in light of the political-economic processes that may leave young men and women vulnerable to experiences of exploitation in Samoa, as argued in the previous section.

However, neither the globalization of the herbicide paraquat nor the increased out-migration and experiences of exploitation could explain the rise in suicide rates in Chuuk or elsewhere in Micronesia (Lowe 2019; Rubinstein 1992, 1995). Unlike Samoa, where as much as half of the gross domestic product (GDP) in the 1970s came from the export of a few agricultural commodities (O'Meara 1990), Chuuk and the other Micronesian island groups exported little of their agricultural product during this time. Poisoning as a means of self-harm is rare. Rather a regionally particular form of self-asphyxiation by leaning into a rope has been the dominant mode of attempted suicide for decades (Rubinstein 1983). Also, out-migration was strictly limited by the USTTPI colonial government until the Compacts of Free Association with the United States went into effect in 1987 (Rubinstein 1992).

The major historical factor that did correlate with the rise in suicide rates not only in Chuuk but in all of the USTTPI island groups was a massive increase in US development aid targeted directly at raising levels of bureaucratic employment, household incomes, and local consumption of imported commodities (Hezel 1995; Lowe 2019). The increasing availability of cash translated into a well-documented case of escalating competitive exchange and gift giving at ritual events, new and competitive construction of houses and churches, and a rapid increase in the importation and consumption of industrially produced foods and drinks. Among these, there was a rapid increase in the availability and excessive consumption of alcohol concentrated among older boys and young men and associated bouts of drunken brawling and community disturbances (Marshall 1979). The combination of these factors is strongly associated with the sharp rise in suicides during the 1970s and into the 1980s. This influx of cash may have contributed to a condition of disjunctive "status inflation" in Chuuk and elsewhere in Micronesia, generating new sites of tension and conflict between older boys and young men and their families in particular. Interestingly, as levels of economic aid and a new fervor for neoliberal reforms emerged in Chuuk and elsewhere in the region after 1987, suicide rates decreased (Lowe 2019).

To summarize this section, by comparatively considering how the different historically contingent variables (e.g. the levels of the importation of a lethal herbicide in Samoa versus the level of direct foreign aid in Chuuk) were associated with the rapid rise and decline in suicide rates in Samoa and Chuuk, we are able to more effectively identify and explain the historically contingent intersections of different local-global processes that may have given rise to the suicide epidemics in Chuuk and Samoa in the 1970s and 1980s. This adds a dimension of explanation that is not possible in the admittedly "thicker" incommensurate comparative examination of the ethnopsychological understandings of emotion and personhood that situate acts of self-harm in the wider moral worlds that obtain in Chuuk and Samoa. Scaling up also helps us to distinguish the insights we gained into how political-economic processes can produce disparities in levels of vulnerability and resiliency from those that reflect the larger global-local intersections that contribute to changing epidemiological patterns at a society-wide scale.

But more than this, this variation-finding comparative strategy helps us see that different, often disjunctive (Lazar 2012), configurations of global-local intersections can articulate in particular ways for each historical case, producing an apparently similar pattern in empirical indicators such as the change in suicide rates over time. In the Samoa epidemic case, it was the intensified movement of people through migration that increased labor loads for young adults and the importation of a new herbicide and techniques designed to promote increased agricultural output – and to serve an ideology of "development" – that contributed to the epidemic pattern. In the case of Chuuk, it was the increased inflow of money, its entanglements with a US-based ideology of "dependency-development," and flows of globalizing consumer commodities that contributed to the rising suicide rates (see Lowe 2019).

Conclusion

The main objective of this chapter was to demonstrate how explicit comparative methods in anthropology can be an effective means of developing middle-range theories of the phenomena we study. Unlike theories that attempt to describe and explain social phenomena in universal, context-free ways, middle-range theories attempt to explain them in ways that can be both historically interpretive and causally analytic (Ragin 1987). This chapter has examined the historically particular cases of late-twentieth-century suicide epidemics in Chuuk and Samoa. Theoretical insights that remained sensitive to the contexts of each case required three analytic moves. First, an incommensurate comparison that compared the ethnopsychological understandings of emotion, personhood, and suicidal behavior in Chuuk and Samoa was used to destabilize existing middle-range theories of suicide that have been developed primarily in the globalizing psy-disciplines. Drawing on the ethnopsychological insights, the second strategy involved "drilling down" to compare the similarities and differences in the political-economic processes and social organization in Chuuk and Samoa that create structural positions of differential vulnerability and resilience with regard to suicidal acts as a means of protest over perceived unjust actions of one's social superiors. The third strategy involved "scaling up" to compare and contrast the particular historical intersections that contributed to the epidemic patterns of suicide death rates in both Chuuk and Samoa in the 1970s and 1980s. These three analytic moves provide a more satisfying middle-range explanation for the suicide epidemics in Samoa and Chuuk in the last decades of the twentieth century than any of the comparative approaches would have if used alone.

References

Bell, Richard. 2011. "Weeping for Werther: Suicide, Sympathy and the Reading Revolution in Early America." In *The History of Reading, International Perspective c. 1500–1990*, vol. I, edited by Shafquat Towheed and William R. Owens, 49–63. Basingstoke: Palgrave Macmillan.

Booth, Heather. 1999. "Pacific Island Suicide in Comparative Perspective." *Journal of Biosocial Science* 31 (4): 433–48.

Bourke, Terry. 2001. "Suicide in Samoa." *Pacific Health Dialog* 8 (1): 213–19.

Bowles, John R. 1985. "Suicide and Attempted Suicide in Contemporary Western Samoa." In *Culture, Youth and Suicide in the Pacific: Chapters from an East-West Center Conference Center for Pacific Islands Studies*, edited by Francis X. Hezel, Donald H. Rubinstein, and Geoffrey M. White, 15–35. Working Paper series. Honolulu: Pacific Islands Studies Program, Center for Asian and Pacific Studies, University of Hawaii at Manoa.

Bowles, John R. 1995. "Suicide in Western Samoa: An Example of a Suicide Prevention Program in a Developing Country." In *Preventative Strategies on Suicide*, edited by René F. W. Diekstra, Walter Gulbinat, Ineke Kienhorst, and Diego de Leo, 173–206. Leiden: E. J. Brill.

Chua, Jocelyn L. 2012. "Tales of Decline: Reading Social Pathology into Individual Suicide in South India." *Culture, Medicine, and Psychiatry* 36 (2): 204–24.

Durkheim, Emile. 1951. *Suicide: A Study in Sociology*. Translated by John A. Spaulding and George Simpson. Glencoe, IL: Free Press.

Fischer, Michael M. J. 2018. *Anthropology in the Meantime: Experimental Ethnography, Theory, and Method for the 21st Century*. Durham, NC: Duke University Press.

Gerber, Eleanor R. 1985. "Rage and Obligation: Samoan Emotion in Conflict." In *Person, Self, and Experience: Exploring Pacific Ethnopsychologies*, edited by Geoffrey M. White and John Kirkpatrick, 121–67. Berkeley: University of California Press.

Gingrich, Andre. 2002. "When Ethnic Majorities Are 'Dethroned': Towards a Methodology of Self Reflexive, Controlled Macrocomparison." In *Anthropology, by Comparison*, edited by Andre Gingrich and Richard Gabriel Fox, 224–47. London: Routledge.

Gingrich, Andre, and Richard G. Fox, eds. 2002. *Anthropology, by Comparison*. London: Routledge.

Goodenough, Ward H. 1978. *Property, Kin, and Community on Truk*, 2nd ed. Hamden, CT: Archon Books.

Hallowell, Alfred I. 1955. *Culture and Experience*. Philadelphia: University of Pennsylvania Press.

Handler, Richard. 2009. "The Uses of Incommensurability in Anthropology." *New Literary History* 40 (3): 627–47.

Henrich, Joseph, Steven J. Heine, and Ara Norenzayan. 2010. "The Weirdest People in the World?" *Behavioral and Brain Sciences* 33 (2–3): 61–83.

Hezel, Francis X. 1976. "Micronesia's Hanging Spree." *Micronesian Independent*, December 31. Accessed [January 3, 2019]. www.micsem.org/pubs/articles/suicide/frames/microhangspreefr.htm

Hezel, Francis X. 1984. "Cultural Patterns in Trukese Suicide." *Ethnology* 23 (3): 193–206.

Hezel, Francis X. 1995. *Strangers in Their Own Land*. Honolulu: University of Hawai'i Press.

Hirsch, Jennifer, Holly Wardlow, Daniel J. Smith, Harriet Phinney, Shanti Parikh, and Constance A. Nathanson. 2009. *The Secret: Love, Marriage, and HIV.* Nashville, TN: Vanderbilt University Press.

Hollan, Douglas. 1990. "Indignant Suicide in the Pacific: An Example from the Toraja Highlands of Indonesia." *Culture, Medicine and Psychiatry* 14 (3): 365–79.

Hollan, Douglas. 2001. "Developments in Person-Centered Ethnography." In *The Psychology of Cultural Experience*, edited by Carmella C. Moore and Holly F. Mathews, 48–67. Cambridge: Cambridge University Press.

Jackson, Michael. 2013. *Lifeworlds: Essays in Existential Anthropology*. Chicago, IL: University of Chicago Press.

Lazar, Sian. 2012. "Disjunctive Comparison: Citizenship and Trade Unionism in Bolivia and Argentina." *Journal of the Royal Anthropological Institute* 18 (2): 349–68.

Lowe, Edward. D. 2002. "A Widow, a Child, and Two Lineages: Exploring Kinship and Attachment in Chuuk." *American Anthropologist* 104 (1): 123–37.

Lowe, Edward. D. 2003. "Identity, Activity, and the Well-Being of Adolescents and Youths: Lessons from Young People in a Micronesian Society." *Culture, Medicine and Psychiatry* 27 (2): 187–219.

Lowe, Edward. D. 2018. "Kinship, Funerals, and the Durability of Culture in Chuuk." In *Advances in Culture Theory from Psychological Anthropology*, edited by Naomi Quinn, 75–108. Cham: Palgrave Macmillan.

Lowe, Edward. D. 2019. "Epidemic Suicide in the Context of Modernizing Social Change in Oceania: A Critical Review and Assessment." *The Contemporary Pacific* 31 (1): 105–38.

Lutz, Catherine. 1985. "Ethnopsychology Compared to What? Explaining Behavior and Consciousness among the Ifaluk." In *Person, Self, and Experience: Exploring Pacific Ethnopsychologies*, edited by Geoffrey M. White and John Kirkpatrick, 35–79. Berkeley: University of California Press.

Lutz, Catherine. 1988. *Unnatural Emotions: Everyday Sentiments on a Micronesian Atoll & Their Challenge to Western Theory*. Chicago, IL: University of Chicago Press.

Macpherson, Cluny. 2010. *The Warm Winds of Change: Globalisation and Contemporary Samoa*. Auckland: Auckland University Press.

Macpherson, Cluny, and La'Avasa Macpherson. 1987. "Towards an Explanation of Recent Trends in Suicide in Western Samoa." *Man* 22 (2): 305–30.

Marsella, Anthony J., Ayda Aukahi Austin, and Bruce Grant. 2005. "Introduction." In *Social Change and Psychosocial Adaptation in the Pacific Islands*, edited by Anthony J. Marsella, Ayda Aukahi Austin, and Bruce Grant, 1–8. New York: Springer.

Marshall, Mac. 1979. *Weekend Warriors: Alcohol in a Micronesian Culture*. Palo Alto, CA: Mayfield Publishers.

Matangi Tonga. 2014. "Suicide Rate in Pacific Islands among Highest in the World." August 14. Accessed [March 1, 2019]. www.pireport.org/articles/2014/08/15/suicide-rate-pacific-islands-among-highest-world

Mead, Margaret. 1961. *Coming of Age in Samoa*. New York: William Morrow.

O'Meara, Tim J. 1990. *Samoan Planters: Tradition and Economic Development in Polynesia*. Fort Worth, TX: Holt, Rinehart and Winston.

Ragin, Charles C. 1987. *The Comparative Method: Moving beyond Qualitative and Quantitative Strategies*. Berkeley: University of California Press.

Rose, Nikolas. 1996. *Inventing Our Selves: Psychology, Power, and Personhood*. Cambridge: Cambridge University Press.

Rubinstein, Donald H. 1983. "Epidemic Suicide among Micronesian Adolescents." *Social Science & Medicine* 17 (10): 657–65.

Rubinstein, Donald H. 1992. "Suicide in Micronesia and Samoa: A Critique of Explanations." *Pacific Studies* 15 (1): 51–75.

Rubinstein, Donald H. 1995. "Love and Suffering: Adolescent Socialization and Suicide in Micronesia." *The Contemporary Pacific* 7 (1): 21–53.

Salzman, Michael. 2005. "The Dynamics of Cultural Trauma: Implications for the Pacific Nations." In *Social Change and Psychosocial Adaptation in the Pacific Islands*, edited by Anthony J. Marsella, Ayda Aukahi Austin, and Bruce Grant, 29–51. New York: Springer Press.

Strathern, Marilyn. 1988. *The Gender of the Gift: Problems with Women and Problems with Society in Melanesia*. Berkeley: University of California Press.

Stromberg, Peter. G. 2015. "Wesleyan Sanctification and the Ethic of Self-Realization." *Ethos* 43 (4): 423–43.

Tcherkezoff, Serge. 2015. "Sister or Wife, You've Got to Choose." In *Living Kinship in the Pacific*, edited by Christina Toren and Simonne Pauwels, 166–85. New York: Berghahn Books.

Widger, Tom. 2015. *Suicide in Sri Lanka: The Anthropology of an Epidemic*. London: Routledge.

Part II

Regional Comparisons

4 The Comparison of Structures and the Comparison of Systems

Lévi-Strauss, Dumont, Luhmann

Guido Sprenger

Comparison of cultural configurations springs from the experience that people behave, live, and communicate differently in any context that an observer is not familiar with. By a long, peculiar, and contingent process, this has resulted in a modern concept of culture and an academic discipline called anthropology. This development has been shaped by the values of enlightenment, which demand that the implicit becomes explicit and that what may have been "between the lines" should be spelled out directly. For this reason, anthropology needs to be explicit about the shock of difference from which it emerges, which also means that it should reflect upon and systematize the means of comparison that underlie its discourse.

I broadly see two attitudes to comparison as an asset. In the first, scholars are confronted with at least two different sets of complex empirical data that represent some significant social reality. They then proceed to apply certain analytical methods that reduce the complexity of these datasets according to particular procedures in order to make them comparable – identify indicators, quantify them, and so forth. As a result, they are able to tell how the two sets of data are similar to or different from each other. This requires a generally positivist stance: there are matters out there that can be known to us and that follow particular rules that we can capture with our analytical apparatus. Of course, we may admit that this apparatus is far from explaining everything and only approaches the truth – but saying this implies that explaining everything and capturing the truth is the yardstick of success.

The second attitude addresses both this positivist stance and its opposite, a relativist skepticism regarding the possibility of adequately rendering social life or cultural concepts in scholarly models at all, not to talk about comparison. This second position is currently found mostly in the anthropology of ontologies but is not restricted to it. It does not so much aim at comparing real entities "out there" and is thus not interested in particularly positivist results. Rather, it intends to elicit thought and extend the range of reflection by confronting conventionalized Western modern ideas with unexpected but plausible possibilities, drawn from ethnography. It is then not so much an attempt to "grasp the native's point of view" or to analyze cultures and systems as objects. Rather, comparison produces a provocative and fertile tension between concepts and ideas that expands thought, practices, and possibly politics. This implies that anthropology is separated neither from other discourses of modernity nor from the local worlds it explores. Feeding new ideas into anthropology changes discourse in general.

In this latter view, comparison operates not so much by measuring similarities and differences but by the strategic exaggeration of alterity. The works of Tim Ingold (2000) and Eduardo Viveiros de Castro (1998, 2013) belong to this type of comparison, but so too do those of a number of earlier scholars, including Marilyn Strathern (1988) and, as I argue, Louis Dumont (1991). Claude Lévi-Strauss in some respects unites both types of comparison: within a positivist framework, Lévi-Strauss sought out those themes and issues from ethnography that would reinvigorate modern philosophy. It is no wonder then that proponents of the anthropology of ontologies such as Philippe Descola (2011) and Viveiros de Castro (2016) find inspiration in his work (see Kohn 2015, 316).

I am aware of the merits and limitations of both approaches. In the following discussion, I am thus trying to operate with both frameworks in mind: thinking about comparison as grounded in solid and complex ethnographic fieldwork but with a sense of conspicuous, even exaggerated contrasts. In this sense, comparison is not so much about finding similarities as about systematizing differences.

I compare three different ways of comparing, based on the work of Claude Lévi-Strauss, Louis Dumont, and Niklas Luhmann. In my own work, I have fused these three approaches when comparing the way local societies relate to the outside in upland Southeast Asia (see Conclusion).

Functions and Attributes of a Comparative Language

The craft of anthropology lies in uniting the necessity of comparison with the notion that cultural representations are contingent, culturally specific, and qualitatively different from one another. The terms "emic" and "etic" put this difference into stark contrast, but nothing in ethnographies is fully "emic," and insofar as even general analytic terms are shaped by handling ethnographic data, they are not fully "etic" either. Therefore, it seems to me that comparison and the understanding of specificities are indeed the same project rather than two incompatible enterprises. The recognition that cultural/social configurations differ demands an examination of their (internal and local) systematicity as well as how they compare to one another.

This raises the question of how the terms of comparison are organized and how they relate to local concepts.[1] The aim is to establish a systematic relationship between local terms and concepts, on the one hand, and disciplinary strategies of generalization, on the other. This raises the problem of comparing entities that appear to be qualitatively different – almost a contradiction in terms. One strategy to accomplish this is to compare not so much the local terms themselves but rather the relationships between them, i.e. the way they are organized. Therefore, comparison should pay attention to formal qualities of the compared entities and at the same time heed the meaning of local concepts. By operating with local terms, comparison keeps pointing at a complexity that stays beyond its grasp; this way, it remains reflexive of its own strategies for reducing complexity. Comparison can account for its limitations by using local terms, thus constantly reminding readers of a uniqueness that exceeds comparison.

In the following discussion, I compare three different but interrelated ways of approaching this issue. All of them are concerned with the comparison of relationships and therefore represent attempts to systematize difference. Relationships, here, are processes that establish differences as mutually dependent, as complementary, antagonistic, or in some other way necessarily related. All of them provide space for local and specific concepts.

For Claude Lévi-Strauss, the comparison of select features of different societies is based on relational, often contrasting terms (oppositions), which are organized in codes and then patterned across codes. The variations of these patterns across cultural configurations are called transformations. Lévi-Strauss usually identifies the cultural representations he compares as belonging to ethnic groups or societies – the masks of the Salish, the myths of the Kwakiutl – but he does not claim to compare these societies as such.

Louis Dumont, in contrast, asks how societies can be compared as wholes and which parts of them appropriately represent these wholes. This raises the question of how the wholeness of societies that this assumes comes about in the first place. Dumont focuses on the comparison of hierarchically organized value systems (ideologies).

Both theories implicitly or explicitly compare societies on the basis of part-whole relationships. While this approach, I argue, does not lose its epistemological value simply through an increase in global relationships, as some of its critics suggest, it is hardly able to take such entanglements into account. Niklas Luhmann's theory of autopoietic social systems offers potentials to combine the analysis of local coherence and of translocal relations. Luhmann replaces the part-whole relationship at the core of functionalist (and some structuralist) approaches with the relationship between system and environment. In this view, systems are operatively both closed and open, reproducing themselves through their relationship with the environment. This, as well as Luhmann's attention to contingency and process, offers comparisons that are appropriate for an anthropology in a globally entangled world.

While relationships are the subject of comparison in all these approaches, they are conceptualized in three different analytical languages. For Lévi-Strauss, the notions of model, code, structure, and transformation are central. Dumont addresses the part-whole relationship more explicitly, relating it to the terms "value" and "hierarchy." For Luhmann, the system-environment relation is determined by semantics and guiding differences between the respective systems. For all three authors, comparison consists in creating a set of terms that can be fruitfully applied to different cultural configurations without denying their difference; in other words, comparison elicits different answers to the same questions.

Coding Differences: Claude Lévi-Strauss

Above I have referred to two types of differences. The first type is the difference *between* two cultural configurations, which, I suggested, is rooted in the experience that people behave, live, and communicate differently in different contexts. This difference-between is the object of comparison. The second type of difference is situated *within* each configuration, system, or society. The various representations (practices, institutions, ideas, etc.) making up one configuration need to be different from one another. Furthermore, their differences have to be organized in relational and systematic ways in order to enable communication within society – communication seen here as creating and cultivating difference as the condition of relationships. A mountain is different from the sky; that much seems obvious. But it would be unsystematic to say that a mountain is different from the sky because the mountain is made of rock and the sky is blue. Rather, in relational terms, one could say that the mountain is below and the sky is above. This expresses their difference in terms of a code of spatial relations. Therefore, the systematic organization of any configuration is based on relationships, not beings. Claude Lévi-Strauss connects both types of differences, those *within* and those *between* configurations, through his notions of code, structure, and transformation.

In order to analyze the systematic organization of representations, Lévi-Strauss developed the notion of codes: a shared set of terms that were more abstract than the data but at the same time inherent to them – like "above" and "below" in the example given. Lévi-Strauss suggested that any myth, ritual, or exchange system would be incoherent or meaningless without such abstract codes unifying the bits and pieces they consist of. Comparison then addresses the question of whether these codes work transculturally and, ultimately, if they are universal or not. It is important to note, however, that Lévi-Strauss drew codes from the ethnographic material and then asked for the range of data to which they could be applied.

This is less obvious in Lévi-Strauss's first grand attempt at comparison, *The Elementary Structures of Kinship* (1969). Here, the code is kinship and is taken to be universal, as was appropriate to anthropological theory of its time. It thus seemed unnecessary to point out that "kinship" and "exchange" performed the same function in his argument as the codes he identified more explicitly in his later analyses of myth.

Examples of the latter feature in his early articles, "The Structural Analysis of Myth" (Lévi-Strauss 1963) and "The Story of Asdiwal" (Lévi-Strauss 1976e). Here, he demonstrates how different episodes of a story appear as contrasts within a given code: sky and earth, valley and mountain, above and below constitute a code of space; in-laws and descendants, wife and son, a code of kinship; hunting and agriculture, a code of livelihood; and so on. Thus, concrete terms such as "mountain" become meaningful only when related to a more general notion of space. A code appears as a set of terms in differentiated relationships that exhaust a particular field of experience or ideas – both the field and the terms being culturally defined on the basis of concrete local experience. The combination of codes produces specific meaning (Leach 1976e, Chapters 8 and 13). However, the ways in which terms are related are universal, thus making comparison possible.

Analyzing a myth – to take Lévi-Strauss's most prominent field of study – along such lines suggests a number of questions: First, does the same code structure other representations of a given society, i.e. its rituals, kinship, and cosmological notions? This is crucial for establishing the existence of the code in the first place. Second, can the same code be found in neighboring groups? Third, is the code, which represents one step into abstraction, subject to a larger, even more encompassing code, on a higher scale of generalization? This last question immediately refers to the second: When one code reaches its limits of diffusion in a particular region, and a different code gains prominence among its neighbors, do these two codes provide a larger framework for the comparison of the regions they appear in, and are they thus transformations of each other, just as neighboring myths are such transformations?

This approach to comparison suggests certain presuppositions. First, it operates with a difference-based notion of intercultural relationships. Scholars who tried to reduce the Galton effect considered those case studies optimal for comparison that had no historical connection and therefore provided the anthropological equivalent of laboratory conditions in experimental sciences. They were thus treating "cultures" as individuals and sought to isolate universal laws (Schnegg 2014).

In contrast, Lévi-Strauss preferred case studies where such connections are present. A major example is that of the Amerindian myths whose transformations he followed through the four volumes of his *Mythologiques* (1976a, 1976b, 1976c, 1976d). Starting with the Bororo in Brazil, he slowly expanded comparison to their neighbors until he had covered the entirety of South America. In the fourth volume, *The Naked Man* (1976d), he ventured to compare these findings with the mythological complex of North America, in, as he wrote, an "expanding galaxy" of myths (Lévi-Strauss 1976a). Besides a strong belief in the importance of diffusion, this approach betrays a different concept of intercultural relationships than that held by Galton and his successors. For Lévi-Strauss, their relationships do not make societies more similar to one another but rather more different. He assumes that neighboring groups tend to differentiate from one another by developing transformations based on similar codes and structures. A transformation is present when elements of a structure are exchanged for others and thereby affect the entire structure (Lévi-Strauss 1963).

His analysis of masks and myths in *The Way of the Masks* (1983) serves as an example. Here, he focuses on closely related societies of the American Northwest Coast whose cultural representations appear as reversals of one another. The Swaihwé masks of Salish-speaking groups are connected to two contrasting sets of myths. The versions from Vancouver Island seem incoherent – their storylines strangely unresolved. However, if their separate episodes are compared with the myths on the mainland, each episode appears as a reversal of the corresponding episode of the neighboring myth (Lévi-Strauss 1983, Chapter 1).

Lévi-Strauss then goes on to compare the Swaihwé masks with the Dzonokwa masks of the Salish's northern neighbors, the Kwakiutl. The Swaihwé masks have protruding eyes and their tongues are sticking out, while Dzonokwa masks have hollowed-out eyes and their mouths have protruding lips. Both sets of masks are not isolated – Swaihwé masks were adopted by Kwakiutl, while the mythical character of Dzonokwa is present among the Salish as well. However, the relation between masks and myths is reversed among the Kwakiutl (Lévi-Strauss 1983, 56–60, 83). Thus, Lévi-Strauss compares both myths and masks as transformations of transculturally shared codes and argues for a pattern that integrates stories and things across several societies into a single set of transformations.

These transformations are not necessarily unconscious, as Lévi-Strauss argues in "Relations of Symmetry between Rituals and Myths of Neighboring Peoples" (1976e). Here he demonstrates how the Hidatsa and the Mandan cultivated their differences by linking similar rituals in the two societies with oppositionally structured myths. This is, he suggests, the result of a conscious politics of proximity and distance, similarity and difference at the foundation of the relationship between the two groups. Comparison is thus also a productive act of cultural elaboration (see Sprenger 2017c). Only the formation of ideas for such a politics of difference follows universal nonconscious patterns.

Thus, external relationships appear as constitutive of the specific internal order of myth and ritual, and the two types of differences mentioned earlier depend on each other – a point to which I return in my discussion of Luhmann. Here, I want to point out that this approach challenges functionalism in the sense that function denotes the relationship of a part to the whole. Lévi-Straussian structuralism shares with Radcliffe-Brownian functionalism the idea that structure is a set of related elements that change when one of them changes. This implies that the range of elements affected is limited and that the structure thus has boundaries. If Hidatsa and Mandan myths are functions of each other, what is the whole? Is it restricted to these two groups only or is it larger? Here, Lévi-Strauss suggests that the operation of codes and the structure of relationships work on different levels of the social in the same way.

However, Lévi-Strauss does not aim to compare societies; he is not taking myths or rituals to represent the given society as a whole. He conventionally refers to certain representations as belonging to this or that society and insists that the context of a given representation is crucial for its understanding. But his argument does not necessitate the idea that societies are distinctive wholes or should be units of comparison. This is a way to reduce the complexity of comparison that allows Lévi-Strauss to sideline the question of boundaries. The differences between masks or myths are structured, but it remains open as to whether this indicates differences between societies. In this respect, Lévi-Strauss predates current approaches that do not take societies and their boundaries for granted.

Lévi-Strauss's reflections on dualist organizations move a step closer to the comparison of societies but also further develop his ideas of encompassing codes. Here, he explores the relation between binary and ternary relationships and finds comparable structures in different societies in different parts of the world – albeit in different codes. "To put it yet differently, what a given society 'says' in terms of marriage relations is being 'said' by another society in terms of village layout, and in terms of religious representations by a third, and so on" (1976e, 77). Here, the specific codes of kinship, space, religion, and so forth are transcended by an encompassing structure consisting of relations between binary and ternary structures – a kind of meta-code of relational forms.

For Lévi-Strauss, structural differences are a matter of scale, not of quality. The comparison of two myths from the same society follows the same procedures as the comparison of the entirety of North America with South America. "Society" as a unit of comparison appears as wholly contingent and heuristic. Therefore, structural analysis as a method that reveals connections and coherence within the data is difficult to disentangle from structuralism as a general theory of mind and society. The same modes of difference-making pertain potentially everywhere, even though Lévi-Strauss has pointed out that structural analysis works best for small-scale societies (Lévi-Strauss 1980, 254).

Lévi-Strauss's most important successor today, Philippe Descola, operates probably on the highest scale of comparison. His *Beyond Nature and Culture*

(2011) provides a prime example of a specific feature of Lévi-Strauss's work, as found in, for example, his study of the atom of kinship (1963, Chapter 1); that is, the limitation of possible combinations. Insofar as codes contain a limited number of terms, the combinations within one code can be exhausted. If they are reduced to two dimensions with two terms each – as in a graph with x and y axes – four variations result. In Descola's work, the code is referred to in terms of "modes of identification" and is concerned with the way humans identify nonhumans. It consists of combinations of two pairs of oppositions: physicality versus interiority and identity versus difference. If beings are identified to have the same physicality as, but different interiority from, humans, this is called "naturalism" by Descola. In turn, he denotes same interiority but different physicality as animism, same interiority and physicality as totemism, and different physicality and interiority as analogism. This fourfold scheme basically exhausts all possible modes and is thus formally identical with Lévi-Strauss's analysis of the atom of kinship. Although exciting and timely in the current nexus of ecological crisis and anthropological theory, Descola does not offer any advance in comparative methodology. In fact, Viveiros de Castro (2016) finds that this exhaustible, "grammatical" type of comparison is only one mode of structural analysis in Lévi-Strauss. The other, "analogic" form posits complex transformations that only slightly diverge from one another in a possibly endless series. This second type is characteristic of Lévi-Strauss's *Mythologiques* but atypical of Descola's work.

In sum, I want to point out the following features of Lévi-Straussian comparison: the aim of comparison is not to prove causality (*pace* Pickvance 2001) but rather to demonstrate how differences in cultural representations relate to one another. The strength of this procedure is its reliance on local codes that appear in myths, rituals, relationship terminologies, things, and so forth. While comparisons of, say, kinship or residence structures always raise the question of whether the items compared are actually of the same kind (Schneider 1984), the comparison of representations from neighboring societies presumes similar codes and classifications.

Lévi-Strauss encompasses the concrete terms of the data with more abstract and general ones. But he develops the latter from the ethnographic material and less so from disciplinary analytical toolkits. Lévi-Strauss has been criticized, since early on, for the choice of his abstractions, in which he sometimes seems to construct oppositional terms, i.e. codes, instead of revealing them, giving them an air of arbitrary invention (Douglas 1973). This raises the question of which terms of comparison would be valid. A code of, say, negation/confirmation of human autochthony, as in Lévi-Strauss's analysis of Oedipus (1963, Chapter 11), might seem arbitrary, but to what extent are codes such as "kinship,""gender," or "class" any better? At least Lévi-Strauss's codes emerge from relating data to his own analytical devices, in a way that allows the data to determine the terms of the code while theory provides its structure. In this respect, analysis references the complexity of local terms and keeps the work of reducing complexity open to scrutiny.

At the same time, Lévi-Strauss's stress on the importance of context and his avoidance of the notion of societies as stable, functional wholes emerge from his notion of transformation. Transformations occur between different versions of myths or marriage rules, and while the bounded society appears as a convention in Lévi-Strauss's work, there is no necessity for it. Indeed, in the *Mythologiques*, he considers the entirety of the (precolonial) American continent as a whole of which all local representations are parts. The strong interest in diffusion both in Lévi-Strauss's framework and in current studies of a globalized world suggests fertile reassessments of his comparative apparatus.

The questions for comparison that his work provides are thus the following:

- How are cultural representations locally organized by codes, and how are these codes related to each other?
- How do these systems of codes change relationally across localities or cultural boundaries; that is, how are adjacent or remote cultural representations transformations of each other?
- Which common themes are addressed in these transformations – that is, which combinations do the codes allow for, and what do they "say" about the social realities in which they are enacted?
- What are the consequences of the transformed representations for the cultural configurations in which they exist?

Comparing Value Systems: Louis Dumont

Louis Dumont's approach to comparison appears in some respects as a synthesis of Lévi-Strauss's comparison of structures and transformations and a more British concern with societies as functional wholes. Dumont claims that comparison cannot be restricted to specific cultural representations or subsystems, such as kinship and mythology. Rather, comparison has to address societies as wholes. Thus, the society as a somehow bounded entity is the unit of comparison for him. Kinship, politics, religion, and so forth, he argues, may be considered subsystems, but there is no way from the outset to be sure whether they are "real systems" – internally coherent subsystems within the overall system of society – or just "nominal systems," whose coherence is only assumed by the external observer (Dumont 2006, 13). This is due to Dumont's notion of a whole: "Ultimately and logically, in contrast to a collection, a 'whole' is an ensemble founded on distinctive oppositions which determine a complementarity between its elements" (Dumont 2006, 9).[2]

The relationships on which the whole is based are, first of all, part-whole relationships. These are hierarchical, as the whole encompasses its parts (Dumont 2006, 13). Each element of a system is defined by two types of relationships: those with other elements of the system and that with the system/society as a whole. Therefore, "[t]he comparison is guaranteed only at the level of the global [i.e. entire, bounded, GS] society" (Dumont 2006, 12). The comparison of subsystems such as kinship – which occupy different positions within different societies and have various degrees of coherence – will only divert from the society's "indigenous representations" (Dumont 2006).

From this perspective, the comparison of societies as wholes would seem to be an impossibly complex task. Still, Dumont rejected the notion, which he termed "sociocentrism," that communication and thereby comparison between societies is impossible. Instead, he practiced comparison "relentlessly" (Damon 2009), in particular between India and Western modernity. This raises the question of what type of cultural representation represents the whole and could thus serve as an object of study.[3] This relates to Dumont's notion of hierarchy. If whole and parts constitute each other, then it is possible to identify in any relationship between two elements the one that is superior to the other. This element can be taken to represent the whole – that is, the ultimate superior position – at least in this particular relationship. This is Dumont's answer to Robert Hertz's (1960) question of why the right hand is considered superior to the left – it represents the whole of the body (Dumont 1991, 242–43).

This procedure can now be applied to societies. For Dumont, it is values and their organization as ideologies (systems of values that at the same time are ideas or concepts) that allow us to approach the whole. The ideology is organized into different hierarchically organized levels – not levels of abstraction but levels of representativeness in relation to the whole. Each level is structured by the hierarchical relationship between two value-ideas. The hierarchy between two value-ideas might be reversed on a different level of the ideology. Values that are superior on one level of the ideology might be inferior on a different level. Levels on which the value representing the whole is superior to its opposite are higher than those where it is inferior. Such reversals indicate differences between levels that are fixed in hierarchical relations to one another.

This is where Robbins (2015, 175) – who has, like Kapferer (2010), criticized the notion that Dumont assumes static hierarchies – locates what he calls "Dumont's hierarchical dynamism." Values exist in social life because people are constantly striving to attain them. As the highest value realizes the whole of the system, seeking to attain it equals seeking to realize the whole. This, in turn, allows people to valorize any event they take part in or witness and relate it to the highest value. Each social situation, each decision, judgment, or debate can thus be understood – by actors and observers alike – in terms of the value configuration enacted in it, and thus attributed to a particular level.

I would like to add that Dumont's dynamism emerges even without the drive to transcend a given situation. Each time people have to make a decision or a judgment, they are not only deciding which value is superior in a given situation but also, by extension, deciding which level the situation is part of. The hierarchy of levels and the structure of the ideology thus do not allow one to easily predict the outcome of a decision, as decisions are constantly realizing the ideology. For instance, choosing between a career as an artist or as an accountant implies the hierarchization of two values: individual expression at the cost of financial security or the other way around. If Western modern society places, as Dumont argues, the individual as its paramount value, becoming an artist may realize a higher value than security. This is suggested by the idea that failure to become a successful accountant is failure plain and simple, while failure to become a successful artist can be considered as somewhat heroic, even unjust. Still, this does not foreclose an individual's decision to pursue a specific career. Choosing security over risk realizes a different value at a lower level. For ethnographers, the distinction of levels allows for detailed studies of singular situations or aspects of a given society that can then be situated in relation to the whole. Thus, the comparison of societies as wholes involves a comparison of the structure of the ideology, its central value-ideas, and the organization of its levels (see also Parkin 2003, 50–53).

Similarly, Rio and Smedal (2009) have addressed the question of the whole and its representations by linking Dumont's "ideologies" with Mauss's "total social fact." In their view, a specific total social fact focuses numerous practices and actions into the emergence of society as a whole. The wholeness of the social is not a given. It must be created, time and again, through the enactment of particular values. Those values and acts that create the whole constitute the "total social fact" that permeates or touches upon all levels of life in a particular configuration. Rio and Smedal thus speak of "totalization" as the process that constitutes society as a whole.

As the specific whole, its paramount value, and its total social fact create each other, it is difficult to identify the concrete institutions that should be selected for comparison. Dumont himself chose the Indian caste system as the realization of specific notions of "purity" and "impurity," thus establishing it as the total social fact that represents the central values of society (Dumont 1980). However, when he turned his attention to comparison with European modernity, he did not focus on social hierarchy or religious institutions, but mostly on intellectual history, in order to identify modernity's central value of individualism (Dumont 1977, 1991). The subject of comparison is thus not a specific social institution, but the system of values. Once again, as with Lévi-Strauss's abstract codes, the anthropologist's choice of what to take as representative of the whole may seem arbitrary, thereby also questioning the very assumption of society as a whole.

However, it should be noted that for Dumont, there is no external, third-person perspective inherent in comparison. As he says, "every ideology is relativized *in relation to others*" (Dumont 2013, 310, italics in original), thus suggesting that comparison demands a culturally specific position. His analysis of the caste system demonstrated "how man as a member of caste appears to man as an individual" (Dumont 2013, 236). Consequently, he chose intellectual history as representative of modernity because he conceived of it as the major obstacle that kept Europeans from understanding the caste system (Dumont 1980, Chapter 1).

A group of Dumont's students addressed the question of comparison by choosing a more specific conceptualization of ideology and hierarchy, as they turned to exchange systems as the central institutions that establish the wholeness of societies (Barraud et al. 1994). Such (gift) exchanges are typically enacted in the form of rituals that condense the central values and relationships of a given society (Barraud and Platenkamp 1990). In particular, Daniel de Coppet's (1995) analysis of 'Aré'aré mortuary rituals is an excellent example of how to account for the various levels of an ideology.

For these scholars, exchange makes value apparent. Each exchange is an answer to the question of how two items (objects, services, persons) are valorized in relation to each other. In particular, gift and ceremonial exchanges establish relationships that correspond to Dumont's concept of the whole. The exchange items are defined as parts – i.e. as entities with a particular value respective to the whole – only in relation to each other, as they are being exchanged. Just like society as a whole, an exchange realizes at least two values by assigning values to the exchange items. As values, they are related hierarchically; any employment of two related values must establish one of them as superior in a given situation.

A brief example from my own field will suffice. In marital exchanges among Rmeet, Laos, a bride that will bear children is exchanged for a buffalo that will be sacrificed for the ancestors. Thus, the value of relations with future generations is related to the value of relations with past generations. The exchange is possible because the values are qualitatively different but complementary. At the same time, they are clearly hierarchized: Rmeet insist that wife-givers are superior to wife-takers.

Thereby, gift exchange serves to create long-lasting social relations. In contrast, an exchange in which the items are conceived to be equivalent on a quantitative scale does not require the relationship to last. The hierarchical asymmetry of qualitative values thus assures the continuity of exchange and thereby of society (Sprenger 2017b). For this reason, the analysis of exchange systems provides a powerful operationalization of the comparison of ideologies, a means to make values detectable. At the same time, the extent of an exchange system helps to define the social whole, the unit of comparison.

Thus, the specification of the units of comparison, along a Dumontian line, would ask the following questions:

- How is a social whole conceived? The Dumontian answer would be, through its particular system of values. One crucial problem here is the question of whether these values are explicit as actual local terms (e.g. "the individual", and "equality") or implicit, as in the case of the Orokaiva, for whom Iteanu has identified an unnamed "ritual system" as the highest value (Iteanu 1990)". Another question asks about the range of social relationships for which the value system is valid.
- In which contexts are these central values enacted? This addresses the aforementioned problems raised by the comparison of social structure, intellectual history, or exchange systems. These contexts or institutions constitute total(izing) social facts.

The elegance of this mode of comparison lies in its synthesis of two opposing demands: First, anthropology should be comparative and therefore should identify some *tertium comparationis*; second, anthropology should heed local terms and concepts in their respective complexity and uniqueness. A Dumontian framework integrates these two demands as two levels of analysis. Values are locally specific concepts that can only be understood in the context of their configuration – in their relation with one other, in their relation to exchange (or other) practices, and in their prominence or implicitness in social life. However, the way in which they are hierarchically organized, their formal and structural aspects can be compared. The comparative questions to be answered are thus refinements of Lévi-Strauss's analysis of structure:

- What are the central (pair of) values organizing a social whole?
- How is the ideology organized into levels, and in which social contexts (e.g. exchange) are they enacted and differentiated?
- Where do reversals of central values occur, and what role do they play in the overall system?

At best, this mode of comparison enables an analysis of very concrete empirical situations in relationship to a comparative enterprise, as any specific situation can be taken as representing a particular level of the overall ideology. This kind of analysis even works without assuming, as Dumont does, that there is a highest value in the ideology. A tension between two oppositional values in shifting hierarchical positions would work equally well.

This way, comparison does not require the suspension of cultural specificity but actually depends on it. Of course, comparison demands abstraction, a reduction of the complexity of the model that is designed to approach a specific local reality. Notions of "value" and "hierarchy," for example, need to be taken as generally applicable. However, they do not define an exclusive class of specific phenomena but rather represent empty boxes in a relational matrix for analysis. Dumontian comparison thus does not entail the reduction of local terms and ideas or their omission but rather stresses the specificity of each value configuration.

However, there is a central problem in Dumont's approach. How do we determine the boundaries of a social whole? How do we know what belongs to it and what does not? Dumont never, to my knowledge, addressed the question of how system boundaries emerge. For this reason, I turn to Niklas Luhmann.

The Comparison of Systems in Their Environment: Niklas Luhmann

Niklas Luhmann's theory of autopoietic (i.e. self-reproductive) social systems, although rarely employed in anthropology, offers a potential for the systematic comparison of cultural configurations encompassing "internal" and "external" relationships. At the same time, it addresses the specific values and ideas of a given context. This is particularly useful in a region like that of my specialization, upland Southeast Asia. Here, a clear sense of boundaries and the distinction between internal (endosocial) and external (exosocial) relationships – based on village, ethnic, religious, national, or other cultural identities – prevails and continues to shape research up until today (Leach 2001; Moerman 1966; Scott 2009, Chapter 6; Jonsson 2014; see Conclusion). At the same time, this scholarship has stated that cultural identities can be changed and are performative, while boundaries appear as malleable and porous – wordings I found quite unsatisfactory: they made identity look like a project of seeking individual opportunities and boundaries as something that people could not make up their minds about.

Instead of getting stuck in a notion of cultural boundaries as somehow contradictory or incomplete, Luhmann's theory helps us to understand that, in Southeast Asia and elsewhere, external relationships are a condition for the reproduction and stability of internal ones. Therefore, I argue that Luhmann provides analytical tools worth considering in social anthropology. I am fully aware of the reservations anthropologists usually raise regarding Luhmann, and I address some limitations of his approach toward the end of this section.

Luhmann employs an analytical terminology that is deliberately detached from everyday language. Reading Luhmann is an experience of difference that is quite unlike the confrontation of two different cultural contexts but still raises the necessity of translation – a translation that is, in his case, very explicit about its procedure: terms that form a coherent set in one context (i.e. Luhmann's theory) need to be applied to another context that is coherent in a different way (e.g. a particular set of data) (Luhmann 1984, 13). In this respect, Luhmann provides a set of generally applicable terms fulfilling the demands of a language of comparison, as outlined earlier in this chapter.

The following features of Luhmann's approach make it feasible for comparing social systems as entities that are connected with or rather depend on their environment. First, there are different types of social systems; some of them are volatile, while others are more stable and enduring. Their emergence depends on the stabilization of a particular system-environment boundary that is created by the system itself (Luhmann 1998, 623). This is what Luhmann calls "differentiation." What is taken for granted by Lévi-Strauss and Dumont thus becomes a central concern here. (Sub)systems can be classified according to their type of differentiation. Luhmann proposes, for larger societies, the following four dominant types of subsystem differentiation: segmentary, stratified, center-periphery, and functional (Luhmann 1998, 614). However, this list is not supposed to exhaust all possibilities.

Each type operates through a different semantics, although within each type, numerous ways to code the differentiation may be found: the Indian caste system and the medieval system in Europe are both stratified, but their semantics are substantially different, as the caste system operates with the guiding difference of purity and impurity.

Not all systems operate by guiding differences. But Luhmann has designed his theory self-consciously as a theory of modernity, which is dominated by functional differentiation. Therefore, his analysis of semantics has mostly focused on functional systems that are structured by guiding differences – such as true and false for science and legal and illegal for the law (Luhmann 1990, 75). Each operation within these systems – that is, each communication – has to be coded in terms of their respective guiding difference. A more differentiated analysis of a Lévi-Straussian or Dumontian type may yield additional types of semantic structure beyond guiding differences. The analysis of types of differentiation and the internal structure of semantics (with or without guiding differences) provides a first level of comparison for both large-scale societies and for coexisting (sub)systems of smaller scale.

Second, social systems are made up of communications, not persons (Luhmann 1984, 192, 227–29). This avoids the empirically problematic notion that social systems are groups of people and also allows a better understanding of how persons change identities (e.g. ethnicities) situationally. Every communication connects to particular earlier and subsequent communications and not to others. The exclusion of possibilities that this selection of communication entails corresponds to the distinction between communications belonging and not belonging to a specific system. This way, each communication reproduces the boundary between system and environment. Therefore, a change of ethnicity involves a shift toward semantics that reproduce the boundary of a different system. As several systems usually coexist, changes of identity are analytically quite easy to grasp as changes of semantics and thereby redrawings of boundaries.

This view provides a critique of Dumont's distinction between subsystems, of which only some are real while others may be inventions of the observer, and the encompassing society, whose reality is not questioned. According to Luhmann, systems are real because of differentiation, and it is of secondary importance if they are Dumont's "global societies" or subsystems. Rather, it is important that any communication within them (implicitly) references the difference between the respective system and its environment. As the system-environment difference is built into every communication, the comparison of systems actually means to compare the process – structural and semantic – by which this difference comes about.

While social systems are made up of communication, they do attribute communications to persons, which helps us to analyze the way persons are constituted (Luhmann 1984, Chapter 3). But for comparative purposes, the focus on communication raises the question of how the semantics of a particular system are coded. This includes the specificity of the codes, terms, values, and so forth in the comparative analysis – a point that is not elaborated by Luhmann, as he has little concern with cultural difference. But as any communication recreates the boundary between system and environment, boundaries are specific to systems and their semantics. Boundaries can appear as group membership; as institutions such as a state, a church, an office, and a classroom; as communication about a certain cultural repertoire; and so forth (Luhmann 1984, 268–69).

Third, the environment is the source of information that is processed by the system. Only those events in the environment that can be coded in terms of the system's semantics appear as information (Luhmann 1984, 103–04). Thus, the system, as it were, feeds upon its environment – relating to its environment is its only way to reproduce, but only on condition of the maintenance of a boundary (Luhmann 1984, 243). Information processing and boundary maintenance are thus the same process. Systems then are operatively closed and open at the same time. They need an environment as well as coherent semantics and self-reference. Processing information means producing new communications as elements of the system (i.e. autopoiesis). Therefore, social systems constantly change because their elements are temporalized, that is, volatile. This allows the analysis of the stability and coherence of communication systems and, at the same time, addresses their linkage with the external world.

The object of comparison is the process by which the system relates to its environment. Any system only processes select events as information and is thus receptive to only part of its environment. This raises the question of how patterns of reception or processing compare – both in the specific choices they make and in the extent to which external events can be processed (Luhmann 1984, 155, 250; 1990, 42). This allows us to compare case studies of resilience or instances in which local systems relate in often unpredictable ways to globalized forces. A comparison of systems under the aspect of their reception of external factors and their subsequent change, based on their specific semantics, may bring a more qualitative type of comparison to studies of globalization.

Fourth, systems stabilize their relationship with the environment by establishing certain conventionalized translations or relay points – institutions or semantic devices that address specific information and process it in predictable, habitual ways (Luhmann 1995, 32). Among these are what I have called "transcultural communication devices" (Sprenger 2011) or "structured misunderstandings" (Sprenger 2016). The study of globalization is, in many respects, a study of such relay points and translation devices. Among them are the nation, cultural heritage, and world religions as well as shamanism and spirit cults. A comparison of such relay points and the information processing they enable for different systems worldwide would contribute to comparison in a globalized world.

The questions a comparative inquiry can derive from Luhmann are as follows:

- How does a system differentiate from its environment and by which social institutions and semantic devices (like guiding differences)?
- What is the form of differentiation? This by necessity addresses other social systems in the environment.
- How is information selected and processed? What is the resonance of the system? What are its conventionalized relay points?
- How do systems change through the processing of information; how do they emerge and dissolve?

There are, of course, limitations to the application of Luhmann as a comparative theory in anthropology. I only briefly address some of the more conventional critiques here.

There is a common opinion that Luhmann excludes individual agency and "people" (Gershon 2005, 99). This point seems to assume that individual agency is self-evident and irreducible. It, therefore, resembles more a value statement from an individualist perspective than a theoretical argument. Individual agency, however, is difficult to integrate into anthropological comparison anyway and belongs to those detailed data that comparison can only hint at.

A second critique draws attention to the fact that applying Luhmann may result in redundant formalization that consists merely of highly detached descriptions instead of real insights. This is indeed a problem, which I personally deal with by being quite eclectic about Luhmann. I recommend keeping in mind which question one wanted to answer in the first place and thereby drawing limits on the use of Luhmann.

A third point addresses issues of comparison. The notion of a system differs from that of structure in the sense that a system does not presume stability but rather continuous, conditioned reproduction. If a system is defined by the fact that its elements change when one element is changing, systems only reveal their systematicity through change. Social systems, as Luhmann (1984, 157) argues, are improvisatory and constantly in flux. The task of comparing them – that is, comparing process instead of structure – thus increases the complexity of the comparative endeavor (Luhmann 1984, 388). As in the case of Dumont, this demands precise strategies for the reduction of complexity. A comparison of systems will thus be part snapshot of fleeting states, and part comparison of the conditions of the autopoiesis of semantics and institutions. However, if done well, it will reveal significant insights into the way sociality emerges and reproduces through differences.

In this respect, the work of comparison appears as continuous with social processes in general: both are reductions of complexity. Any operation within a social system, any communication, begins by reducing the complexity of a given situation. Anthropological comparison thus does not happen outside the normal social process but is rather characteristic of it – another argument against the position that it is impossible.

Conclusion

In my own comparative work on ethnic differentiation and identity in upland Southeast Asia (Sprenger 2008, 2011, 2013, 2015, 2017c), I have combined ideas from Lévi-Strauss, Dumont, and Luhmann. From Lévi-Strauss, I have derived the notion that systematic oppositions shape difference in a multiethnic field and that codes communicate this difference. From this perspective, recent "inventions" of tradition appear as instances of regional and global codes of ethnic identity (Sprenger 2017a).

In addition, a combination of Dumont and Luhmann provided me with the possibility of comparing processes of the inclusion of the external and the maintenance of cultural distinctiveness. I initially ventured into system-environment relationships in Southeast Asia in an attempt to compare identity formation. I constrained my use of Luhmann with the question: If anthropology has produced good models for the comparison of kinship systems, is there something similar for systems of cultural identity? After all, both are aspects of social structure – the first endosocial and the second exosocial.

Luhmann's framework, in my admittedly peculiar reading, allowed me to approach the apparent paradox of the stability and permeability of boundaries in upland Southeast Asia. I did so in a way that emphasizes the specifics of each cultural situation and at the same time compares patterns of endosociality and exosociality. Ethnic identity formation thus appears as part of social structure (Sprenger 2011). This enabled me to analyze how some systems – marked with ethnonyms and thus commonly seen as ethnic groups – tend to replicate the cultural representations of their dominant neighbors, while others relate to them by emphasizing contrast and reversal. In both types of ethnicities, the respective other way of dealing with the environment is equally present, albeit in a subordinated, minor way. These two types of information processing relate to each other as hierarchically organized levels of value in the structure of exosociality (Sprenger 2013).

Comparison thus involves a central question: What exactly is being compared? I do not see any way to go back to a universal definition of "culture units" (e.g. Naroll 1964) or other such entities. Equally unsatisfactory is a view that states that we are actually not comparing societies or cultures but just ethnographies – models written in a shared language of modern academia that guarantees their comparability but reveals little about the relationships between the empirical realities beyond them. The models presented in ethnographies and other sources are not just academic games that facilitate comparison simply because they belong to the same discourse. I think that local models own a certain resilience, based on their internal coherence, that goes into the ethnographies and shows up as a difficulty in comparing them.

Thus, a present-day approach to comparison has to operate on at least two levels: besides a classical concern with the question of how different social entities are internally organized, it also has to consider the constitution of entities. It can do so, I propose, by considering the way systems make differences between what constitutes them and what does not belong to them. Systems are not necessarily societies or organizations, but emerge contingently, through different types of differentiation. Especially in contexts of multisited ethnography, when the researcher follows a person, a story, or an object (Marcus 1995), the extent of the relevant data in different locations might vary significantly. However, anthropologists working in translocal or globalized settings were possibly too quick to dismiss the notion of bounded entities, as if there was no alternative to the classic concepts of ethnic groups as isolated integrated wholes. Instead, when the units of comparison are considered as processual, a notion of system that necessarily relates closure and openness appears as a workable alternative to both the idea of ethnic groups and the denial of boundaries. Anthropologists do not need to deny the existence of systems or "societies" just because their boundaries only exist as volatile, temporalized elements, i.e. communications. Boundaries are means to reduce complexity and transform events into something one can communicate about. Therefore, boundaries and systems are constantly communicated into existence.

For this comparison of processes, I consider it more promising to focus on difference than on similarity. Similarity demands that we ignore many of the variations in the ethnographic record in order to find what is identical. A focus on difference that does not restrict itself to particular entities will make all kinds of varieties productive. It applies to variations between groups and ethnicities as well as to variations between contexts, classes, and other systems. Thus, comparison by difference is closer to the production of the social as we find it in the field. This is true even though comparison is always framed by notions of similarity, at least regarding the analytic language employed. This assumes that the items being compared are of the same nature, starting with a somewhat debatable notion of "anthropos."

As I have mentioned in the beginning, the stress on difference in the authors portrayed here is currently reinforced by a strategy employed in the anthropology of ontologies, although not confined to it. This consists of drawing those elements from the ethnographies that best serve to challenge conventional modern or academic thinking. Superficially, this might look like a return of exoticism, but its intention is different. Rather, this strategy builds upon the reflexivity asked for by post–Writing Culture anthropology. It aims at the reconstruction of an external perspective based on concepts drawn from foreign cultural configurations. However, these concepts or perspectives are not confined to their local contexts but experimentally given a universal value, similar to that of philosophy (Viveiros de Castro 2013). This procedure retains the distinction between reality and model, established by Lévi-Strauss, but now explicitly employed as a means to reduce complexity. Proponents of this approach also follow Lévi-Strauss in treating indigenous myth and ritual as valid contributions to humanity's intellectual history. At the same time, they dispense with the assumption of a universal arbiter, a superior position from which, for example, epistemology (knowing the world) and ontology (being in the world) could be distinguished. What remains is a contrastive dialogue of incommensurable positions as a permanent enactment of comparison (Holbraad and Viveiros de Castro 2016). Comparison is thus not just a means to detect shared codes or meanings as discoveries, but also to help create them in a transcultural conversation that is not only a scientific inquiry but also a moral project of cultural relationships.[4]

The eclecticism of this strategy with regard to data, however, collides with Dumont's (and others') demand that we compare complex wholes – a collision not devoid of irony, as Dumont's attempt to view Western modern ideology from an Indian perspective (Dumont 1977, 1991) is an early example of the reflective strategy.

The exaggeration of difference is probably not what anthropologists should do most of the time. However, it is undeniable that the greatest impact anthropology had on the intellectual history of the West in the past century – those instances that woke people up to the importance of cultural comparison – came from much-maligned cases of exoticism such as Mead's *Coming of Age in Samoa* (1928) or Malinowski's *The Sexual Life of Savages* (1929). However, these were not simply colonial attempts to fix the foreign in the exotic, to keep it at bay, as a postcolonial critique would rightly have it. They also functioned as openings, as relay points that enabled the processing of the unknown and the provocative in the anthropological encounter. Here, a Luhmannian perspective reveals the similarities between the academic enterprise of comparison and the process of sociality in general. Anthropological comparison is just one mode of operating in a modern social system that is both closed and open, and insofar as anthropology is part of this larger system, it can provide relay points that select and process information from other systems in unpredictable ways and with unpredictable consequences.

There is thus a need to synthesize the provocations of contrastive comparison with the demands of carefully raising the complexity of comparison on the basis of detailed ethnography. This requires that constant attention be paid to the various types of systems that emerge in the flow of social life. Anthropological comparison thus should heed both agendas: a detailed account of different social and cultural formations in their relation to one another, with a clear awareness of the reduction of complexity this entails, and a bold sense of difference as a fertile force in social life, here as elsewhere.

Notes

1 Paradoxically, during the colonial era, anthropologists drew comparative and generalizing terms such as *mana, totem,* or *shaman* from local languages and cultures, while the postcolonial era prefers Graeco-Roman terms such as "hybridity" or "transculturality" (Graeber 2004, 97–98).

2 Kapferer (2010, 196) has argued that this definition of "whole" does not equal a bounded society in the functionalist sense. Dumont's late work complies better with Kapferer's understanding than the work I am quoting here.

3 I understand representing here not in the sense of symbolizing but as "making present anew" (de Coppet 1992, 65).

4 The ongoing debate about the politics of this approach asks if it supports foreign realities by releasing them from being mere objects of superior scientific scrutiny – or if it rather subordinates foreign lifeworlds to the needs of academic intellectual play (Todd 2014).

References

Barraud, Cécile, Daniel de Coppet, André Iteanu, and Raymond Jamous. 1994. *Of Relations and the Dead: Four Societies Viewed from the Angle of Their Exchanges.* Oxford: Berg.

Barraud, Cécile, and Josephus D. M. Platenkamp. 1990. "Rituals and the Comparison of Societies." *Bijdragen tot de Taal-, Land- en Volkenkunde* 146 (1): 103–23.

Damon, Frederic. 2009. "Afterword: On Dumont's Relentless Comparativism." In *Hierarchy: Persistence and Transformation in Social Formations*, edited by Knut Mikjel Rio and Olaf H. Smedal, 349–59. New York and Oxford: Berghahn.

de Coppet, Daniel. 1992. "Comparison, a Universal for Anthropology: From 'Re-presentation' to the Comparison of Hierarchies of Value." In *Conceptualizing Society*, edited by Adam Kuper, 59–74. London: Routledge.

de Coppet, Daniel. 1995. "'Are'are Society: A Melanesian Socio-Cosmic Point of View. How Are Big Men the Servants of Cosmos and Society?" In *Cosmos and Society in Oceania*, edited by Daniel de Coppet and André Iteanu, 235–74. Oxford: Berg.

Descola, Philippe. 2011. *Jenseits von Natur und Kultur.* Translated by Eva Moldenhauer. Frankfurt am Main: Suhrkamp. First published in 2005.

Douglas, Mary. 1973. "Die Bedeutung des Mythos, mit besonderer Berücksichtigung von 'La Geste d'Asdiwal'." Translated by Elmar Hoffmeister. In *Mythos und Totemismus: Beiträge zur Kritik der strukturalen Analyse*, edited by E. Leach, 82–108. Frankfurt am Main: Suhrkamp. First published in 1967.

Dumont, Louis. 1977. *From Mandeville to Marx: The Genesis and Triumph of Economic Ideology.* Chicago, IL: University of Chicago Press.

Dumont, Louis. 1980. *Homo Hierarchicus: The Caste System and Its Implications – Complete Revised English Edition.* Chicago, IL: University of Chicago Press.

Dumont, Louis. 1991. *Individualismus: zur Ideologie der Moderne.* Translated by Una Pfau. Frankfurt and New York: Campus. First published in 1983.

Dumont, Louis. 2006. *An Introduction to Two Theories of Social Anthropology: Descent Groups and Marriage Alliance.* Edited and translated by Robert Parkin. New York and Oxford: Berghahn. First published in 1971.

Dumont, Louis. 2013. "On Value: The Radcliffe-Brown Lecture in Social Anthropology 1980." *HAU: Journal of Ethnographic Theory* 3 (1): 287–315.

Gershon, Ilana. 2005. "Seeing Like a System: Luhmann for Anthropologists." *Anthropological Theory* 5 (2): 99–116.

Graeber, David. 2004. *Fragments of an Anarchist Anthropology.* Chicago, IL: Prickly Paradigm Press.

Hertz, Robert. 1960. *Death and the Right Hand.* Translated by Rodney Needham and Claudia Needham. Glencoe, IL: Free Press. First published in 1906.

Holbraad, Martin, and Eduardo Viveiros de Castro. 2016. "Ideas of Savage Reason: Glass Bead in Conversation with Martin Holbraad and Eduardo Viveiros de Castro." *Glass Bead: Site 0.* Accessed [May 22, 2019]. www.glass-bead.org/article/ideas-of-savage-reason-glass-bead-in-conversation-with-martin-holbraad-and-eduardo-viveiros-de-castro/?lang=enview

Ingold, Tim. 2000. *The Perception of the Environment: Essays on Livelihood, Dwelling, and Skill.* London and New York: Routledge.

Iteanu, André. 1990. "The Concept of the Person and the Ritual System: An Orokaiva View." *Man* 25 (1): 35–53.

Jonsson, Hjorleifur. 2014. *Slow Anthropology: Negotiating Difference with the Iu Mien.* Ithaca: Cornell University Press.

Kapferer, Bruce. 2010. "Louis Dumont and Holist Anthropology." In *Experiments in Holism: Theory and Practice in Contemporary Anthropology*, edited by Nils Bubandt and Ton Otto, 187–208. Oxford: Wiley Blackwell.

Kohn, Eduardo. 2015. "Anthropology of Ontologies." *Annual Review of Anthropology* 44: 311–27.

Leach, Edmund. 2001 [1954]. *Political Systems of Highland Burma: A Study of Kachin Social Structure.* London and New York: Continuum.

Leach, Edmund. 1976. *Culture and Communication: The Logic by Which Symbols Are Connected.* Cambridge: Cambridge University Press.

Lévi-Strauss, Claude. 1963. *Structural Anthropology.* Translated by Claire Jacobson and Brooke Grundfest. New York: Basic Books. First published in 1958.

Lévi-Strauss, Claude. 1969. *The Elementary Structures of Kinship.* Translated by James Harle Bell, John Richard von Sturmer, and Rodney Needham. London: Eyre Spottiswode. First published in 1949.

Lévi-Strauss, Claude. 1976a. *Mythologica 1: Das Rohe und das Gekochte.* Translated by Eva Moldenhauer. Frankfurt am Main: Suhrkamp. First published in 1964.

Lévi-Strauss, Claude. 1976b. *Mythologica 2: Vom Honig zur Asche.* Translated by Eva Moldenhauer. Frankfurt am Main: Suhrkamp. First published in 1967.

Lévi-Strauss, Claude. 1976c. *Mythologica 3: Der Ursprung der Tischsitten.* Translated by Eva Moldenhauer. Frankfurt am Main: Suhrkamp. First published in 1968.

Lévi-Strauss, Claude. 1976d. *Mythologica IV: Der nackte Mensch.* Translated by Eva Moldenhauer. Frankfurt am Main: Suhrkamp. First published in 1971.

Lévi-Strauss, Claude. 1976e. *Structural Anthropology II.* Translated by Monique Layton. New York: Basic Books. First published in 1973.

Lévi-Strauss, Claude. 1980. *Mythos und Bedeutung: fünf Radiovorträge. Gespräche mit Claude Lévi-Strauss*, edited by Adelbert Reif. Frankfurt am Main: Suhrkamp. First published in 1978.

Lévi-Strauss, Claude. 1983. *The Way of the Masks.* Translated by Sylvia Modelski. London: Cape. First published in 1975.

Luhmann, Niklas. 1984. *Soziale Systeme: Grundriß einer allgemeinen Theorie.* Frankfurt am Main: Suhrkamp.

Luhmann, Niklas. 1990. *Ökologische Kommunikation: Kann die moderne Gesellschaft sich auf ökologische Gefährdungen einstellen?* Opladen: Westdeutscher Verlag. First published in 1985.

Luhmann, Niklas. 1995. *Soziologische Aufklärung 6: Die Soziologie und der Mensch.* Opladen: Westdeutscher Verlag.

Luhmann, Niklas. 1998. *Die Gesellschaft der Gesellschaft Bd. 2.* Frankfurt am Main: Suhrkamp. First published in 1997.

Malinowski, Bronislaw. 1929. *The Sexual Life of Savages in Northwestern Melanesia.* London: Routledge.

Marcus, George. 1995. "Ethnography in/of the World System: The Emergence of Multi-sited Ethnography." *Annual Review of Anthropology* 24: 95–117.

Mead, Margaret. 1928. *Coming of Age in Samoa.* New York: Morrow.

Moerman, Michael. 1965. "Ethnic Identification in a Complex Society: Who Are the Lue?" *American Anthropologist* 67 (5): 1215–30.

Naroll, Raoul. 1964. "On Ethnic Unit Classification." *Current Anthropology* 5 (4): 283–312.

Parkin, Robert. 2003. *Louis Dumont and Hierarchical Opposition.* New York and Oxford: Berghahn.

Pickvance, Christopher G. 2001. "Four Varieties of Comparative Analysis." *Journal of Housing and the Built Environment* 16 (1): 7–28.

Rio, Knut M., and Olaf H. Smedal. 2009. "Hierarchy and Its Alternatives: An Introduction to Movements of Totalization and Detotalization." In *Hierarchy: Persistence and Transformation in Social Formations*, edited by Knut Mikjel Rio and Olaf H. Smedal, 1–64. New York and Oxford: Berghahn.

Robbins, Joel. 2015. "Dumont's Hierarchical Dynamism: Christianity and Individualism Revisited." *HAU: Journal of Ethnographic Theory* 5 (1): 173–95.

Schnegg, Michael. 2014. "Anthropology and Comparison: Methodological Challenges and Tentative Solutions." *Zeitschrift für Ethnologie* 139 (1): 55–72.

Schneider, David M. 1984. *A Critique of the Study of Kinship.* Ann Arbor: University of Michigan Press.

Scott, James C. 2009. *The Art of Not Being Governed: An Anarchist History of Upland Southeast Asia.* New Haven and London: Yale University Press.

Sprenger, Guido. 2008. "The Problem of Wholeness: Upland Southeast Asian Cosmologies in Transition." *Zeitschrift für Ethnologie* 133 (1): 75–94.

Sprenger, Guido. 2011. "Differentiated Origins: Trajectories of Transcultural Knowledge in Laos and Beyond." *Sojourn* 26 (2): 224–47.

Sprenger, Guido. 2013. "Transcultural Communication and Social Order: Comparisons in Upland Southeast Asia." *Asian Ethnology* 72 (2): 299–319.

Sprenger, Guido. 2015. "Idiome von Zentrum und Peripherie: Transkulturalität in einer asiatischen Grenzregion." In *Transkulturelle Dynamiken: Aktanten – Prozesse – Theorien*, edited by Jutta Ernst and Florian Freitag, 227–54. Bielefeld: Transcript.

Sprenger, Guido. 2016. "Structured and Unstructured Misunderstandings: Thoughts Towards an Anthropological Theory of Misunderstanding." *Civilisations* 65 (1&2): 21–38.

Sprenger, Guido. 2017a. "The Connectivity of Ethnic Displays: New Codes for Identity in Northern Laos." *Asian Ethnicity* 18 (1): 95–116.

Sprenger, Guido. 2017b. "Goods and Ethnicity: Trade and Bazaars in Laos from a Gift Perspective." *Heidelberg Ethnology Occasional Papers 6.* Accessed [January 3, 2019]. https://journals.ub.uni-heidelberg.de/index.php/hdethn/article/view/42017

Sprenger, Guido. 2017c. "Local Comparisons: Buddhism and Its Others in Upland Laos." *Zeitschrift für Ethnologie* 142 (2): 245–64.

Strathern, Marilyn. 1988. *The Gender of the Gift: Problems with Women and Problems with Society in Melanesia.* Berkeley: University of California Press.

Todd, Zoe. 2014. "An Indigenous Feminist's Take on the Ontological Turn: 'Ontology' Is Just Another Word for Colonialism." *Urbane Adventurer: Amiskwac^ı Blog*, October 24. Accessed [May 24, 2016]. http://zoeandthecity.wordpress.com/2014/10/24/an-indigenous-feminists-take-on-the-ontological-turn-ontology-is-just-another-wordfor-colonialism/

Viveiros de Castro, Eduardo. 1998. "Cosmological Deixis and Amerindian Perspectivism." *Journal of the Royal Anthropological Institute* 4 (3): 469–88.

Viveiros de Castro, Eduardo. 2013. "The Relative Native." *HAU* 3 (3): 473–502.

Viveiros de Castro, Eduardo. 2016. "Claude Lévi-Strauss, Begründer des Poststrukturalismus." In *Die Unbeständigkeit der wilden Seele*, 406–23. Translated by Oliver Precht. Vienna: Turia and Kant.

5 Regional Comparison in Historical Anthropology

Three Case Examples from South Arabia

Andre Gingrich

There is a particularly long record of regional versions of anthropological comparison within the field's history. To an extent, regional comparison may indeed be addressed as the version of qualitative and explicit comparison that is best established in anthropology's methodological record of comparing (Gingrich 2012a). Even at times when other forms of comparison were not considered truly useful or had fallen out of fashion for some other reasons, one or the other form of regional comparison nevertheless continued to be practiced. In that sense regional comparison can be thought of as representing, until recently at least, the enduring core of anthropology's wider, pluralist comparative inventory. Seen from another angle, however, regional comparison has survived those various fashions and paradigmatic changes in anthropology's history so well because it can be a potentially useful tool in any epistemological or theoretical approach. To a considerable extent, this is related to its basic feature of spatial proximity. This certainly makes it difficult for any approach to flatly ignore parallels and differences that are so visibly at hand or to fail to inquire into those very parallels and differences. From evolutionism through German diffusionism to Boasian cultural relativism, and from British functionalism to neo-evolutionism to French structuralism, all major directions in the various quasi-national trajectories of anthropological approaches before the 1970s and the 1980s therefore used regional comparison in their respective ways and for varying purposes. However, together with the emergence – since the turn of the last century – of a transnationally oriented and globally contextualized anthropology of the present, that era during which regional comparison was everybody's methodological darling may gradually be coming to an end.

This chapter is a partial outcome of several Austrian Science Fund (FWF) research projects, in particular the FWF project (1979–83) directed by the late Walter Dostal, the Wittgenstein project I directed from 2000 to 2007, and the SFB VISCOM I currently continue to codirect (2011–19). The FWF's generous support is hereby acknowledged. In addition, I wish to thank those colleagues who were helpful in discussing earlier versions of this text. They include the publishing house's anonymous reviewers; Ted Lowe and Michael Schnegg as this volume's coeditors and as hosts of the conference preceding this volume; Christina Lutter (Department of History, University of Vienna) and Johann Heiss and Mehmet Emir (Institute for Social Anthropology, Austrian Academy of Sciences).

In the current era of increasing deterritorialization, migration processes, global interconnectedness, and worldwide climate change, the relevance, for anthropological studies of the contemporary world, of any spatially distinct sociocultural phenomena is obviously decreasing (Gupta and Ferguson 1992). This state of affairs is also inspired by the gradual vanishing of earlier quasi-national theoretical metanarratives that had upheld the enduring status of one or the other form of regional comparison throughout much of the twentieth century. New epistemological and theoretical horizons, as well as the global transformation of empirical relations, therefore seem to jointly promote the gradual decrease in contemporary anthropological relevance of regionally distinct phenomena. This does not imply that regionally specific phenomena are no longer occurring at all, whether in well-known established forms or in newly emerging constellations. Still, since contemporary anthropological priorities clearly seem to be set otherwise, regional forms of comparison tend to lose their primary importance for the anthropology of the present and thus will begin to become less relevant within anthropology's methodological inventory.

Consider, for instance, the qualitative assessment of "neo-nationalism in Europe and beyond" that Marcus Banks and I carried out together with a group of scholars shortly after the turn of the century (Gingrich and Banks 2006). In terms of both its approach and its results, this was basically a contemporary project conducted over a decade, focused on Western Europe while including contrasts from Australia and India. The outcome did yield some useful insights into a particular moment in time when neo-nationalism, in its more recent versions, was beginning to move beyond its first phase of regional emergence in some countries of Western Europe. Predictably, many of the ensuing core anthropological insights from 2006 are no longer applicable to those global contexts that have profoundly changed fifteen years later. Today, the same phenomena would have to be studied primarily by means of comparative devices other than regional comparison – including, for instance, aspects of distant and global comparison, together with elements of virtual anthropology, and so forth.

This certainly does not imply that regional comparison has lost all its potential for contemporary purposes. In whatever way a region is defined (a question that will be addressed again at the end of this chapter) for specific purposes, it may still display at some level a certain combination of homogeneity and heterogeneity with respect to one or several social fields, such as the family system, religious rituals, or political preferences. Researchers may be interested in exploring and explaining any of these fields, investigating how changes are occurring in them, or understanding how they may affect other cultural practices. In turn, this might mean that regional comparisons are still rewarding within certain limits.

If regional comparison is potentially losing some of its previous significance for anthropological studies of the contemporary world, it nevertheless tends to retain an enduring importance in historical anthropology. For late precolonial and early colonial times (on different continents), for instance, wider factors of influence can certainly be identified – but still, local and regional phenomena had a more lively and enduring relevance. Long-distance trade, enforced or voluntary migration, and cross-regional and intercontinental military, commercial, and religious interests certainly were essential if not defining characteristics in many parts of the world during these eras. Yet the temporal rhythms by which those factors were pursued and implemented, e.g. during the fifteenth or seventeenth century, were of a different kind than those in the late twentieth and early twenty-first century. Simultaneously, local and regional agents and phenomena, although never isolated from the wider world, displayed a more enduring perseverance. At times, these contrasts between the relevance of local and regional phenomena in the late precolonial/early colonial period and those of the present may be seen as differences of degree rather than of kind and quality. In general, however, the importance of regional factors was higher in early and precolonial eras of history. Consequently, regional comparison will maintain some of its core relevance for historical anthropology among the field's overall spectrum of comparative procedures.

This chapter discusses and summarizes three examples of regional comparison in the historical anthropology of Arabia to substantiate these introductory points. At the same time, the discussion of these three examples provides an opportunity to assess how regional comparison in historical anthropology may be usefully combined with other methodological procedures, where some basic caution is indispensable while pursuing it and some methodological precision is not only required but also possible.

Rock Art

The first example discusses rock art from West and Southwest Arabia, based on two previous publications (Gingrich and Heiss 1986; Gingrich 2017) and a corresponding visual archive in Vienna. The actual visual documentation was carried out between 1979 and 1983, directed by Walter Dostal (1929–2011) and a team in which I participated as of 1980. The sample in the Vienna archives (Institute for Social Anthropology at the Austrian Academy of Sciences) relates to twelve actual sites in southern Hijaz and northeastern Asir (both located to the south of Mecca, in the southwestern parts of Saudi Arabia), as well as in Sa'da province (northern Yemen).

Visiting, identifying, and documenting those twelve rock art sites was not a systematic element of our main ethnographic documentation project (Dostal 2006). Instead, this became a more or less accidental by-product of our main work, whenever our respective hosts would sense that their academic visitors were interested in "old local" and "traditional" things. They would then indicate that such rock art sites existed in the wider vicinity, and if we had the time, we accepted their invitation, accompanying two or three of them (first by car and then always on foot) to the respective sites. None of the twelve sites was directly associated with any substantial set of local myths, folklore, or oral history. In all cases except one our local guides referred to those rock art items as being left over by "Bani Hilal," as they said, a term indicating residents of ancient times who were already gone when the ancestors of today's tribal inhabitants had settled in the area. Given the historical depth of genealogical reasoning in these parts of Arabia, such statements about Bani Hilal contexts thus would refer back to an era some time before the twelfth century CE. In the northern Yemeni case, locals' time reference to the particular rock art site in question was to "Himyar," i.e. to ancient pre-Islamic South Arabia: indeed, that rock art site came with ancient South Arabian scriptural graffiti. Only one other site in the entire sample was also accompanied by scriptural evidence. In that second case, the writing was in Arabic and occurred in one of the sites closest to Mecca, i.e. in southern Hijaz.

Three decades elapsed between the original rock art documentation and the current phase of its analysis and discussion, during the course of which the main ethnographic documentation was analyzed and published. Many of the technical devices that are methodologically standard today for documenting rock art were not yet available to our teams in the late 1970s and early 1980s. This fact provided an additional rationale for making extensive use of all other methodological tools available to classify, analyze, and interpret those visual rock art examples. In turn, this is where and how comparative procedures became important.

To begin with, today's efforts toward territorial and geographic location of those twelve sites have made it much clearer than it had ever been during our fieldwork periods that all sites share a common general feature in terms of location. They are all positioned in the barren, barely accessible transition zones between West and Southwest Arabia's mountain ranges or plateaus and inner Arabia's steppe and desert regions. Our four fieldwork campaigns had been carried out in many other zones and subzones of the overall area as well (e.g. shoreline and coastal plain and isolated mountains). The common adherence to West and Southwest Arabia's barren eastern zones became apparent and demonstrable only in hindsight (for an overview of the ethnographic present, see Gingrich 2012b). Furthermore, similar techniques and styles of drawing or engraving occurred together with the more important commonality that all examples were found in two basic kinds of locations within their respective immediate environments: either on rock walls at higher elevations or on isolated rock blocks in low-lying positions. Those locations offered protection from the sun and wind, thereby providing good qualities as hunting outposts that could also be combined with the conspicuous display of artful imagery.

Indeed, the one graphic theme across each and every example was hunting. All these factors taken together suggested that it would be fruitful to analyze the twelve examples as representing a single regional group of rock art and to analyze it accordingly. Consequently, the scriptural evidence at the northwestern and the southeastern tips of that regional group permitted a provisional dating frame of around fourth to ninth century CE. In the climate history of West and Southwest Arabia, these late pre-Islamic and early Islamic centuries are characterized by elements of the Late Antiquity Little Ice Age (LALIA), with correspondingly higher precipitation and more wildlife than, say, in the fifteenth or twentieth century CE.

Based on these three crucial steps of analysis, regional comparison of rock art imagery in the Vienna sample then led to a focus on those hunting scenes as the entire sample's cross-cutting visual theme. In the strictly inductive and empirical process of regionally comparing these visual materials, the ensuing results provided interesting fragments. They indicated a visual emphasis upon a limited number of wildlife groups – ibex and other wild goat at higher elevations and antelopes in more lowland zones. These were hunted by groups of humans mostly on foot (exceptions being rare riders on horses or donkeys), armed with lances, spears, and slingshots; dogs occasionally assisted them. If our provisional dating frame is correct, then this would indicate for the LALIA-era horizontal seasonal movements of some of these groups of wildlife and vertical seasonal movements of others and seasonal movements of small human hunting bands in line with that. It should be added at this point that archaeological inquiry has developed its own methodological criteria and procedures for regional comparison, based on its empirical, descriptive, and analytical assessment (for Arabia, see e.g. Bednarik 2017). Dialogical cooperation between archaeological and anthropological regional comparison certainly is important and, in fact, indispensable in such fields of intersecting relevance as the study of rock art. Still, I would argue that the pursuit of regional comparison by (historical) anthropologists at first preferably is pursued independently from other disciplines in order to fully exploit anthropology's specific resources, before subsequently entering direct cooperation between both disciplines.

From general anthropological perspectives, the inductively derived and regionally compared results as discussed so far by no means exhaust what this field is able to say about such sets of evidence. In fact, anthropologists have much more to say about foragers. This is where the results from the regional comparison then had to be more fully contextualized by comparison-saturated general anthropological expertise about hunters and gatherers, both past and present, living under comparable conditions (i.e. not under the very different environmental constraints of e.g. the circumpolar zones). A number of methodological and epistemological challenges are of course implied whenever attempts are made to translate comparative insights derived from ethnographic analyses in recent centuries so as to interpret much earlier historical contexts. Although not impossible, this demanding task requires the complex subtlety of historical specification and *recontextualization* for those regionally relevant insights that are derived from recent and contemporary comparison of foragers at various wider regional and intercontinental levels (Gingrich and Schweitzer 2014).

From existing, empirically saturated, general insights, we know that hunting is very rarely if ever pursued as the only subsistence activity by local groups or bands. So, *despite* the rock art images' exclusive depiction of large wild animals, general anthropological expertise translates those as largely symbolic representations, while also taking the imagery as indicating mixed local economies in which hunting was merely one among several practical fields of agency – i.e. collecting plants and small animals, semispecialized craftsmanship, and barter as well as gift exchange. In some cases, these regional economies could also include simple forms of cultivation, together with animal husbandry, as indicated by those rare horses and donkeys in the rock art images.

The pragmatic content of rock art images, compared in regional terms and also through topic-specific general comparison, therefore has suggested regional economies of the fourth to ninth centuries, in which wildlife hunting had great symbolic significance: internally, it could promote meritocratic positions, while externally, its best products could enter processes of gift exchange and barter. Those regional economies could be semiautonomous, but they could also represent the peripheries to wider, centralized entities that existed in the region during those centuries. In fact, this is precisely what is indicated by the scriptural evidence in some of the examples, testifying to the existence of elite minorities of people with reading and writing skills in centralized complex constellations. Some of the hunting trophies from the local peripheries thus could also be delivered as occasional tribute.

In sum, as indispensable, though complicated, regional comparison for historical analysis sometimes turns out to be, this may still not be sufficient. Inductive results from regional comparisons still may require some completion by means of comparison-saturated, topic-specific, generalized anthropological expertise. Yet in turn, this may shed some light on those sectors and corners of history that are difficult to determine for philologists or archaeologists through their own sources and insights. The results are bottom-up perspectives from the peripheries, by means of regional comparison in the service of historical anthropology.

Indian Ocean Connections

The second example concerns South Arabian and Gulf navigators between the tenth and the fourteenth century CE. In that regard, as with the first example, I shall confine myself to a partial summary of a more extensive publication

(Gingrich 2018) to make a few additional methodological points about regional comparison in historical anthropology. In this example, the task concerned the question of what historical anthropology might be able to contribute toward a better understanding of maritime interactions and forms of connectivity across the Indian Ocean, as seen from "medieval" South and East Arabian perspectives and activities.

From the outset, the term "region" in this second example is embedded in a quite different setting of academic scholarship than it was in the previous section. For hunting scenes in West and Southwest Arabian rock art, it took some considerable research effort to identify, and also to a certain extent to "construct," the historical region – i.e. the transition zone to the east – within which comparison could then take place. For the Indian Ocean between the tenth and the fourteenth century, however, no such special efforts are required: archaeologists, epigraphers, and philologists of various languages, historians and geographers accomplished this long ago through a sequence of debates and other mutual professional interactions. Historical anthropologists in this case have every reason to admire the results and insights of their colleagues' work and to benefit from it when embarking upon regional comparison.

Within the Indian Ocean world's medieval setting, the actual "object" or theme of regional comparison in this second example is that of the major forms of maritime interaction, as recorded in Middle Eastern sources from those centuries. This requires the elaboration of a provisional inventory of major forms of agency, of maritime networks and nodes across time, and finally, the outlining of what distinguished some, among the more specific forms of strategic maritime interactions, from the rest in these waters during the centuries under scrutiny.

From the tenth and early eleventh century CE, South Arabian ship crews were regularly navigating East African and South Asian shores, largely by sailing along the shorelines. Most of these ships were owned and sent by private merchants. Star lore and stellar charts as well as navigational handbooks had already been in use for much longer, but the range of South Arabian navigation expanded considerably with the introduction of the magnetic compass after its invention in eleventh-century China. Together with innovations in techniques of ship and sail construction and usage, the risks of sailing across the open sea thus could be substantially decreased. By consequence, the extent of West Asian and South Arabian maritime influence across the Indian Ocean expanded considerably, especially after the mid-thirteenth century. By then, Omani and Yemeni trading vessels transported regular visitors, part-time residents, and early emigrants to East Africa, South Asia, and Southeast Asia.

In a way, these were indeed decades and centuries of "Arab" navigational hegemony in the northwestern, western, and central part of the Indian Ocean world, but these vessels had a more contested presence in its northeastern and eastern coastal and insular zones. If we use "Arab" in these contexts, then this is based on the main language in most sources from the northwestern Indian Ocean shorelands and on the apparent fluency of most of the actors mentioned in those sources in Arabic as a first or second language. "Arab" navigational hegemony nevertheless also included Iran-based actors, and beyond Muslim majorities, it also comprised Christians, Jews, and followers of South Asian and African religions. There is a wide spectrum of bibliographic materials available (e.g. Goitein and Friedman 2008) about these captains, navigators, tradesmen, and traveling interpreters. The leading crew members on these ships, leaving from and returning to South Arabia and the Arab/Persian Gulf, therefore spoke Arabic as a first or second language; they could speak or at least understand a second and third language, and they were familiar with the expertise of translators and local interpreters. They were born in Arabia or Persia – or they had backgrounds and relatives in Arabia or Persia, whereas they were born elsewhere such as India, East Africa, or Southeast Asia. They belonged to the growing intercontinental elites who had mastered reading and writing skills, together with an understanding of the increasing relevance of communicating across long distances. They were experienced travelers used to spending long seasons abroad, since they depended on the rhythms of the monsoon winds. Some of them were married and had families in different locations. By and large they preferred sailing together with the same small groups of leading crew companions across the years, including junior disciples who would learn these professional skills from them through practical participation.

From the perspectives of historical anthropology, it is not too challenging to suggest that we consider these social groups of actors in their times and in these specific Indian Ocean world contexts as "cosmopolitans" (Hannerz 1990). If we carefully and critically translate that concept from its main contemporary and globalized usage back into the precolonial regional Indian Ocean world of the tenth to fourteenth centuries, then we arrive at useful insights: Cosmopolitans entertain, and engage in, a plurality of relationships with representatives of cultural settings other than their own by developing a personal ability to make their way into other sociocultural contexts. "Being on the move" is part of their professional lifestyle, usually distinguishing them from refugees, exiles, diplomats, migrants, and other expatriates. Cosmopolitans on the move and abroad regularly achieve their personal transformation from suspicious intruders to acceptable guests, while when at home they tend to remain at some distance from the locals (Hannerz 1990, 239, 241, 246–48).

Regarding the cross-cultural elite members in these maritime interactions, it is thus fairly evident to suggest, for these historical regional contexts, a comparative anthropological concept that provides further depth and substance for the dispersed but rich and widely available source evidence. Tasks become much more complicated and challenging, however, once we ask about one or the other among these cosmopolitans' local counterparts at their various stopovers or destinations. What is particularly relevant for maritime interactions is a specific type of local actor who would assist the cosmopolitan crew leaders in carrying out their respective maritime missions whenever they encountered navigational challenges.

The focus therefore zooms in on those local counterparts who are professionally linked to local maritime knowledge and expertise, which becomes a precious and indispensable service if located in strategic passages of navigation. Dangerous or dire straits and other challenging passages, particularly of the eye-of-a-needle type, would clearly mark those points of maritime interactions where navigators from distant regions would have to rely on local experts. Network analysis in its graph-theory version emphasizes the same point by clarifying that so-called cut vertex points have the "eye-of-a-needle" quality that sets them apart from all other possible nodes within our maritime regional arena in medieval times. This is where the comparative distinction of "cut vertex" interactions from other forms of connectivity across the medieval Indian Ocean can be made productive for actual research purposes. Ethnographic insights from islands with dangerous outer shorelines (such as the Maldives) and from river deltas that were crucial for stopover anchoring (such as those of southwestern Sri Lanka) provide further arguments about the same issue. Navigators from far away could not possibly have safely entered or crossed eye-of-a-needle types of dangerous passages without the help of experienced local pilots.

In the previous section's discussion of the first example, comparative regional insights were enhanced and completed by topic-specific insights from general anthropology. By contrast, this discussion of the second example in historical regional comparison requires input from ethnography and from the graph-theory version of network analysis, i.e. from other methodological inventories. Consequently, if such additional input comes from other methods (and not from conceptual insights gained elsewhere), it helps to fine-tune upcoming, additional research (but does not complete existing evidence by means of additional insights). The additional methodological input therefore encourages researchers to scrutinize existing sources more selectively and more closely. In contrast to the frequent mention of cosmopolitan personalities in the available source materials, it is very hard to find references to local pilots. Still, a few do become visible once the focus is set precisely on nothing but maritime passages of the "eye-of-a-needle" type.

For instance, a few Arabic sources mention pilots when speaking about the island of Qays/Kish near the Straits of Hormuz. This small island state was ruled by sultans who managed to expand their influence far beyond the island's immediate vicinity. Between the late eleventh and the early thirteenth century, "Kish became the major entrepot in the Gulf." Ibn al-Mujawir, in his famous thirteenth-century travelogue, underlined this role of the island, together with its market and the local role of ship building. In addition, the local ruler awarded a special premium for all persons with maritime expertise who were ready to settle there (Margariti 2008, 556–58). As soon as a sufficient number of additional sources with such references to local maritime expertise and/or pilots become available, it is also possible to suggest an anthropological concept for this type of group. "Expert cultural brokers" come to mind – locals with a long experience of dangerous waters in the region, who benefited from regular visits by incoming ships and who were more at ease in communicating with foreigners and visiting strangers in order to translate their interests back to their local communities (see Gingrich and Knoll 2018 for additional case examples).

For assessing certain historical Indian Ocean connections from South Arabia and the Gulf (tenth to fourteenth century), regional comparison is thus helpful for focusing on intercontinental crew leaders and on local pilots as one group among their various counterparts. Applying the anthropological concept of cosmopolitans, and in addition, that of (local expert) cultural brokers, helps us to analyze and theorize about existing source materials and to selectively focus on some of the data more closely. Regional comparison therefore is helpful when scrutinizing and conceptually theorizing about available but dispersed source materials, as in the case of cosmopolitans, while in the case of local pilots, it helps us to reexamine, filter, and focus on a special selection of sources. Condensation of existing sources and scrutinizing a selection of sources are thus both encouraged and promoted by regional comparison in historical anthropology.

Rural Highland Architecture

The third example relates to multistorey domestic architecture in southern Hijaz and Asir (Southwest Saudi Arabia), as documented in a number of previous publications (Abdulfattah 1981; Gingrich 1983, 2006, 2013). In this case, identifying the region for which such an ethnographic comparison would be relevant observed the twofold set of emic and etic criteria. The less complicated etic criterion relied on material and constructional characteristics by asking about multistorey domestic stone and mud buildings that had been built using nonindustrial methods by local and/or regional craftsmen. The somewhat more complex emic criterion asked for local opinions about what was considered as typical architecture for the region and why. In the final analysis, the ethnographic pursuit of both criteria led to almost identical results. The etic criterion delivered the fuzzy outer limits of an overall region of strong internal diversity, with clear links to neighboring regions to the southeast, i.e. in Yemen. The emic criterion delivered the same fuzzy outer regional limits, but while it played down any links to Yemeni architecture, it emphasized internal diversity only to the extent that it upgraded one particular form to the superior status of a cultural landmark for the entire region.

In many ways, elaborating and identifying what the "region of comparison" might be in this particular case turned out to be less of a puzzle than in the first example on rock art but more complicated than the second example about the Indian Ocean world. In regional comparison, the "region" is therefore never an a priori given but something to be elaborated and critically assessed and constructed, including a respectful inclusion of local and indigenous views.

Regarding domestic architecture, local views on what "traditional" meant in terms of historical background would usually refer to Ottoman times and therefore to periods between the mid-sixteenth and the late nineteenth/early twentieth centuries. Quite obviously, architectural remains of Ottoman fortifications near the regional capital Abha, and along that city's connecting road to al-Qunfidha as the region's main port along the Red Sea coast, seemingly supported these local views, while also influencing and shaping them. Quite a few among the rural and tribal elites in the region, however, would occasionally remark that "the Ottomans came and went, but our people have built houses like this much longer than that" or make similar statements to the same effect – thus implicitly referring to tribal ancestors already living in the region for centuries before the first Ottoman presence. In addition, some among these educated local elite members had read one or the other book by contemporary local historians who had indicated early references to multistorey architecture in the region at least since the tenth century. Since the Arabic and vernacular term for "house" also has semantic connotations of "family," "honor," and "ancestry," these identifications between "our houses" and "our tribal origins" were in fact readily suggested by anybody with some education and some regional pride. In this regard, source criticism would have to carefully distinguish between the normative and the descriptive value of such statements. Still, emic and academic assessments could to an extent substantiate most of these local views, not only by pointing out architectural innovations of Ottoman times, such as in sanitation or military installations, but also by revealing a systematic set of references to multistorey architecture in the region through Arabic sources from the tenth to the twelfth century. In addition, academic assessments based on archaeological and epigraphic evidence would point out that, all across West and Southwest Arabia, those regions in which multistorey domestic architecture had survived until the 1980s largely coincided with those historical regions where multistorey architecture had already flourished in the late pre-Islamic era.

The main results of regional comparison led to an emphasis on regional diversity but in a manner that did not correspond to the emic priority for a "landmark" form. Actually, research analysis had to deconstruct that landmark form to an extent by demonstrating that it represented a simple combination of various elements from two adjacent architectural versions while responding to certain climatic challenges. Instead, the academic analysis distinguished according to the criteria of construction and symbolism between the main Asiri versions (closer to the Yemen in the south) and those of southern Hijaz (i.e. closer to Mecca and North Arabia). Asiri architecture featured clusters of single defensive dwelling houses, with three to five floors built around an inner supportive wall with the staircase around it. By contrast, southern Hijazi architecture displayed clusters of dwelling houses with two to three floors, around an uninhabited defense tower (around five floors) that was shared by the village. In an Asiri house, the inner walls of the main upper room (majlis) would be decorated with women's paintings using local colors. In contrast, the main upper room in a southern Hijazi house had a central wooden pillar to support the roof. The pillar was usually decorated with patterned wood carvings made by mobile regional carpenters.

In a final step of analytical comparison, these main results of regional comparison in domestic architecture could then be associated with central elements of social and symbolic life. The decorated wooden pillar in southern Hijazi architecture thus was seen as symbolizing gender hierarchy and the more elaborate patrilineal ideologies characteristic of northwestern and northern Arabia. By contrast, the women's paintings on the inner walls in domestic Asiri architecture were analyzed as symbolizing the somewhat more balanced gender relations and stronger cognatic kinship elements that characterized certain parts of Southwest and southern Arabia.

Conclusion

In this chapter we argue that regional comparison may continue to remain highly relevant for historical anthropology, while its significance for studies of the contemporary world may be somewhat diminishing. Three case examples have been discussed to substantiate this point and to demonstrate the ways in which such continued relevance may be enacted usefully for historical anthropology. On an abstract level, "region" remains a useful and potentially productive concept for anthropological comparison in its historical dimensions, as long as its volatile and fluid contextualized characteristics are observed. From anthropological perspectives, a region therefore designates an environmentally grounded human habitat within shifting spatial and temporal boundaries that are defined by cognitive and pragmatic interactions between insiders and outsiders. These dynamically changing interactions include all dimensions from the intentional to the unintended, from the practical to the symbolic, and from the local to the intercontinental. By way of concluding, the results of these discussions may be highlighted through three main points.

First, like all comparisons, and in fact like all methodological activities, regional comparison does not represent any *l'art pour l'art* principle but serves the pursuit of research questions for addressing and solving research problems. This is why there is absolutely no reason to pursue regional comparison as a sole method, or even as a primary method. Sometimes it may be merely a minor intermediate step in the overall research process, and sometimes it may represent one among a few core methodologies. By consequence, *combining* regional comparison in one way or another – for instance, by means of *triangulation* (Flick 2004) – with other methodological procedures does not represent an exception but rather the rule. This was demonstrated in the second example when ethnographic fieldwork and network analysis helped to substantiate and specify a point when regional comparison alone did not provide any further advances of insight. The triangulation of three methodological procedures including regional comparison, however, made substantial research advances possible.

Second, an inherent weakness in regional comparison is constituted by the danger of reifying the "region" once it has been explicitly or implicitly identified. To my mind, Bourdieu's early treatise on representing one version of "the house" in Berber cultures of Northwest Africa is a well-known example of how an implicit regional comparison may result in singling out one form only, which comes close to stereotyping while disregarding local and regional diversity (Bourdieu 1970). That negative potential of reification can be counterbalanced by methodological triangulation, as indicated earlier. The self-reflexive awareness about regions being constructed, in sociocultural ways by local actors as much as by research activities, is also helpful in minimizing the risks of reifying the regional factor. As the third example demonstrated, a critical inclusion of both emic and etic perspectives on what constitutes a region for a given historical period is crucial in maintaining the term's current usage as flexibly as possible. This allowed us, for instance, to establish the wider mountain and plateau region of West and Southwest Arabia for multistorey domestic architecture for the late pre-Islamic period while identifying internal diversity among southern Hijazi and Asiri domestic architecture for the Ottoman and post-Ottoman period.

Third, the necessity of skeptical caution with regard to reifying and stereotyping notions of the region is therefore not an argument in favor of shying away from regional comparison in historical anthropology but, on the contrary, is an argument for its improvement. Explicitly addressing why a specific concept of regionality is preferred to alternatives, how emic and etic perspectives are included in the elaboration (and "construction") of what constitutes a region for a given period of time, while keeping the concept fuzzy and flexible, has already been pointed out as a helpful and essential device in processes where "regions" actually are the units of comparison in history. The three examples have demonstrated that the specific challenges involved in achieving this aim may differ considerably. They ranged from minimal through mid-level to maximal difficulty in the three examples. One may go as far as to use the critical theory's version of Hans Reichenbach's original distinction to clarify this point somewhat further. According to such a rationale, it does make a difference whether we "discover" a region of comparison for a period of time for which the task of dating was ours, as in the first example. By contrast, in the third example, we were primarily preoccupied with the "justification" of how existing but competing notions of region were or were not useful for different tasks in different periods. Finally, a well-established interdisciplinary discourse informing the second example helped us to accept the existing notions of region for that purpose. In turn, this enabled us to move beyond contexts of "discovering" or "justifying" the region in question and to focus our attention on "applying" comparison within given regional contexts.

In the end, my argument for an improved employment of regional comparison in historical anthropology therefore emphasizes a self-reflexive, critical, and empirical usage of region as a methodological concept embedded in shifting spatial and temporal contexts. It may be helpful in inductively sorting out and classifying evidence; it is useful in the condensation of existing evidence as well as in selectively scrutinizing sources for new evidence, and it is open to discussions of comparative regional results by means of wider comparative insights. Anthropologists' awareness of the weaknesses and the limits of regional comparison is the decisive prerequisite for improving and applying this useful set of methodological procedures in the pursuit of qualitative goals in historical inquiry.

References

Abdulfattah, Kamal. 1981. *Mountain Farmer and Fellah in 'Asir Southwest Saudi Arabia: The Conditions of Agriculture in a Traditional Society.* Erlangen: Erlanger Geographische Arbeiten.

Bednarik, Robert G. 2017. "Scientific Investigations into Saudi Arabian Rock Art: A Review." *Mediterranean Archaeology and Archaeometry* 17 (4): 43–59.

Bourdieu, Pierre. 1970. "The Berber House or the World Reversed." *Social Science Information* 9: 151–70.

Dostal, Walter, ed. 2006. *Tribale Gesellschaften der südwestlichen Regionen des Königreiches Saudi Arabien: Sozialanthropologische Untersuchungen.* Vienna: Verlag der Österreichischen Akademie der Wissenschaften.

Flick, Uwe. 2004. *Triangulation: Eine Einführung*. Wiesbaden: VS Verlag.

Gingrich, Andre. 1983. "Traditional Architecture." In *Ethnographic Atlas of 'Asīr: Preliminary Report*, edited by Walter Dostal, 74–124. Vienna: Verlag der Österreichischen Akademie der Wissenschaften.

Gingrich, Andre. 2006. "Wohnarchitektur im südwestlichen Saudi Arabien: Lokale Zeugnisse historischer Interaktionen mit Nachbarn, Herrschern und Fremden." In *Tribale Gesellschaften der südwestlichen Regionen des Königreiches Saudi Arabien: Sozialanthropologische Untersuchungen*, edited by Walter Dostal, 207–406, 576–613, 630–37, 676–82. Vienna: Verlag der Österreichischen Akademie der Wissenschaften.

Gingrich, Andre. 2012a. "Comparative Methods in Socio-cultural Anthropology Today." In *Handbook of Social Anthropology*, edited by Richard Fardon et al., vol. II, 201–14. London: SAGE.

Gingrich, Andre. 2012b. "Paradise Lost, or Paradise Regained? Conceptions and Ideologies of Himah as a Ritual Site in the Highlands of South-Western Arabia." In *Ritual, Conflict and Consensus: Case Studies from Asia and Europe*, edited by Gabriela Kilianová, Christian Jahoda, and Michaela Ferencová. Veröffentlichungen zur Sozialanthropologie, 16, 65–74. Vienna: Verlag der Österreichischen Akademie der Wissenschaften.

Gingrich, Andre. 2013. "Wooden Pillars and Mural Paintings in the Saudi South-West: Notes on Continuity, Authenticity, and Artistic Change in Regional Traditions." In *Debating Authenticity: Concepts of Modernity in Anthropological Perspective*, edited by Thomas Fillitz and Jamie A. Saris, 142–59. Oxford: Berghahn.

Gingrich, Andre. 2017. "Rock Art from West and South West Arabia: Socio-Cultural Anthropology's Insights for the Region's Eastern Transition Zones." *Mediterranean Archaeology and Archaeometry* 17 (4): 71–83.

Gingrich, Andre. 2018. "Small Island Hubs and Connectivity in the Indian Ocean World: Some Concepts and Hypotheses from Historical Anthropology." In *Connectivity in Motion: Island Hubs in the Indian Ocean World*, edited by Edward A. Alpers and Burkhard Schnepel, 57–91. London: Palgrave Macmillan.

Gingrich, Andre, and Johann Heiss. 1986. *Beiträge zur Ethnographie der Provinz Ṣa'da, Nordjemen: Aspekte der traditionellen materiellen Kultur in bäuerlichen Stammesgesellschaften*. Vienna: Verlag der Österreichischen Akademie der Wissenschaften.

Gingrich, Andre, and Marcus Banks, eds. 2006. *Neo-nationalism in Western Europe and Beyond: Perspectives from Social Anthropology*. Oxford: Berghahn.

Gingrich, Andre, and Peter Schweitzer. 2014. "Barter and Subsistence: Insights from Social Anthropology for Anatolia's Prehistory." In *Prehistoric Economies of Anatolia: Subsistence Strategies and Exchange (Proceedings of a Workshop Held at the Austrian Academy of Sciences in Vienna, November 13–14, 2009)*, edited by Celine Wawruschka, 27–31. Rahden: Marie Leidorf Verlag.

Gingrich, Andre, and Eva-Maria Knoll. 2018. "Pilots of History: Ethnographic Fieldwork and Anthropology's Explorations of the Past." *ANUAC, Rivista della Società Italiana di Antropologia Culturale* 7 (2): 27–48.

Goitein, Shlomo D., and Mordechai A. Friedman. 2008. *India Traders of the Middle Ages: Documents from the Cairo Geniza (India Book)*. Leiden: Brill.

Gupta, Akhil, and James Ferguson. 1992. "Beyond 'Culture': Space, Identity, and the Politics of Difference." *Cultural Anthropology* 7 (1): 6–23.

Hannerz, Ulf. 1990. "Cosmopolitans and Locals in World Culture." *Theory, Culture & Society* 7: 237–51.

Margariti, Roxani. 2008. "Mercantile Networks, Port Cities, and 'Pirate' States: Conflict and Competition in the Indian Ocean World of Trade before the Sixteenth Century." *Journal of the Economic and Social History of the Orient* 51: 543–77.

6 Scaling Ethnography Up

Michael Schnegg

When the American Museum of Natural History was about to be built, in the middle of the 1880s, a fierce debate arose as to how its exhibitions should be arranged. On one side of the controversy, which unfolded over a series of articles in *Science*, stood Otis T. Mason, who was then the director of the Smithsonian Institution. He argued that museums should communicate a sound scientific message about the processes that governed the development of human societies. Mason argued that exhibitions at the new museum should show that people everywhere, under the same stress and with the same resources, made similar inventions. Moreover, he held that "the explorer who goes among a people to study their entire creed and activity will do his work better by having in his mind the determination to bring each industry into comparison with the same activities in other times and places" (Mason 1887). In practical terms, Mason (1886, 1887) proposed that the ethnographic objects like throwing-sticks, basketry, and bows should each fill the museum's rooms to communicate that universal principles are responsible for the cultural differences and similarities we observe among human technological achievements.

On the other side of the debate was Franz Boas. Boas was critical of generalizing explanations of cultural variability and change and instead urged the planners to design a museum that displayed different artifacts from one ethnic group in their respective societal and historical contexts. To make the difference between the two approaches clear, Boas used musical instruments as an example. He argued that one could not derive conclusions about music by comparing a symphony orchestra with the Kwakiutl's means of making music.

Without the continuous support of numerous people and communities in Kunene, this research would not have been possible. The results presented in this chapter are the product of the research project LINGS (Local Institutions in Globalized Societies), directed by Michael Schnegg (Universität Hamburg) and Michael Bollig (University of Cologne). Kathrin Gradt, Thekla Kelbert, Richard Kiaka, Theresa Linke, Diego Menestrey, Elsemi Olwage, and David Parduhn work(ed) on the project and collected part of the ethnographic data. They all provided valuable ideas, partly incorporated into this chapter. Martin Dallek manages the data of the LINGS project. Julia Pauli and Edward Lowe have offered critical and extremely constructive comments on an earlier draft of this chapter. The DFG (Deutsche Forschungsgemeinschaft) has funded this research generously since 2010. I am indebted to all of them.

Rather, any serious attempt to understand Kwakiutl music required that the instruments used be considered in the context of other instruments used by the same people at that time. In practical terms this meant that the rooms of the museum should be arranged according to ethnic groups (Dall and Boas 1887).

Boas's position did not go unchallenged. John Wesley Powell, the founding director of the Bureau of American Ethnology, wrote that the ethnic groups Boas imagined did not exist. To provide an example, Powell argued that during the 100 years prior to that time, many Native American groups had merged, formed, or disappeared. Consequently, the objects the museum had collected during these years could not be allocated to the well-known Native American groups that the public knew at the time. Neither could these artifacts be assigned to the groups that had existed a century earlier. Powell agreed with Mason that only a context-free, scientific classification of the objects to be displayed at the museum should be used (Powell and Boas 1887).

In the argument about the American Museum of Natural History, two interpretations of anthropology – one relativist and the other universalist – opposed each other, a debate that is still relevant to the discipline today (Buettner-Janusch 1957). Both approaches have valid points. On the one hand, the relativist position enables an in-depth and highly contextualized understanding of social and cultural phenomena, often produced through ethnography. A shortcoming of the relativist, ethnographic approach is that it is hard to assess whether the phenomena described in the ethnographic study might also be found elsewhere and what are the implications about the processes that generate those social and cultural phenomena across time and space. On the other hand, those who favor more universalist approaches in anthropology advocate for comparative means that offer the opportunity to describe scientifically more general and even universal patterns. The most widely recognized comparative strategy, the variable-oriented approach used in cross-cultural comparison, typically erases the local variations, conflicts, disagreements, and power dynamics that are so important to the contextualization of social and cultural phenomena in ethnography. Thus, when using a variable-based comparative strategy, we lose one of anthropology's biggest strengths: its capacity to place things into a wider social, cultural, and historical context.

Against this background, the discipline became deeply skeptical about explicitly comparative research strategies. This is especially true for larger-*N*, variable-based comparative strategies. However, this skepticism is not restricted to the kind of variable-based, cross-cultural comparison that George Peter Murdock advocated. Comparisons of only a few cases have received similar criticisms. At the same time, whether or not it is used as an explicit method, most anthropologists do compare data, at least informally. For example, in conference sessions and edited volumes, we place "our" cases in relation to those of other researchers in the collection. Indeed, casual exchanges among colleagues at professional meetings can hardly occur without references to how things are where "you" and "I" work.[1] Possibly, our intuitive approach to comparison implies that the two positions – finding common ground among a range of cases and appreciating the specificity of each case – are less antagonistic than they are typically considered to be in disciplinary debates.

The aim of this chapter is to further this disciplinary dynamic between the particularity of ethnography and the more generalizable understandings that formal comparative methods allow. To that end, I propose a methodological strategy, *ethnographic upscaling*, that combines in-depth ethnography of a small number of cases with larger-*N* regional comparisons that use formal, variable-based approaches. In the section "On Comparison," I typically refer to larger-*N* (more than ten cases) comparisons that use systematic methods for reducing the information and the relationships they contain. While the in-depth ethnography provides valid observations that can be used to identify factors that might contribute to variability of a particular phenomenon among a larger sample of cases, regional comparison allows the hypothetical associational patterns that are derived from ethnographic observations to be tested on a regional scale through the analysis of indicators taken from a larger number of cases.

The ethnographic upscaling approach proposed here has been developed in the collaborative research project that I codirect, titled Local Institutions in Globalized Societies (LINGS). The aim of LINGS is to explore how global policies have shaped the micropolitics of water in rural, arid Namibia. Guided by the notion of community-based natural resource management (CBNRM) policies, over the past two decades, Namibian pastoralists have had to develop new rules governing how to share water and distribute the costs involved in providing it. While all communities in rural Namibia were exposed to similar CBNRM blueprints and designs, distinct local institutions and practices have emerged. From the early stages of our research, the discussions among the ethnographers revealed that regional variations in rulemaking had existed, yet we had no well-supported explanation for these variations. In our discussions, many possible explanatory factors were identified, but we had no means to separate them and estimate how much they mattered for the emergence of different rulemaking regimes. In order to make these estimates and develop a robust explanation for the variability in rulemaking, we needed a larger number of observations than were available from the ethnographic cases. To provide such an explanation, the idea of comparing a larger number of cases in the region, and hence that of ethnographic upscaling, was born.

On Comparison

As a formal methodological strategy, comparison requires (1) the definition of the cases that are to be compared, (2) the selection of the activity, process, or system that is to be analyzed within each case and compared across cases, and (3) the methodological operation that determines whether the patterns observed among the cases are different or the same. When applied in anthropology during its founding years, "cases" were understood to be distinctly bounded cultures, societies, or nations. The features that defined these cases, such as kinship, subsistence strategies, political organization, and religious beliefs and practices, were described for each group that anthropologists encountered. These cultural features were then treated as distinct, independent variables that were distributed among all human societies or cultures. Cross-cultural analysis in this mode resulted in tabulations of many cases to reveal whether two variables, e.g. horticultural production and a specific form of descent, generally correlated (Boas 1887; Tylor 1889). It was already clear in the late nineteenth century that there were two problems with this approach. First, as Powell had argued in the debates about the design of the American Museum of Natural History in the 1880s, cultures were not stable, bounded groups that could be treated as definite units of analysis. Second, and equally present in the debate about the American Museum of Natural History, cultures influenced one another, often borrowing from or imposing on their neighbors (see Chapter 4, by Sprenger), which made it difficult for researchers to treat the cases to be compared as independent entities. The second problem is referred to as the Galton problem in anthropological comparison.

The reflexive debates of the 1970s and 1980s made the severity of the first problem even more evident. The controversy over the social construction of cultural groups and traits led to a significant improvement of ethnographic methods and writing. Anthropologist Lila Abu-Lughod, for example, proposed "ethnographies of the particular" that allowed anthropologists to describe individuals and their often conflicted and contested lived experiences without treating them as representatives of some larger, coherent group (i.e. a culture; Abu-Lughod 1991, 1993). Alternatively, George Marcus proposed that ethnography might "follow the flows" of culture across sites instead of writing about cultures as timelessly bounded to a particular place. Both research approaches avoid using traditional notions of a culture as a coherent, distinct social group. Instead, they place the individual, linkages, flows, or particular phenomena at center stage.

I find these solutions unsatisfying. Even in times of unprecedented globalization and translocal livelihoods, locally rooted social groups remain salient for understanding many social processes. Local communities, associations, organizations, and households act collectively to pursue common interests and goals. To capture these social dynamics, we need refined theoretical concepts that allow us to continue studying social groups.

One solution to the problem is given in the approaches that represent culture as sets of overlapping fields (called *social fields*, or *semiautonomous fields*). Moore (2000, 57) defines a semiautonomous field as a social setting, including different social actors, that can generate rules and coerce individuals into compliance with these rules. Moore calls these fields semiautonomous to denote that they are not bound and isolated but embedded in larger social and political frameworks and connected to one another. If individuals simultaneously belong to a set of social fields, such as a rural water-point association, a religious organization, and a state, those fields can overlap and shape one another (Schnegg 2018). If fields overlap, the boundary problem is more adequately addressed.

As Galton pointed out over a century ago, the comparison between groups (and individuals as well) poses a second important problem (Naroll 1961; Tylor 1889). It is easy to see that groups live in similar ecological environments and have similar subsistence strategies. But does this really mean that a specific environment has causal effects on how people make a living? Could it not also be that one society has adopted or "learned" the subsistence strategy from the other? In a previous article, I have shown how the processes that lead to similarities between cases can be identified and distinguished (Schnegg 2014). Instead of abandoning larger-*N* comparison as methodologically flawed, identifying and separating the within-case and between-case factors that can influence variables can provide insights into the processes we observe. To overcome the problem Galton first identified, I have proposed *multilevel comparison* as an analytical tool. To seek comparative explanations, multilevel comparison differentiates between the dynamics that take place within cases, the dynamics that emerge from embeddedness in larger-scale institutional structures, and the dynamics that are present in the networks that connect cases together. To make this clear, we might consider the relationship between two phenomena, such as the degree of economic stratification and sharing as the preferred local distributional norm (as opposed to reciprocity). The three conditions that could lead to the occurrence of both phenomena in two cases are as follows:

1. *Within-case dynamics:* One phenomenon can be considered as the cause of the other, e.g. low economic stratification causes sharing to be the normative rule for distributing goods.
2. *Embeddedness in larger-scale institutional structures:* Either or both of the two phenomena may have been shaped by the same larger context, e.g. sharing as a distributional norm and socioeconomic equality are both influenced by the religion the groups have in common.
3. *Networks and learning:* Either of the two phenomena may have been transmitted and/or negotiated from one case to the other (networks and

diffusion); e.g. sharing as a distributional norm became the rule in one community after people saw how well it worked for a neighboring community and how happy it made them.

Multilevel comparison recognizes that each type of co-occurrence leads to a different substantial interpretation. Only in the situation of within-case dynamics can the observation of two instances of the same pattern be taken as confirmation that an internal process is the cause of the outcome variable (i.e. low economic stratification causes the adoption of a norm of sharing). In both the second and third situations (i.e. scalar embeddedness and diffusion within networks), other noninternal processes have led to the co-occurrence of the two phenomena in the two locales. So, internal processes cannot be the cause of the similarities or differences between the two cases.

In the following case study, I address these two problems – how to define the relevant social groups for comparison and how to deal with the relationships that exist among those groups – by relating them. To address the first problem, we compare communities of practice that jointly manage water and design rules for doing so. At the same time, and to address the second problem as well, I do not treat those groups as bounded units but show whether and how internal and external dynamics contribute to variations in institutional regimes. In other words, multilevel comparison overcomes the very criticism of cross-cultural approaches that tend to treat social groups as homogeneous (bounded units governed by universal processes or principles) by bringing ethnography back in.

Sharing Water in Rural Namibia

In the arid environment of northwestern Namibia, pastoralism is the dominant livelihood, and almost all households own cattle and small stock. Water and land for grazing are the two central natural resources. Until the 1990s access to both was regulated by the South West Africa administration under the jurisdiction of the colonial South African state. Since the colonial state covered the costs of running and maintaining the infrastructure, little local coordination was required. Water was basically free to its pastoral users.

Starting in the early 1990s, water governance in rural Namibia changed profoundly. After independence, and in accordance with global environmental policies, it became a central theme of Namibia's environmental legislation to transfer the responsibility, costs, and benefits of resource management to local user associations. The legislation is founded on concepts like community-based natural resource management (CBNRM) and integrated water resources management (IWRM), which contain clear premises about the nature of resources and their appropriate uses. The implementation of CBNRM and IWRM led to a drastic reconfiguration of the institutional landscape in rural Namibia, and hundreds of communities had to find "new" ways to govern one of their two main natural resources: water (Linke 2017; Menestrey Schwieger 2017).

Sharing the costs of water production through borehole maintenance is one of the most important problems in water governance. Groundwater is typically pumped up from wells as deep as 300 m, and most pumps operate with diesel. Thus, the price of water is largely determined by the amount of water and the price of diesel required to pump it. In practice, the institutional solutions to cover the costs of water oscillate between two extremes: per head of cattle (PHOC) and flat-rate rules. In the first case, contributions are regulated according to the amount of water used. In the second case, payment for water is a fixed sum and more independent of usage.

During the process of implementation, emerging institutional arrangements are negotiated with representatives of the Ministry of Agriculture, Water and Forestry, or contracted NGOs. Representatives visit the communities and call for meetings during which many pertinent questions are discussed. Since discussions about the payment schemes are typically conflictual, the process often requires a number of meetings that stretch over months (Schnegg and Bollig 2016; Schnegg et al. 2016; Schnegg 2016; Schnegg and Linke 2015). During the meetings state representatives play an active role. They go through sections of a handbook and sensitize community members to the issues they have to resolve. While they do not provide any material incentives to apply a PHOC rule, or penalize communities that opt for a flat-rate rule, the state's representatives clearly articulate in public meetings that the PHOC rule is what the state favors and what they perceive to be just and fair (Schnegg 2016).

At the end of this process, possibilities for applicable rules are negotiated, and each community agrees upon a management plan, officially signed by the members of the Water Point Committee, the community group responsible for managing water distribution. As we will see later, the outcome of this process varies, and some communities decide on a flat-rate rule, and others on a PHOC rule. The aim of this comparison is to explain why this is so.

Doing Ethnography and Comparison

The data analyzed here were collected in northwestern Namibia by a team of anthropologists between 2010 and 2018 (M. Bollig, M. Schnegg, Th. Kelbert, D. Menestrey, Th. Linke, and K. Gradt), as part of the German Research Foundation (DFG)–funded research project LINGS (Schnegg 2016, 2018, 2019; Schnegg and Bollig 2016; Schnegg et al. 2016; Schnegg and Linke 2015). The two principal investigators, Schnegg and Bollig, have been conducting ethnographic fieldwork in the region since 2003 and 1994, respectively, and are responsible for the overall design and comparative analysis of the data.

In the first phase of the fieldwork, each of three anthropologists (D. Menestrey, Th. Linke, and K. Gradt) stayed for roughly one year between 2010 and 2011 in one part of the research area – southern (Fransfontein), central (Otwani), and northern (Okangwati) – to gain an in-depth understanding of processes involved in negotiating and crafting new institutions through daily routines. Since the pastoral communities in the area were relatively small (ten to twenty-five households), the three fieldworkers together were able to explore the dynamics in seven communities during their year-long stay. The qualitative data presented in the following were collected as part of their ethnographic fieldwork and derived from all three research sites (Menestrey Schwieger 2015, 2017; Linke 2017).

After returning from the field, an initial analysis of the data revealed that the range of institutional solutions in the seven communities was comparably small. One of the institutional fields that turned out to be especially interesting concerned the ways costs were covered. While some communities asked all households to pay the same amount, others required payments according to the number of cattle owned or applied an attenuated form in which the rich paid more than the poor. We observed and discussed these variations in our regular team meetings. At the same time, we had no definite answer to explain the variations observed. This had to do with the relatively small number of cases ($N = 7$) and the many independent variables that were thrown into the discussion. Soon it became clear that only a larger number of observations could provide an answer.

On the basis of our initial observations, we decided to develop a number of hypotheses to account for the differences we observed. Initially, we envisioned a relationship between the wealth distribution in the community, the number of people who would profit from either rule, and the likelihood that one of the two payment regimes would emerge. At the same time, we had observed that over time many communities that started off with the PHOC rule slowly slipped into the flat-rate regime. This gave rise to the hypothesis that the involvement of the state and NGOs could also explain the dynamics. In addition, we formulated a number of alternative hypotheses involving the size of the community, its heterogeneity, and its social cohesion as potential factors. While this chapter focuses on water-sharing rules, the LINGS project has identified a number of other phenomena as dependent variables, including different measurements of sustainability and success. For those phenomena, hypotheses were formulated in similar ways.

Thus, after our initial analysis of the ethnographic data, we designed a comparative research project to test for the distribution of the phenomena observed in the seven communities. Since our analysis treated communities as cases, it was methodologically challenging to gain the relatively large number of observations that would permit comparisons. To achieve this end, we designed an interview guide to elicit the variables identified previously on a community level.

For geographical areas of approximately 250 km^2 surrounding Fransfontein, Otwani, and Okangwati, sixty-three communities were sampled concentrically around the localities we had researched in depth in the preceding years. We decided against a representative sample of the entire Kunene Region owing to its size, bad road infrastructure, logistical constraints, and the lack of a list of communities that could serve as a sampling frame. In addition, our approach made use of the fact that fieldworkers were already known and trusted in the target areas. The logic of this nested comparative approach is summarized in Figure 6.1.

During community visits, we elicited rules of water management and the composition of community-based organizational structures for water governance. Focus group discussions took place in the open and included both female and male participants, some of whom were active in the group responsible for community-based water resource management, the Water Point Committee. The focus group discussions were semipublic so that people could join in during a session. In most cases, it took one or two days to complete a focus group discussion in any one community. In total, we visited sixty-three communities. Since information remains incomplete for some of them, the quantitative analysis presented here includes fifty-six cases. In addition to the focus group discussions, we conducted interviews with selected individuals. These covered more sensitive issues, e.g. conflicts and perceived success. The selection of individuals was guided by the need for representation of a mixture of important social categories, including gender, age, and wealth.

Some variables were already coded in the survey, while others had to be coded on the basis of open responses transcribed during the research. Two variables in this analysis were not coded a priori: the rules for water management and the involvement of the state. To code these variables from open responses, I categorized the rules for contributions from community residents into instances of proportional use and those instances where this was not the case. The coding was cross-checked by the other members of the research team. To measure the involvement of the state, we used two indicators based on information collected in the focus groups. First, we asked about the frequency and purpose of visits by state officials to a community during the past two years. When state officials had visited a community at least once during the previous year for consultations and activities other than urgent repairs of broken infrastructure, this served as an indication of greater-than-average state involvement. Generally, we found that state officials wanted to push communities in certain directions, above all concerning the payment schemes for water use. Second, our ethnographic observations showed that some employees of the ministry or commissioned NGOs lived in the communities in question. In these cases, the impact of the state was significantly greater, because those people typically wanted their communities to be flagship cases for the state's mission and ideology and thus worked consistently with other residents in the

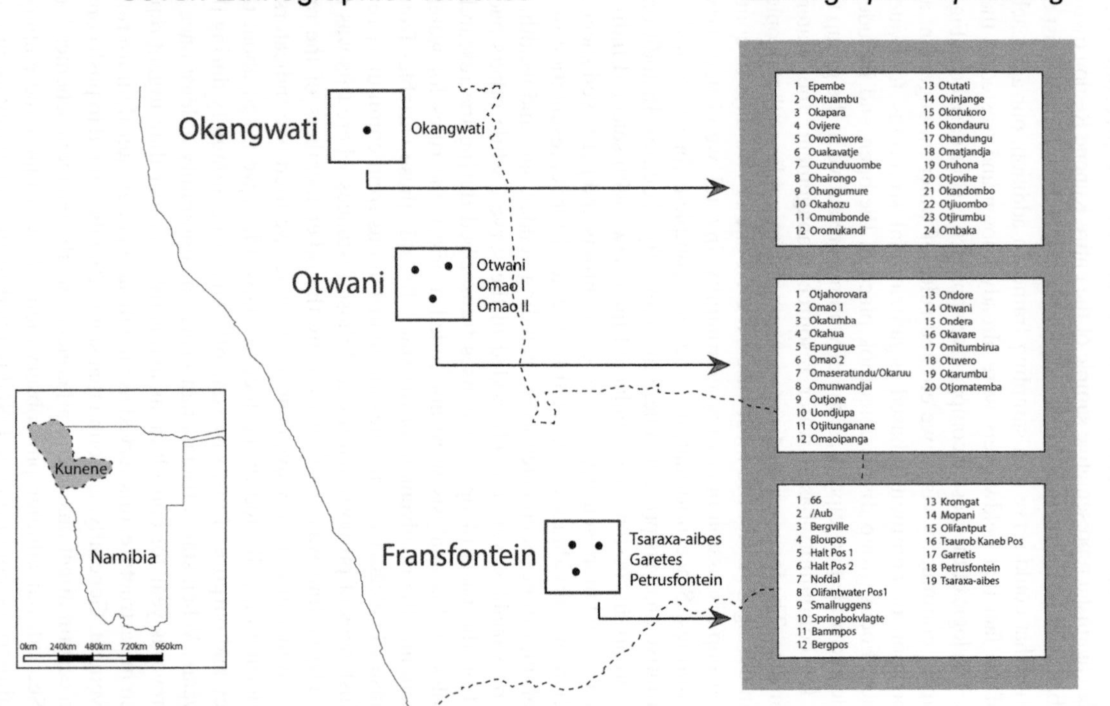

Figure 6.1 Ethnographic upscaling as a comparative research design.

hope of achieving this. For the analysis, we coded state involvement to be above average if either of the two indicators (more than one visit per year or a state authority member in residence) was applicable.

The Social Life of Water, by Comparison

As we have seen, the government promoted a proportional PHOC rule through the participation of its bureaucrats in the negotiation of water-governance schemes. At the end of the process in which those rules were locally negotiated, all communities had to agree upon a management plan, which was officially signed by the members of the Water Point Committee. The management plan gives a tentative budget for a water point and specifies rules for how each member should contribute financially. In the vast majority of the management plans, communities formally subscribed to a PHOC rule; that is, all households should pay according to the number of livestock they own.

However, we found that, in many communities, the PHOC rule was never applied, or if it had been, it was altered relatively soon thereafter. When we conducted the ethnographic upscaling research in 2012, out of the fifty-six communities, only twenty-five (44.6 percent) had continued with a PHOC rule.[2] In addition, seven communities (12.5 percent) used an attenuated form in which the rich pay more, but not exactly according to their number of livestock (e.g. rich = N$200, poor = N$100). This difference in payments is not as significant as the differences that emerge with exact livestock counts. In twenty-four communities (42.9 percent), the proportional rule, promoted by the state and NGOs, was never practiced. It was replaced instead by a rule that required equal payment for all households (Schnegg 2016; Schnegg et al. 2016). In some of these cases, money was collected, and a trusted person bought diesel with it. In equally many cases, the households had agreed that each household would pump for a month or that the households in charge during that specific month would provide the diesel to a caretaker in charge of pumping the water. All solutions led to equal payment (i.e. a flat-rate rule).

The results from the upscaling research support our initial observations that variations exist. The following analysis attempts to explain why this is so.

Internal Dynamics: Micropolitics of Water

The communities in Kunene are relatively small, and different domains of sharing overlap extensively (Schnegg 2015, 2018; Bollig 2000). As a consequence, sharing water is socially and culturally embedded. Dense and multiplex social networks constitute a specific social fabric with far-reaching consequences for building and maintaining institutions, as the following instance of Justus and his uncle reveals.

In Vingerklip,[3] a community in the Fransfontein area, Alfons, the head of the wealthiest household, refused to pay more than the rest and thus refused to support a PHOC rule. His nephew Justus was the chairperson of the Water Point Committee. Once when discussing water together, Justus complained bitterly to me about his uncle's refusal to pay according to the number of cattle he owned. When I asked Justus why he, as the elected chairperson acting with the majority of the households, could not push his uncle into accepting a just and fair rule, he explained,

> Since we were young, we knew exactly who is who, and that you have to have this respect for, let us say, "this is my uncle, I can't talk to my uncle like that." He is the big one in the family who's running the house, is the one making the decisions. I must not talk against my uncle. So, if my uncle says something, whether it is right or whether it is wrong, I have to follow the rules. So, that causes a lot of problems in the community, because now, the families were afraid to talk to their uncle, because they were keeping this respect.[4]

In Kunene, kinship, generation, and gender structure social interactions to a large degree. As the preceding example reveals, water management is part of the wider social field of kinship. As Justus explains, the dense kinship network and normative expectations make it impossible for him to force his uncle to accept a particular position. Among all kinship ties, that between a nephew and his uncle (mother's brother) is the most salient. A man will inherit property (especially cattle) from his maternal uncle, and therefore he is supposed to be subordinate, helpful, and respectful to his uncle.

In a series of articles, Cleaver has shown that resource governance is not only socially but also culturally embedded (Cleaver and de Koning 2015; Cleaver 2002, 2012). This implies that the rules that govern one domain are transferred to another domain. This becomes evident in considerations of water governance when we examine the justifications people bring forward for making households the central cultural unit for rulemaking (Otjiherero: *eanda*; Khoekhoegowab: *||gaus*), instead of the number of animals a household owns. As Pete explains,

> All we normally do is to contribute per household. Therefore, for us it is never a problem, because we are used to the issue of receiving something per household or paying, contributing per household. Even as we are talking now, if I slaughter cattle and I divide this meat among the households, I will divide it per household without considering how many people there are. Many of the things or activities, we do it per household. That is our normal routine. That's why it was never a problem for us, since we are used to this practice of per household.[5]

Pete heads a relatively rich household, and in our conversation, he argues that the rules that count for food should count for water as well. When benefits are shared, all households receive the same.

Our conversations with Pete and Justus indicate that institutions are socially and culturally embedded. We can hardly understand the variations that emerge at the institutional level if we do not take these dynamics into account. Given such micropolitics and the role of power in negotiations, we would expect all communities to shift from the PHOC to a flat-rate rule in the long run. However, and as we have seen, this is often not the case.

Embeddedness in Larger-Scale Institutional Structures: State Involvement

To answer why not all communities shift to a flat-rate rule, I ask when the institutions that the majority claims to be just and fair emerge. A closer examination of the twenty-four cases that do apply a proportional rule reveals that they share a key characteristic. The ministry and NGOs contracted by the state maintain strong involvement in the local water governance in these cases. As we have already seen, not only do local actors have different interests and bargain for what each sees as the proper institutional solution but the state and its local representatives also advocate for particular rules (Menestrey Schwieger 2015; Schnegg et al. 2016; Schnegg 2016). An interview with Christa, who works for the ministry in charge of the rural water supply and is responsible for roughly 100 water points, shows the state at work. When we talked about my observation that most communities switch to a flat-rate rule, she claimed, "It is not fair. But as soon as we turn our back, the community big men come and tell the rest what to do." In the course of the conversation, she repeatedly stated how frustrated she was that she, the official from the ministry, could not even implement the rule in the community where she herself was farming. When asked where the PHOC rule was actively working, she started talking about the community of Duurwater, where an active young woman was the chairperson. To support her, Christa drove early in the morning, when the cattle drink, to Duurwater to count the animals with the other committee members. "Then, we approached the poor households and talked to them about the different rules and encouraged them to stand up and talk in the meeting. In the meeting we would support them."[6]

Much of the institutional reconfiguration takes place in a social environment where the state has explicit preferences and some means to pursue them. The institutional regimes that emerge can only be understood if we simultaneously consider both the distribution of power at the local level and the role of the state. Recognizing this allows us to formulate a hypothesis, which combines the arguments and observations made so far: communities will employ a flat-rate rule unless the state actively supports the less wealthy pastoralists and their interests.

Table 6.1 tests this hypothesis and shows the correlation between the institutional regime (flat-rate versus PHOC rule) and the involvement of the state,

Table 6.1 *Engagement of the state and institutional regimes*

State/NGO Involvement	Flat-Rate Rule	PHOC Rule	Total
Strong	4	20	24
	16.7%	62.5%	
Weak	20	12	32
	83.3%	37.5%	
Total	24	32	56

Note: $N = 56$, phi = −0.478, sig. = 0.000.

coded as discussed earlier. The results show that the involvement of the state can explain, to a significant degree, the institutional outcome (phi = −0.478, sig. = 0.000).[7] This confirms that, in communities where the state is only weakly involved, a flat-rate rule is more likely to emerge. In those communities, the three dynamics analyzed earlier push the institutional regime toward a flat-rate rule.

An institutional form that deviates from the main pattern offers additional insights into the dynamics observed. In seven communities, an attenuated PHOC rule is practiced, and the rich pay twice as much as the poor. A closer examination of these communities reveals that the state is comparably inactive (coded as "weak") in six of them (85.7 percent). They thus lack the external support to establish a PHOC rule. In Table 6.1, all six cases fall into the category of proportional rule and weak state involvement and make up half of the twelve communities here.

Networks: Local Learning

Information and experiences are negotiated in social networks, and network effects have long been recognized as important for explaining individual behavior, e.g. the willingness and timing of individuals' adoptions of new technologies and innovations (Rogers 2003; Valente 2005). It is much less recognized that networks can have an effect on the behavior of larger units, equally connected in a system, as well (Jahn 2006; Dow et al. 1984). In our research, we do not have precise information on how the fifty-six communities shared information, nor do we know who might have interacted with whom. Given their livelihoods and the fact that most people rely on animals for transportation, it is reasonable to assume that people discuss such matters most intensively with their local neighbors, who are often also their kin.

An ethnographic vignette can exemplify this. I was sitting at the water point with a group of community members, and we were waiting for the pump to fill the dam sufficiently to give water to the almost fifty cattle surrounding us, partly patient, partly aggressive, especially the younger bulls aiming to challenge their elder peers. The community only started pumping water this morning because they had run out of diesel and had to wait until Harold, the teacher from nearby Fransfontein, brought some the previous evening. While we were waiting, chatting, and watching the animals attentively, Justus, the young man from the neighboring community (Vingerklip) discussed previously, stopped by. He was riding his donkey cart on the way to Fransfontein to drop children off at school. As almost always the case at the water point, conversation soon turned to the hardship of providing water for one's animals. Justus explained that they just had another meeting with the people from the Ministry of Agriculture, Water and Forestry to update the technical infrastructure so that it could not be destroyed very easily by elephants. In that same meeting, the extension officers had assisted in implementing a rule according to which each household would pump for one month, except the households with less than ten livestock, which did not have to pump at all but instead contribute some labor for cleaning or repairing the infrastructure. The people at the water point – mostly rather poor, just like Justus – were impressed and soon agreed that they would ask the chairperson of the Water Point Committee to call a meeting. That same afternoon a group went to the chairperson's house and requested that he ask the ministry to update their infrastructure, hoping that this would trigger debates and solutions for the payment regime as well.

This particular episode is unique in my observations in Namibia. Nonetheless, it expresses how physical proximity, in combination with specific means of transportation and casual conversations, can lead to an exchange and evaluation of experiences and information in a larger group. These extended talks are typically held in public places, such as water points or the open fireplace, where the cooking is done and most household members sit for many hours at night to chat among themselves and with visiting neighbors.

The significance of this observation is supported by a social network survey that we conducted in the seven communities studied ethnographically. In this survey, we asked people about with whom they would discuss important matters concerning the water point. In more than 90 percent of the cases, people from the immediate neighborhood were named.

To test the consequences of the communication and network effects, we developed a model that located each community on the geographical map. Then we asked whether the communities in immediate geographical proximity came up with the same rule (regardless of the content of the rule). If a network effect was observed, we would expect the local homogeneity to be higher than average.

Table 6.2 reports the percentage of communities in immediate proximity within varying radii that use the same rule. The results indicate that proximity

Table 6.2 *Similarity of rules within selected concentric geographical zones around the community*

Radius (km)	Communities with Same Rule (%)
5	65.2
10	55.9
15	55.2
20	56.6

Note: $N = 47$.

plays a role. The communities in the immediate network environment are significantly more likely to employ the same rule than the average 50 percent that would be expected to do so by chance alone. Moreover, nearby communities are more likely to come up with similar solutions than widely dispersed groups.

Conclusion

I started this chapter by referring to a historical debate that highlighted an enduring disciplinary tension in anthropology. At the core of the controversy between Boas, Mason, and Powell was the antagonism between a universal and a relativistic approach to anthropology. Often, ethnography and systematic comparative methods are kept separate by adherents of each side of this debate, greatly limiting the different strengths that these approaches can bring to anthropological research. As a way forward, the first aim of this chapter was to show how the LINGS project combined in-depth ethnography with a comparative approach to overcome some of the particular problems each approach had on its own. The second aim of this chapter was to demonstrate that the methodology we developed – ethnographic upscaling – enabled ethnographically sound generalizations and explanations, at least in the middle range of theoretical generality. These concluding remarks discuss the lessons we learned, both substantially and methodologically.

In LINGS, we wanted to know how new institutions of water governance emerged at the intersection of global policies and micropolitics. Our ethnographic work indicated early on that different water-governance regimes had emerged across communities. We wanted to understand what might contribute to this variability. In the early ethnographic work, we were able to propose possible explanations, but the relatively small number of cases we observed did not permit us to identify the most likely explanations from among the many hypotheses we had. Therefore, we decided to scale the ethnography up. We did so by taking our in-depth ethnographic understandings of seven communities to formulate hypotheses and then developing a survey instrument that allowed our researchers to describe the distribution of some of the observations made in the ethnographic work across a larger sample of cases. We could then statistically test for the relationships we had specified in our hypotheses.

Many anthropologists are critical of larger-*N* comparison as an explicit research strategy for a number of reasons. These include whether or not it is possible to define distinct cultural groups as cases without understating the degree of interrelatedness among them as well as the degree to which they are embedded in larger social and cultural institutions and processes. In a previous article, I developed multilevel comparison to overcome some of these problems (Schnegg 2014). Multilevel comparison investigates how patterns of similarity and difference among a set of cases can be the result of processes internal to each case, processes that reflect the way the cases are similarly embedded in larger structures, or processes that reflect the way the cases are networked together. Multilevel comparison acknowledges that within-community dynamics are essential for understanding the patterns and relationships we observe. At the same time, they cannot explain the distribution alone. Only if we take their embeddedness in larger institutional structures and networks into account can we understand why communities manage water in one way or another.

In the LINGS project, the boundary problems of social groups are addressed by treating them as social fields that are embedded in larger structures and related to one another through networks. Social fields group around specific foci (here water) and may or may not overlap with other such fields. The more the social fields overlap, the more we might speak of cultural groups. These social fields can best be understood through in-depth ethnography. The external linkages and effects, including the state and between-community networks, also become evident in ethnography. Multilevel comparison allows us to systematically study how these external contexts and internal dynamics might differentially explain the variations in rulemaking that we observed. In other words, ethnographic upscaling overcomes the criticism that comparative approaches tend to treat social groups as bounded and homogeneous by embedding and linking cases together.

Specifically, the micropolitics of water, the influence of the state, and network effects explain the institutional variation to a large degree. Left alone, local power dynamics – that is, internal processes in kin relations – shape the process of water management and are likely to push in a direction where communities end up with a flat-rate rule. However, if the state maintains an active role, one is likely to find a solution that favors the poor and in which the water consumption of the rich is not subsidized. Thus, external embeddedness plays an equally important role. Moreover, we find a tendency toward local homogeneity, which indicates that communication, adaptation, and learning among regionally proximate communities are also important.

As I have shown, the ethnographic upscaling approach allows us to go beyond narratives about the ethnographers' community of interest and identifies relationships and causal explanations on a larger regional scale. In doing this, we overcome a common shortcoming of ethnography – the lack of knowledge about the reach of an observed phenomenon to other cases – without sacrificing the strength derived from in-depth and highly contextualized explanations. The ethnographic upscaling approach is especially suited for investigations that treat social groups, and not individuals, as central units of analysis. Research that deals with human-environment interaction and the management of tangible resources, such as water, land, game, and forests, seems especially well suited to this approach. The studies of religious or political organizations could be equally promising fields for this methodological strategy. I hope that I have contributed to the value of comparison in anthropology by providing a research design that combines two of the unquestionable strengths of anthropology, instead of adopting only one while highlighting the weaknesses of the other. Such an approach will hopefully strengthen the voice of anthropology in public debates and eventually create the conditions where anthropology can fulfill its public responsibility to inform others of empirically documented patterns of human variability and the processes that can explain them – much as both Boas and Mason had in mind a century and a half ago.

Notes

1 Boas did not dismiss comparison per se. Rather, he advocated an approach to comparison that is regionally and historically rooted, to avoid universalizing fallacies.
2 Seven communities were excluded from this comparative analysis because some of the necessary information could not be collected in a sufficiently reliable way.
3 All community names are pseudonyms.
4 Interview conducted by Michael Schnegg, March 20, 2014 (Fransfontein area).
5 Interview conducted by Kathrin Gradt, October 26, 2011 (Otwani area).
6 Interview conducted by Michael Schnegg, March 25, 2014 (Fransfontein area).
7 The analysis treats the six cases with an attenuated PHOC rule, where the richer people pay more but not exactly according to the number of cattle owned (as in the cases of a PHOC rule). If they were treated as the cases of a flat rate or excluded from the analysis, the correlation would be even higher.

References

Abu-Lughod, Lila. 1991. "Writing against Culture." In *Recapturing Anthropology*, edited by Richard G. Fox, 137–62. Santa Fe: School of American Research Press.

Abu-Lughod, Lila. 1993. *Writing Women's Worlds*. Berkeley: University of California Press.

Boas, Franz. 1887. "The Occurrence of Similar Inventions in Areas Widely Apart." *Science* 9 (224): 485–86.

Bollig, Michael. 2000. "Production and Exchange among the Himba of Northwestern Namibia." In *People, Cattle and Land-Transformations of a Pastoral Society in Southwestern Africa*, edited by Michael Bollig and Jan-Bart Gewald, 271–98. Köln: Rüdiger Köppe Verlag.

Buettner-Janusch, John. 1957. "Boas and Mason: Particularism versus Generalization." *American Anthropologist* 59 (2): 318–24.

Cleaver, Frances. 2002. "Reinventing Institutions: Bricolage and the Social Embeddedness of Natural Resource Management." *The European Journal of Development Research* 14 (2): 11–30.

Cleaver, Frances. 2012. *Development through Bricolage? Institutions and Natural Resource Management*. London: Earthscan.

Cleaver, Frances, and Jessica de Koning. 2015. "Furthering Critical Institutionalism." *International Journal of the Commons* 9 (1): 1–18.

Dall, Wiliam H., and Franz Boas. 1887. "Museums of Ethnology and Their Classification." *Science* 9 (228): 587–89.

Dow, Malcolm M., Michael L. Burton, Douglas R. White, and Karl P. Reitz. 1984. "Galton's Problem as Network Autocorrelation." *American Ethnologist* 11 (4): 754–70.

Jahn, Detlef. 2006. "Globalization as 'Galton's Problem': The Missing Link in the Analysis of Diffusion Patterns in Welfare State Development." *International Organization* 60 (2): 401–31.

Linke, Theresa. 2017. *Kooperation unter Unsicherheit: Institutionelle Reformen und kommunale Wassernutzung im Nordwesten Namibias*. Bielefeld: transcript Verlag.

Mason, Otis T. 1886. "Resemblances in Arts Widely Separated." *The American Naturalist* 20 (3): 246–51.

Mason, Otis T. 1887. "The Occurrence of Similar Inventions in Areas Widely Apart." *Science* 9 (226): 534–35.

Menestrey Schwieger, Diego A. 2015. "An Ethnographic Analysis of the Role of Power in Institutional Arrangements: Borehole Cost Recovery within a Pastoral Community in North-Western Namibia." *Environmental Policy and Governance* 25 (4): 258–69.

Menestrey Schwieger, Diego A. 2017. *The Pump Keeps on Running*. Münster: LIT Verlag.

Moore, Sally Falk. 2000. *Law as Process: An Anthropological Approach*. Oxford: James Currey.

Naroll, Raoul. 1961. "Two Solutions to Galton's Problem." *Philosophy of Science* 28 (1): 15–39.

Powell, John W., and Franz Boas. 1887. "Museums of Ethnology and Their Classification." *Science* 9 (229): 612–14.

Rogers, Everett M. 2003. *Diffusion of Innovations*. London: Simon & Schuster.

Schnegg, Michael. 2014. "Anthropology and Comparison: Methodological Challenges and Tentative Solutions." *Zeitschrift für Ethnologie* 139 (1): 55–72.

Schnegg, Michael. 2015. "Reciprocity on Demand: Sharing and Exchanging Food in Northwestern Namibia." *Human Nature* 26 (3): 313–30.

Schnegg, Michael. 2016. "Lost in Translation: State Policies and Micro-politics of Water Governance in Namibia." *Human Ecology* 44 (2): 245–55.

Schnegg, Michael. 2018. "Institutional Multiplexity: Social Networks and Community-Based Natural Resource Management." *Sustainability Science* 13 (4): 1017–30.

Schnegg, Michael. 2019. "The Life of Winds: Knowing the Namibian Weather from Someplace and from No Place." *American Anthropologist*. doi: 10.1111/aman.13274.

Schnegg, Michael, and Michael Bollig. 2016. "Institutions Put to the Test: Community-Based Water Management in Namibia during a Drought." *Journal of Arid Environments* 124: 62–71.

Schnegg, Michael, Michael Bollig, and Theresa Linke. 2016. "Moral Equality and Success of Common-Pool Water Governance in Namibia." *Ambio* 45 (5): 581–90.

Schnegg, Michael, and Theresa Linke. 2015. "Living Institutions: Sharing and Sanctioning Water among Pastoralists in Namibia." *World Development* 68: 205–14.

Tylor, Edward B. 1889. "On a Method of Investigating the Development of Institutions; Applied to Laws of Marriage and Descent." *The Journal of the Anthropological Institute of Great Britain and Ireland* 18: 245–72.

Valente, Thomas. 2005. "Network Models and Methods for Studying the Diffusion of Innovation." In *Models and Methods in Social Network Analysis*, edited by Peter J. Carrington, John Scott, and Stanley Wasserman, 98–116. Cambridge: Cambridge University Press.

Part III

Distant and Fluid Comparisons

7 Best, Worst, and Good Enough

Lessons Learned from Multisited Comparative Ethnography

Jennifer S. Hirsch, Holly Wardlow, Daniel Jordan Smith, Harriet Phinney, Shanti Parikh, and Constance A. Nathanson

Comparison is one of the fundamental elements of critical thinking. We teach our students to ask, "How is what this author writes about this topic different from what other authors write?" We push, with those comparisons, to teach them to think abstractly, to go beyond the descriptive (people like flat pizza in New York; they like deep-dish pizza in Chicago) to the abstract. This requires learning to see beyond the particulars, to go beyond the uninteresting observation that things are different in different places, and to reach a level of explanation that focuses on why categories of social phenomena differ in social salience between places or how processes of social change differ. Comparison and synthesis of work in a field of inquiry represent a – if not *the* – critical intellectual skill we seek to cultivate in our students. We know students are ready for independent research when they can survey a field of knowledge, sort work according to different approaches to the topic, and identify the key *conceptual* gaps in the literature, i.e. not descriptive gaps (X has been studied in Taiwan but not in Indonesia).

Further, there are ways in which our basic ideas about the advancement of knowledge involve comparison. Both theory formulation and substantive knowledge advance by formulating questions based on prior research in that setting. Questions are generated through the comparison of one's underlying conceptual framework, which lays out the terrain of what one seeks to know against what is currently revealed and foregrounded by the conceptual frameworks that others use. But with ethnographic research, this comparison is folded back on itself a second time or multiple additional times. First, questions worth asking are born from a survey of extant knowledge: What are the things that we do not yet know about X? Then, ethnographic research changes shape while in process, responding both to emerging data and to how these data fit into the broader field of knowledge: again, comparison generates understanding.

So, there are clearly ways in which conventional single-sited ethnography is intrinsically comparative. That differs, however, from research that is

The authors gratefully acknowledge support from the Eunice Kennedy Shriver National Institute of Child Health and Human Development, R01 HD041724.

explicitly and emphatically comparative – that is, which sets out to examine a common set of research questions across distinct settings, with each project realized by a separate person or team. Comparative ethnography that takes place in different settings, which we explore in this chapter, is one tool for the interrogation of a common set of questions. In comparative ethnography, researchers approach multiple sites with a shared analytical framework and then strive to distinguish between observations that are unique to a particular field site and those that have broader theoretical relevance. We use the case study of a once-in-a-lifetime opportunity – a large, National Institutes of Health (NIH)–funded comparative ethnographic study – to discuss in detail (1) elements of the process that were key to the undertaking's success, (2) ways in which comparative research could have been even more powerful or productive, (3) things that future comparative research should strive to avoid, (4) recommended best practices, and (5) what we would call "minimum adequate" approaches to comparative ethnography. We also discuss, in closing, more virtual approaches to comparative work. In telling the story of our project, we illustrate how shared concepts both at the macro level (a general culture and political economy approach) and at the meso level (the notion of extramarital opportunity structures) grounded our shared work from the beginning, as well as how two of the key concepts that frame our subsequent written work (sexual geographies and social risk) emerged from the comparative work itself.

Love, Marriage, and HIV: The Origin Story

Origin of the Idea and Collaboration

The project's genesis dates back to the connections initially forged among three of us (Hirsch, Smith, and Wardlow) through the Emory University Department of Anthropology's dissertation-writing seminar in the 1997–98 academic year. Wardlow and Smith were Emory University's doctoral students in anthropology, and Hirsch was a PhD student at Johns Hopkins University who had done fieldwork in Atlanta and then joined the Emory University Department of Anthropology's dissertation-writing seminar seeking intellectual community during dissertation writing. As we shared and discussed our chapters, we noted the surprising resonances in terms of people's engagement with discourses of companionate marriage across the Igbo (Nigeria), Huli (Papua New Guinea), and Mexican field sites. Although, without question, the meaning of companionate marriage varied in each place, we were struck both by the power that notions of love and marriage had across these very distinct contexts and by the cross-site differences in what this meant on the ground for men's and women's experiences of intimacy. Initially, what brought us together was this shared interest in changing ideas about love and changing forms of marriage.

One of us entered into this conversation about comparison fresh from the field research that had included a comparative element for strategic, pragmatic, and intellectual reasons. Hirsch's training at the intersection of public health and anthropology culminated in an ethnographic dissertation research project that relied on comparison between two sites and a much more explicit sampling strategy than anthropologists typically use (Hirsch 2003; Hirsch and Nathanson 1998). This was an intentional strategy in order to make the work intelligible to (and seem rigorous enough for) a department that had never before approved a dissertation without any quantitative research component. The comparative approach was also intended to problematize the notion of "transnational community" (Basch et al. 1994). That fieldwork resulted in a firsthand understanding of how working across sites can facilitate a move toward abstraction (in that case, an understanding of how the intimate experiences of women from a shared cultural context were shaped by the varying social and economic resources to which they had access). These were certainly not insights that could only have been generated through cross-site comparison; Jane and Peter Schneider's elegant cross-class comparison of the pace of fertility change and the meaning of family limitation practices in nineteenth-century Sicily was a critical intellectual influence, as was the growing literature from diverse locations about the emergence of a companionate ideal (e.g. Collier 1997; Inhorn 1996; Schneider and Schneider 1996). Clearly, the axes of comparison are not limited to geography. This prior experience with cross-site comparison, however, demonstrated both its intellectual potential and its usefulness as an element of research design that would appeal to a more positivist public health audience.

An American Anthropological Association (AAA) panel on Love and Marriage, organized by Hirsch and Wardlow, led to an edited volume (Hirsch and Wardlow 2006) and enabled the recruitment of Phinney and Parikh (who, coincidentally, participated in another AAA panel on global romance that same year, organized by Parikh and Bonnie Adrian) to the nascent project, Love, Marriage, and HIV. At least two of us (Hirsch and Wardlow) faced an additional element of the academic reward structure: along with academic productivity, securing external funding was an expectation in terms of meeting the bar for tenure. Moreover, the team concluded that the level of funding available from NIH was important for making a multisited, comparative ethnographic project viable. The NIH funds basic biomedical and clinical research and in very limited and specific ways also supports behavioral and social science research. It seemed unlikely that by itself work on changing ideas of love and marriage would be competitive as a proposal. However, the November 2000 request for applications for research on Gender and HIV (National Institutes of Health and Human Development [NICHD] and National Institute of Mental Health [NIMH] 2000; accessed May 13, 2016) opened a window of opportunity.

The Quest for Funding and the Work of Designing the Project

In 2002, our team of five (Hirsch, Smith, Wardlow, Parikh, and Phinney) received approximately $1.5 million from the Eunice Kennedy Shriver National Institute of Child Health and Human Development for a four-year comparative ethnographic study of the social roots of married women's vulnerability to HIV in five countries: Mexico, Nigeria, Vietnam, Uganda, and Papua New Guinea (NIH R01 HD041724). Also on our project team were four "senior project advisors": Bruce Knauft, an anthropologist; Carlos del Rio, an infectious diseases doctor and global health researcher; Marjorie Muecke, a medical anthropologist and nurse; and Connie Nathanson, a sociologist.

Looking back, several factors contributed to our ability to successfully generate a comparative research project of this scale: prior existing social relations with a core group of colleagues who shared an interest in understanding how the globalization of companionate marriage and romance unfolded into local settings, liked and trusted one another, respected one another's work, had easy proximity to one another, and faced similar expectations in terms of scholarly productivity; a way of framing our research to articulate the social value of the knowledge we would produce; the availability of funding for our topic; and a reward structure that created a strong incentive for Hirsch to do the work of leading a large, externally funded research project in addition to continuing to press forward with single-authored publications.

It was a long road between the initial formulation of the idea in November 2000 and our first project meeting in 2003. One critical challenge along the way was designing a comparative ethnographic project that maintained the context-specific focus of anthropology yet would appeal to a scientific audience interested in generalizability and not necessarily familiar with ethnographic methods. At NIH, what is denoted "behavioral or social science research" related to HIV and AIDS is reviewed by study sections that include scientists from across multiple disciplines (the more than two dozen people on the study section that reviewed and scored Love, Marriage, and HIV included only one anthropologist and one sociologist), as well as people trained in pediatrics, human sexuality, HIV prevention, addiction science, and many other areas. This required articulating the project's theoretical framing, scientific importance, and methods in a way that was accessible across disciplines rather than taking for granted that the reviewers would understand, for example, what it meant to take a "culture and political economy" approach to vulnerability to HIV or how structural-level and site-specific findings could be both generalizable and translated into tangible recommendations.

In order to appeal to this audience, we ultimately chose to focus our project around a specific health-related question that required social analysis: What puts married women at risk of HIV? This highly relevant public health question allowed us to explore social domains that were of broad interest to social scientists in

The project's **specific aims** include theoretical, methodological, and applied components. Research aims are:

1. *to compare across five developing country sites (Papua New Guinea, Mexico, Vietnam, Nigeria, and Uganda) (a) the relative penetration of ideas and practices associated with companionate marriage, and (b) the specific forms of marital and extramarital relationships;*
2. *to understand and explain the ways in which these ideas about and practices of intimacy are shaped and constrained by gender unequal structures and ideologies, local forms of economic organization, and cultural change;*
3. *to evaluate the implications of these ideas and practices for HIV prevention within and outside of marriage.*

The methodological aim is:

4. *to use multi-sited comparative ethnographic research to generate findings of broad theoretical and public-health significance.*

The applied aim is

5. *to present research findings to appropriate local and international agencies and professionals in order to contribute to the development of gender-sensitive, culturally specific interventions to limit marital HIV transmission in each field site.*

Figure 7.1 Love, marriage, and HIV aims.

general and to each of us. Key areas of interest for us as researchers were marital ideals that emphasize social and emotional intimacy, gender inequality, changing occupational structures, underemployment and poverty, and labor migration and how these diffuse worldwide. Thus, we opted to examine how cultural, social, and economic contexts create vulnerability to HIV among married women and enable men's extramarital liaisons, thereby increasing the risk to women. This entailed an examination, at each field site, of the similarities and differences in emerging forms of marriage, the gendered meanings of sexual intimacy and fidelity, and the similarities and differences in sexual and HIV risk practices. A key question was how marital relationships, in each field site, reflected the relative penetration of ideas and practices associated with companionate marriage and how those practices and ideas may or may not drive or curtail HIV risk. Other questions and ideas, such as about sexuality, public respectability, and social risk, emerged over the course of the ethnographic research as key shared intellectual touchstones. The project's specific aims are listed in Figure 7.1.

Through months of regular conference calls, we developed a conceptual framework summarizing the range of social processes of interest to us. Compelling visual aids force those writing the grant to crystallize in the barest possible terms the key domains of interest and provide an easy way for reviewers – frequently tasked with reviewing three, four, or even five lengthy applications, each of which can take hours to get through – to grasp the essential ideas that drive a project. Our conceptual framework (Figure 7.2) was formulated in a way that is typical in public health, with the social and cultural phenomena of focus on the left-hand side, the key social institutions to be explored in the middle, and the "outcomes" of interest on the right-hand side. This graphic representation of a gendered approach to cultural political economy laid out our ideas for an audience that would not be familiar with that formulation.

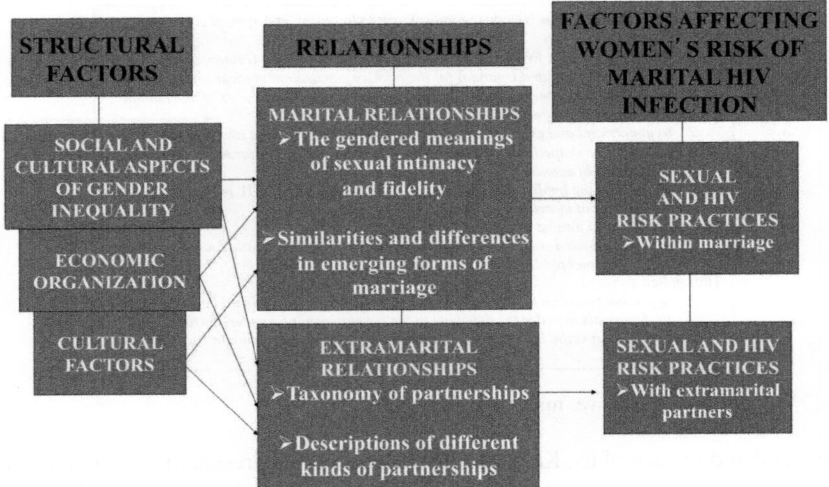

Figure 7.2 Conceptual framework.

Justifying Site Selection

The many months of proposal writing both required and provided an opportunity for the team to work through a number of problems related to cross-site comparison. For the purposes of the grant, we had to justify the selection of field sites, which at first glance might seem like odd locations to compare. The field sites varied along many dimensions and represented vastly different cultural contexts, colonial histories, economic conditions, and religious influences, as well as differences in basic things such as the size of the locations and whether they were urban or rural. For example, Hanoi was a city of millions in the year 2000, whereas the Mexican field site was the capital of a county whose entire population did not surpass 20,000; levels of economic development and literacy, as well as the nature of each location's HIV epidemic (both prevalence and populations most affected), also varied across the five sites. The actual reason for field site selection was that we were working together because we liked one another and because each of us had done extended prior research that suggested the emergence of some form of companionate ideal in our respective field sites. (It is possible, of course, that to the purely anthropological eye, the notion of the companionate ideal might, in and of itself, provide sufficient justification. This is a question to consider: How, beyond existing positive social relations among researchers, do people select locations for comparison?) For purposes of grantsmanship, however, the ex post facto justification of field site selection was framed in terms of "stages" of the HIV epidemic, with Papua New Guinea having a nascent epidemic, Mexico and Vietnam having concentrated epidemics, and Nigeria and Uganda having disseminated epidemics. In the final months of the grant development, for purposes of policy impact, we sought an anthropologist working in the United States, China, or India whose work would fit with that of the team but were unable to find someone who met the three actual criteria (having done prior work on love and marriage; being interested in working on a comparative project; and having a personal relationship with a team member who could vouch for them both scientifically and personally as someone with whom we would like to enter into a long-term professional relationship).

Getting to Work

There were at least five ways in which our research was "comparative": (1) we had a shared "outcome" variable (the thing we were trying to explain); (2) we developed together a shared framework of "explanatory" or conceptual variables as ways of thinking about what might shape the problem at hand; (3) we used the same methods, adapted for each site (in ways that we describe in great detail in Hirsch et al. 2009); (4) we committed to a shared framework for sampling for the marital case studies and key informant interviews; and (5) we were in constant dialogue throughout the process of data collection and analysis, with a great deal of advice seeking, moral support giving, sharing of findings and fieldwork events, and collective editing of one another's writing. The last four of these five elements involved pre-research planning.

Preparing for the Field

In August 2002, we received a notice from NIH that we had been funded by them, with a project start date on January 1, 2003. Immediately, we faced two bureaucratic hurdles. The first, which pushed us back by several months, was caused by an inconveniently timed change in NIH requirements for international HIV research (see Wedland 2008). The second major hurdle was securing institutional review board (IRB) approval from ten institutions in six different countries, during the era in which US practices for ethics review changed, such that IRBs would not give final approval to international research without sign-off by an in-country IRB approved by the US Office of Human Research Protection. Ultimately, it felt like a miracle that it took us only eight months to secure the necessary institutional and research ethics approvals to begin the research.

Finally, between June and October 2003, over the course of intensive three-day meetings as well as regular conference calls, we started to prepare for fieldwork by finalizing research instruments that could be used in all the five field sites. The research proposal contained a concrete set of research questions that we would answer, operationalizing the relatively abstract specific aims. But at this stage of the planning process, we strove to be very detailed and concrete about what specific observable social phenomena we sought to describe in each setting. This was absolutely essential, because we understood that we could only generate data that would serve as the basis for comparison if we started out by asking a shared set of questions. Drawing on the conceptual framework in the grant application, we worked collectively to articulate the corresponding domains of social practice and list the sets of concrete questions for each interview category (married person, health or local expert, etc.) that one might ask about that domain. How would one research or document, for example, the "gendered meanings of sexual intimacy and fidelity"? Where might we observe or ask about that, and what would we look for and ask about? Then, once we'd compiled a full set of potential questions to explore, we went back and pared them down, understanding that we each would only have six months to do the fieldwork. Even though we were all returning to places we had been before, and so in many cases already had a reasonably good idea about things such as the relative shamefulness of men's or women's premarital sexual activity, marriage practices, and the like, we still had to be disciplined in our focus on a shared set of questions.

We had similar but not always overlapping interests: working in Vietnam, where the power of the state to shape people's day-to-day lives was much more explicitly visible, Phinney was far more attuned to those questions than were the rest of us. Among the Huli in Papua New Guinea, the level of interpersonal violence was much greater, and thus a much greater concern both conceptually and practically than it was in other sites. There were funny aspects of this as well; Parikh raised questions about the history of sexual pleasure and gendered knowledge and significance (for instance, women's use of "waist beads" or other "bedroom tricks" in the context of competition among co-wives) that felt less relevant in other places. From the beginning, our shared commitment to the project kept us from spinning off to pursue noncomparable lines of inquiry. Another element of this formulation of a shared conceptual framework involved learning about one another's field sites, with each of us circulating a few key pieces we had written about love, marriage, or sexuality there. We started off the first meeting with a presentation that included both an update on HIV in each field site and a review, for the group, of key social and cultural dimensions. The goal of this first step, thinking retrospectively, was to develop a common conceptual and empirical sensibility so that we could collectively understand both how our shared interests might resonate across sites and what was importantly distinct in each setting.

After settling collectively on what we were trying to learn, it was time to hash out instruments that would generate roughly parallel data in each setting.

The research design, as described in the proposal, involved four primary methods: archival research, key informant (or what we used to refer to as local experts or people with special knowledge) interviews, participant observation, and marital case studies (2009, 42–43). As we worked together to develop very specific plans to move forward with each method, we elaborated thirteen documents to guide us in the field, with each of us rotating through the roles of being the person to develop a first draft, to revise, to cross-check with our research aims, and to edit down, wherever possible, to focus on the highest-priority topics. Part of this involved a conversation about how each method might differ in practice in each setting. For the key informant interviews, for example, there were some types of informants that were common across all five sites (government officials, for example) and others that were particular to one site – in Hirsch's fieldwork, for example, that included psychologists and doctors, as well as a set of interviews with people with locally "troubling sexual reputations" (women and men reportedly engaged in sex work, non-heterosexuals). In another example, in Parikh's site interviewing well-known *ssengas* (literally translated, a paternal aunt who is responsible for providing sexuality education to a niece) provided local insight into marital intimacy and problems. We all focused on an agreed-upon core set of types of key informants, but what an "extramarital sex expert" (or, as we described it in shorthand, "sexpert") meant in practice varied substantially by location.

A particularly crucial element of the commitment to a shared methodological strategy, and to the comparative endeavor more generally, was figuring out how to sample the married couples whose experiences would lie at the heart of our inquiry and would form the basis of what we called a "marital case study" approach. Developing a sampling plan required addressing the noncommensurability of field sites: What it means to be rich in Hela (home to the Huli) is very different from what it means to be rich in Mexico or Vietnam, and so a pig-based metric of wealth made no more sense than a cash- or consumer-goods-based metric of wealth. We eventually ended up with the following (see Table 7.1) as our guide, with the understanding that each of these criteria – with the exception of life stage – would mean different things in different places.

These "axes of diversity" connected back to the conceptual framework graphic (see Figure 7.2). "Generation" was intended to capture people's relative exposure to ideologies of companionate intimacy as well as the length of time they had been married. "Migration status" and "economic status" captured distinct elements of their insertion into and access to resources generated by gendered labor markets; both were highly related to opportunities for extramarital trysts and the possibility of concealing them from marital social networks.

The original proposal actually included four axes of diversity: generation, migration, education, and marital happiness. However, in the process of

Table 7.1 *LMHIV marital case-study sampling table*

		Axis of Diversity: Economic Status	
Axis of Diversity: Generation	Axis of Diversity: Migration Status	Lower Assets and Resources	Higher Assets and Resources
Newlyweds to couples with first young child	NOT M&M: Neither migrant nor mobile after marriage	—Two to three couples	—Two to three couples
	M&M: People whose work has regularly taken them away from home one night/ week or migrants for six months or more	Two to three couples	Two to three couples
Couples w/ children (not yet grandparents)	Not M&M	Two to three couples	Two to three couples
	M&M	Two to three couples	Two to three couples
Grandparents/people with adult children	Not M&M	Two to three couples	Two to three couples
	M&M	Two to three couples	Two to three couples

preparing to do fieldwork, we abandoned "marital happiness." Incorporating a fourth axis would have committed us to an unmanageably large number of marital case studies in the time allotted (somewhere between forty-eight and seventy-two rather than our eventually agreed-upon twenty-four and thirty-six). Furthermore, upon reflection, we agreed that happiness is a culturally contingent concept and that even in very gossipy communities, marital happiness is not an externally observable phenomenon and thus would be a difficult axis to operationalize for sampling. Ultimately, we resolved this by using marital conflict as a domain of inquiry on our interview guides and an analytic criterion comparing high-conflict marriages to lower-conflict ones (while also noting that conflict is not, in and of itself, the only metric along which a marriage's "success" might be evaluated). In any case, the notion of axes of diversity, which Hirsch had used in prior work as a way of making ideas about purposive sampling intelligible to demographers and others accustomed to quantitative approaches to sampling (Hirsch and Nathanson 1998), proved crucial here to operationalizing our shared conceptual framework. Specifically, this sampling strategy enabled both internal and cross-site comparison: it enabled us to show, for example, not only that Huli couples with migration experience differed from Huli couples without migration experience but also that the marital and extramarital experiences of Huli couples with migration experience were similar in important ways to those of Igbo or Mexican couples with migration experience. Seeing that some of the diversity we observed within our field sites was patterned in similar ways *across* field sites led to important hypotheses and ultimately to some of our most theoretically interesting explanations.

There were also a set of logistics to work through: a plan for how we would analyze the data, parameters for individual and group publications, a discussion of the role that research assistants would play in each field site, and figuring out how to stay in touch over the course of the fieldwork.

Challenges Collecting Data in the Field

Once in the field, we encountered some of the challenges characteristic of fieldwork in general (such as how to balance fieldwork with the demands of one's own school-aged children or missing one's own intimate partner) as well as those specific to the topic (four out of the five anthropologists are women, which presented not only some challenges but also unique opportunities in terms of accessing the sites in which married men meet and socialize with women other than their wives). There were site-specific challenges that complicated our adherence to a shared research protocol: in Hela, for example, it turned out to be not only culturally inappropriate but also actually unsafe for both researchers and participants to follow the proposed marital case-study plan to interview married couples about their intimate lives. Specifically, Huli men wanted to be interviewed first, and, once exposed to the interview questions, they refused to give permission for their wives to participate in the research and even threatened the field assistants who gamely tried to convince them otherwise. Their objections included that wives might disparage husbands when interviewed, that talking about sex might inspire a wife to be unfaithful, and that they felt extreme discomfort with not being allowed to know how a wife had answered certain questions. In the end, the Papua New Guinea team interviewed men and women who were married but not to each other. One challenge particular to the work in Vietnam was the state's control over research and the difficulty of securing permissions (which were eventually granted) to interview individuals whom the researchers themselves would select rather than those selected by government officials. For polygynous men in Uganda, the research team had to decide which and how many cowives to interview. Some of these cases resolved themselves, such as distance that prohibited interviewing particular cowives. In other cases, deciding how to handle marital case studies of men with multiple wives led to generative discussions among the team about the reality of marital complexity, such as jealousy among cowives, the slippery concept of "marital duration," and whether secondary households or marriages in which bridewealth was not exchanged should be considered marriages for purposes of this study. The fieldwork was originally planned to take place simultaneously in all five sites, but for personal reasons, one of the five of us was not free to travel that semester, and so Smith's fieldwork in Nigeria took place the following semester.

There were some site-specific challenges in terms of how to define and delineate "marriage" as an analytical object. For example, in Hela, formally a relationship is only a marriage if bridewealth has been given. However, the research project took place during a period when Hela was experiencing a severe economic downturn, young men were giving only partial bridewealth payments or nothing at all, and most people didn't count these relationships as marriage, though the young couples usually did (unless the relationship went awry, and then they didn't). And, at the other end of the age continuum, some older male research participants had three or four wives but lived alone or with male kin and visited only one or two wives regularly and one or two not at all. Wardlow's field assistants asked tiredly whether they were supposed to ask *all* the interview questions about *all* of the wives.

There were also translational challenges in trying to ensure that the interview questions posed to married men and women made sense in each site, could elicit the data we wanted, and were the same across sites (in other words, when we asked an interview question, were we asking the same thing in each site?). One of our initial interview questions asked participants what they did to have a good marriage. We were hoping with this question to elicit information that would speak to what participants understood a "good marriage" to be and how to achieve it. However, we very quickly realized that in some of the sites, this question was too abstract and that there wasn't actually an easy way to say "good marriage." What we meant by "good" (happy, stable, economically successful, respectable in the eyes of others, etc.) was also unclear. This question was modified to "What are things you do to be a good husband/wife?" which was easily understood across all sites and elicited rich data that varied in conceptually useful ways across our axes of diversity.

Similarly, another question asked participants to talk about their feelings for their respective spouses. Here, the underlying goal was to assess what role love, and affect more generally, played in forging and sustaining marriage. This, again, turned out to be an overly abstract question that was both difficult to translate in some sites and left some participants a bit baffled or tongue-tied. For example, in Hela, the English word "feelings" has been adopted into Pidgin English to mean sexual desire, and so the first few Huli men who were interviewed (until we changed the question) thought we were asking them whether they felt sexual desire for their wives. In the end, we determined that what we were after was not the one perfectly phrased and translated question that would work across all sites but rather a question or set of questions that could elicit "emotion talk" about a spouse. We developed different, site-specific strategies for this. In Uganda, for instance, the question "How do you feel about your spouse?" typically elicited the response, "I feel good about my spouse." Using cultural knowledge about love letters as being the medium for emotion from Parikh's previous work (2016), the Uganda team changed the question to "If you were to write a love letter to your spouse, what would it say?" This question was received with excitement and revealed gendered marital emotions toward spouses. While wives' responses were often riddled with complaints, the question elicited long, heartfelt responses from husbands, who often apologized to their wives and praised them for being "patient" and having "perseverance." Two conclusions we reached about these cross-site translational challenges were (1) maintaining communication (made easier by the internet) throughout the field research was crucial to identifying, analyzing, and brainstorming solutions to such challenges and (2) for semi-structured interviews, figuring out the perfect translation to a question can be less important than understanding the research aims of the question and using this knowledge to come up with alternative ways to elicit a participant's thoughts and experiences regarding the topic. We prepared for these translational problems from the beginning, with a process of instrument development that began with the conceptual framework, moved to the domains to describe, and then involved agreeing not just on the general flow of instruments and wording of questions but also on the underlying purpose of each question. For example, the question regarding marital sexuality included the specific objective for asking these questions (purpose: "to understand the role of sex in marriage, especially the extent to which sexual relations are paramount [or not] in the construction of marriage relationship"). This enabled each researcher to ask culturally appropriate questions that would still achieve the comparative research objectives. It was also useful in training research assistants: reviewing the purpose of each question explicitly, and having a shared written record of the intention behind each question, kept us on a shared path while also acknowledging the naturalistic and sometimes improvisational quality of good ethnographic interviewing.

The primary challenge, and one that we managed well, is that of avoiding what we might refer to somewhat figuratively as "cross-site entropy" – failing to adhere to a shared set of research goals and questions. It is hard to understate the role that the group's shared affective commitment played in ensuring that we stayed on track, with enough continued overlap that we produced work that was informed by intensive dialogue, while still having room to do work that produced separate individual publications for each of us. We joked about Parikh's interest in the history of sexual pleasure in her field site, Smith's simultaneous fascination with and abhorrence of the importance of Evangelical Christianity, and Phinney's obsession with the state, and it was perhaps through those jokes that we signaled the boundaries of what did or did not feel to be sufficiently mutually relevant to be a focus of shared inquiry. But we also discussed this very directly, and our collective honesty about where our interests overlapped and diverged was an important part of the conversation – leaving room for each of us to pursue additional complementary interests, as long as it did not detract from our shared project. That honesty was, without question, nourished by our social relations with one another, which started with a foundation of affection and respect and which were nurtured through extensive in-person contact, including many long meals accompanied by wine (none of it paid for with federal funds!) and laughter. This honesty, affection, and respect, in turn, fostered trust – trust in one another, trust that we had a shared agenda, trust that we would be supportive of one another rather than competitive, and trust that we would each do what was necessary to ensure that the project was completed and would prove successful.

Comparative Analysis and Main Findings

Once we all returned from the field, we shared initial findings at two intensive three-day convenings. By sharing photos and compelling stories, we each outlined what we had learned about ideals and practices for marital intimacy and extramarital relations and the social forces that seemed to facilitate (or in some cases discourage) men's engagement in extramarital sex in each site. We had gone into the field with a general sociological notion of "extramarital opportunity structures," first proposed by Connie Nathanson as an extension of the fundamental sociological notion of opportunity structures – the institutionally supported elements that constrain or facilitate behavior and shape differential access to resources – but it was only through the fieldwork that we began to put some ethnographic meat on those bones, filling in what those opportunity structures actually were in a more concrete way in each of the field sites. It became clear that men's extramarital relationships were shaped by certain common institutions, structural factors, and practices across all field sites (men's work-related migration and mobility, men's practices of socializing, and gendered ideologies of intimacy), and so we used this concept to describe the regularities of the circumstances that facilitated (or discouraged) men's access to extramarital sex.

As we discuss in *The Secret*, three extramarital opportunity structures were prominent across all five sites: gendered patterns of migration and mobility, the marital division of labor, and the centrality of homosociality for masculine men's status and reputation. Other extramarital opportunity structures were salient only in some of the field sites. In the Mexican field site, for example, men's same-sex sexual relations were not necessarily subject to greater moral opprobrium that heterosexual dalliances might be, if they were carried out in conformity with local notions of sexual respectability. This was less the case in other field sites (Hirsch et al. 2012). Economic status also played out differently across the sites. While men's access to wealth enabled extramarital activities across sites, in Uganda, men's *lack* of access to wealth, or poverty, drove them into extramarital relationships as they searched for solace from marital conflicts about finances and new ways of obtaining status through liaisons with women. While single-sited research on men's engagement in extramarital relations may have generated the same descriptive material, the jump to a higher level of abstraction, and the recognition of shared underlying social processes, was greatly facilitated by doing the work comparatively.

A little more detail on the role of homosociality in masculinity and its effects in shaping HIV risk further illustrates the value of a comparative approach. Prevalent and highly valued homosociality was one of the three extramarital opportunity structures that was found to be salient across each site. By examining homosociality at each site, we noted that men's extramarital relationships were not just socially produced but they were also socially and in some cases even economically productive. That is to say, men's extramarital sexual behavior was frequently in part a performance of masculinity for other men – a performance through which men used the consumption and display of women as a means to build their relations, ironically, with one another. In some instances, such as in the all-male outings of businessmen in Hanoi or mine workers in Papua New Guinea, peer pressure played a major role in men's decisions to have extramarital sex. In other cases, such as in bars, discos, and social clubs in Mexico and Nigeria, men clearly aimed to affirm their masculinity to fellow men by displaying and entertaining their female lovers in these social spaces. In Nigeria, where men shared stories with one another about their extramarital sexual experiences, the honorific nicknames the men gave to one another that sometimes alluded to sexual prowess exemplified the social rewards of infidelity. In small-town Uganda, given the county's widespread HIV prevention messages warning against sexual networking, and more recent Evangelical messages about the sins of marital immorality, boasting about extramarital liaisons was dangerous because news spread quickly and public gossip about transgressions could sully a reputation. Sexual discretion, or keeping extramarital relationships away from public purview and the gossip mill, was the key to maintaining the reputation of both husbands and wives. However, that did not mean that there was no talk of sexual adventures: men's joking was full of emasculating nicknames for men who did not have additional lovers to take care of their (assumed) multiple needs. In other words, sometimes it was less that extramarital sexuality was actively promoted in men's peer groups and more that men's monogamy was critiqued as being socially unproductive, limiting, and at times almost impossible, given the wider economic and social realities in each setting.

There were two other key concepts that emerged from our cross-site conversations: social risk and sexual geographies. In sharing with one another our descriptive findings, we were struck by the extent to which across all five sites both men's extramarital sexual behavior and the negotiation (or lack thereof) around marital intimacy were shaped by concerns about what we came to call "social risk" in contrast to "viral risk." Through multiple conversations about the reasons why people engaged in unprotected sex, which included things like trusting one's partner and the desire for intimacy, we developed the concept of social risk to describe how in all five sites the fear of losing access to important social resources (e.g. relationships or reputation) was often more compelling and immediate than the fear of illness. Thus, although in each field site, the precise concerns may have been different, across field sites, the logical course of action was to prioritize continued access to these social resources over health.

"Sexual geographies" calls attention to the distinctive spatial dimensions of sexuality. In each of our field sites, there were spaces for the public performance of respectable marital sexuality and other spaces that not only permitted but also actually facilitated men's engagement in extramarital relations. Although the cantinas in rural Mexico differed in many ways from the upscale tennis club in southeastern Nigeria, both were class-specific social institutions that offered gendered opportunities for married men to engage in sexual relations with women who were not their wives as well as to build social relations with other men. These three ideas – extramarital opportunities structures, social risk, and sexual geographies – represent the conceptual scaffolding of our subsequent published work, as well as insights that were facilitated to a substantial extent through the crucible of comparison.

In all of our settings, one of the contradictions we came to recognize was that many men who cheated on their wives did not necessarily see themselves as bad husbands. Indeed, in all of the field sites, plenty of men who cheated on their wives asserted that they loved their wives. Most often, such men associated loving their wives with being a responsible provider, but also sometimes with their discretion with regard to infidelity. And nearly all men thought of themselves as moral actors, at least trying to be good men, however they defined it. Hence, a key finding from our comparative project is that "being faithful" is not a universally understood concept. While global HIV messages and Christian teachings define "fidelity" as having only one sexual partner, we found that people conceived of fidelity as much more related to a husband fulfilling his marital responsibilities and obligations – such as financially providing for the home, protecting his public reputation (hence, the need for secrecy), and the like. In the same way that our work problematized a universal notion of what it means to be married or not, so too did our research call into question the limits of assuming that the definition of "infidelity" that we had started out with was actually meaningful to our informants.

Policy Translation and Publications

A project finding that spoke directly to public health policy was that prevention campaigns emphasizing the importance of avoiding sex that was framed as illicit and immoral did not necessarily have the intended impact and in fact had substantial unintended cultural ripple effects: rather than discouraging people from multiple partnerships, these messages actually made condom use seem even less desirable through linking condoms to stigmatized, casual, and transactional sex. In addition, publicly naming acts and practices as "immoral" does not necessarily motivate people to stop them but rather might drive the behaviors underground, as in the Uganda case, creating new avenues for risk as people attempt to conceal their behaviors. As laid out in the policy brief that we shared with US federal policymakers and key NGO stakeholders during a group visit to Washington in November 2010, the key policy takeaway from our work was that US funding for HIV prevention should step back from its emphasis on fidelity promotion, which is sometimes based on morality. Trying to explain to policymakers that men's participation in extramarital relations was in many cases the socially organized default option and was enabled by larger opportunity structures (migration, mobility, economic inequality, and marital gender expectations), our policy brief on married women and HIV included the following.

Why Do Abstinence and Fidelity-Only Programs Put Women at Risk?

- For most women around the world, marital sex represents their greatest risk for HIV infection.
- Men's extramarital sexual relations are a major element of that risk.
- Abstinence until marriage programs *increase* women's risk by implying that marital sex is safer sex.
- Comprehensive HIV prevention must include programs to protect women from marital HIV infection.

What's Wrong with Promoting Fidelity?

- Fidelity is great – except that many people live in economic and social conditions that make it hard to live up to that ideal.
- Exhorting men to be faithful is not effective in the absence of socioeconomic conditions that make fidelity more possible.
- Evidence-based approaches to supporting fidelity must work at the structural or community level rather than at the individual level.
- HIV prevention programs that imply or state that abstinence and fidelity are the best and most moral options further stigmatize condom use and make suggestions of condom use tantamount to an accusation of infidelity.
- In our five-country, NIH-funded study of married women's HIV risk, we found that men's participation in extramarital sex is a basic aspect of social organization, produced by intertwining factors including labor migration, leisure time activities, masculine ideals, and gender inequality.
- In the absence of community-based efforts to alter the social structures that promote infidelity, public health programs that aim to reduce married women's risk just by telling men to be faithful will not succeed.

There were two primary products of our work: a set of papers published in the *American Journal of Public Health* in 2007 and 2008 (Phinney 2008; Parikh 2007; Smith 2007; Wardlow 2007; Hirsch et al. 2007) and a jointly authored volume, *The Secret: Love, Marriage and HIV.* The multisited, comparative perspective was a vital element of both the written products and the policy translation work. Whether speaking to congressional staff or writing about the findings in scientific journals, one can speak with a much greater level of authority by noting that something is true in very distinct places around the world than one can by merely referring to findings from a single site.

Reflections on the Process

Love, Marriage, and HIV was, without question, one of the most satisfying and invigorating experiences of our professional lives – not just interpersonally but also intellectually. As we wrote in the acknowledgments of our book, over the course of the decade that we worked together – a period that included many wonderful shared meals; the addition of six children across the five of us; the loss of a sister, three fathers, and two mothers; two transcontinental moves; and endless rounds of editing one another's work – we "unexpectedly became family." There was a sixth researcher, Connie Nathanson, who was a sociologist (and who was Hirsch's dissertation advisor) and a "senior project advisor," who remained involved throughout the course of the whole project and was also part of our "circle of love," as we still refer to it.

Beyond the interpersonal dimension, however, we were able to accomplish something intellectually as a team that was far greater than what any one of us would have been able to do individually. There were, to be sure, the midrange theoretical tools that we developed in the course of our work – extramarital opportunity structures, sexual geographies, and social risk. But taking these three midlevel theories as examples, what was fundamentally so satisfying about the comparative aspect of our work was the ways in which it facilitated the jump from the particularities of any one site to the identification of a more general set of conceptual tools, applicable then to many other questions and situations. As five ethnographers with a deep appreciation of ways in which context shapes particularities, our comparative project and the intellectual discussions of our findings enabled us to more fully engage in this context-particularity investigation in ways not typically done with one-site research projects. An unintended result is that we each came away with a deeper understanding of our own sites.

If We Could Do It Again

Upon reflection, there are ways in which the comparative research could have been even more powerful, and there are things that we could have done differently. We tried, at one point, to think about including some of our field assistants in our cross-site conversation with the aim of facilitating their own professional development and global South-South collaborations. For instance, the Uganda local research team was excited to send off emails to the other teams about their experiences on the project and eagerly waited for a response, but there were language barriers (they did not share a common language) as well as cultural differences in assertiveness. There was also very substantial diversity in their educational backgrounds, which ranged from not having completed primary school to having a PhD. In retrospect, the emails that we exchanged while in the field (not all of which were saved) could have been combined with the notes from our project meetings (which we do still have) to identify the emergence at particular moments of conceptual abstraction from fieldwork-specific conversations. Looking back at these communications might have opened a window into how, exactly, abstraction emerges from the particular. And surely lost in those unsaved emails are some other important insights about how we met the challenges of continuing to work in parallel across very different settings. One remaining nagging concern is the problem of scale: How is Hanoi much more "typical" of daily life in Vietnam than Degollado is for Mexico, and if all five of us had worked in the federal capitals of our respective countries, how would our findings have been parallel in different ways? We describe our work as taking place in Mexico, Uganda,

Nigeria, Vietnam, and Papua New Guinea, but it would have been more accurate to describe it as taking place in semirural, migrant-exporting Western Mexico, and in central eastern Uganda (the Iganga region), Igboland, Hanoi, and Hela. We also discussed the idea of visiting one another's field sites, but since this idea arose after the grant was secured and we had not budgeted for doing so, that proved impossible.

Teams forging boldly ahead to craft comparative work would do well to be more thoughtful than we were in terms of planning publications. We did have a discussion up front about authorship and thus avoided conflicts of that sort, but given the enormous effort that went into the project, we ought to have had a more vigorous publication plan, developed in advance. Four cross-cutting conceptual papers could have preceded the book (one on each of our three key theoretical concepts and one on how our work advanced the research on gender and HIV), because – and this seems obvious in retrospect, but we were so eager to get the book out – it is possible to use materials from chapters in books but not vice versa. Another lost opportunity was to critically look at our interactions with the IRBs; we did not keep close, centralized track of the variation across IRBs in the concerns raised and the actions required to address those concerns. With the exception of the question of how we would respond in cases in which we encountered domestic violence, which was raised by several IRBs, there was almost no overlap in the concerns raised and the modifications required by the different institutional and country-level IRBs. Looking back, it feels like a missed analytic opportunity worthy of publication.

Without question, we regret not having had more of an impact on policy. Most social scientists are trained only in the production of good data and not at all in the processes through which one can maximize the impact of evidence on policy with these data. When we began our work, despite the fact that two of us had worked for policy advocacy organizations before gaining our PhDs (Hirsch and Phinney) and that one was actively conducting research on the sociology of public health policy (Nathanson 2007), we did not think to situate our work in the vast literatures on the range of ways in which evidence is more or less likely to have an impact on the world, literature that derives from political science, social work, community-based participatory research, and community organizing. At the same time, the limits of our engagement in policy translation work reflected not only the constraints of our training but also the academic reward structures that we faced as pretenure faculty members.

Our initial success in securing funding for our work, followed by multiple failures to secure grants for subsequent comparative projects, underlines the importance of funding fashions, timing, and problem framing in gaining funding for any kind of work. Our subsequent idea, building on Love, Marriage, and HIV, was to examine gendered patterns of engagement in HIV and AIDS care. The reasons for our failure deserve brief mention in relation to securing funding for comparative research. First, public health, in thrall to the clinical impact of anti-retroviral therapy (ART), was moving decisively away from a focus on social impacts of HIV and AIDS, with every year more funding focused on making ART available, improving adherence, and promoting testing and less funding available for social scientific work on structural drivers of the epidemic. Second, in Love, Marriage, and HIV, our subject was, at least in terms of how the project was framed for a public health audience, the appealingly innocent figure of the married woman in need of protection from the damage done by her husband's philandering. In contrast, our interest in men's more fragile engagement with health care, while conceptually and empirically justified and potentially field-advancing in terms of gender and chronic diseases, repeatedly elicited a sort of bristling response on the part of reviewers, whose primary orientation toward gender and health was about women's disadvantage. So we missed out on the politics as well, failing to frame our work in relation to the same kind of sympathetic subject or how men's disengagement with HIV care adversely impacted women's health and risk. Third, the quantitatively oriented reviewers on the NIH grant-review boards indicated that they preferred large quantitative studies to in-depth qualitative ethnographic research.

But beyond these lessons in terms of publication plans, policy impact, and how to bridge the distance between problems that would benefit from a comparative lens and framings that resonate with funders, there are other more general lessons for comparative research. One thing that any research team seeking US federal funding must contend with now is the question of public access to data. Even as we planned for our fieldwork, it became resoundingly obvious that at least for us, there was no such thing as "data pooling." For each of us, although our field notes were in English, the bulk of our data remained in the language in which it was collected, with none of us fluent in the other field sites' languages, and so the sharing of data meant the presentations we gave for each other, the photos we shared, the emails we sent, the questions we asked, and the tiny bits of quotations that made their way into each of our publications. As the NIH moves toward policies that require researchers to share their data to "enhance rigor and reproducibility," it is worth pausing to think about how profoundly useless it would have been to share any of our primary data, unfiltered through our headnotes, with one another, much less to store it in some publicly accessible data bank, as is increasingly required by funders and even some journals.

A second very real problem to take into consideration is publication pressures and how comparative research affects professional reward structures. Collaboratively produced research does not "count" in the same way in different disciplines for professional advancement. Of the five of us, two had monographs that were already published or well under way when going into the project (Wardlow 2006; Hirsch 2003); one of the other three has published not one but three books in the interim (Smith 2010, 2014, 2017), but the delay in the other two's monographs reflects, in part, their extended involvement with, and huge contributions to, our collective work (Parikh 2016; Phinney's book is forthcoming).

Conclusion

In closing, our experience with the Love, Marriage, and HIV project, while not completely or precisely replicable, has produced a set of general guidelines for best practices in terms of comparative ethnography as well as some considerations about things to avoid. Life is too short to work with people with whom one does not share similar theoretical leanings or likes – not only because doing so is less fun but also because the affective and intellectual dimensions of collaboration are very important in terms of making it effective. Similarly, we were lucky in that there was no "weak link" in our team, and conversations with others who have engaged in comparative work underline the importance of choosing with an eye to work ethic and accountability as well as disposition: we respected one another immensely, everyone pulled his or her weight, and we all felt, all along, as if we were learning from one another, with our collective capacity for insight far exceeding that which any one of us would have alone. The interdisciplinarity, with the additional insight of a sociologist grounded in a more universalizing theoretical tradition, helped to speed us toward a higher level of abstraction, and the fact that overall the team's interests were complementary (love, gender, sexuality, and health) but also pushed in different directions (toward the state, toward same-sex sexuality, focused on adolescents, etc.) was also useful. The question of professional reward structures was important too: we were all in tenure-track positions at research universities where publications were a high priority.

Other features of our approach seem central. First, the intensity and frequency of our personal contact ensured a level of analytic iterative dialogue that might otherwise have been lost. Our collaborative work on a shared conceptual framework, specific aims, operationalized research questions, axes of diversity in sampling, and instruments was critical, as was the trust that enabled each of us to tailor these instruments to suit our respective field sites. It goes without saying – and yet it is critical to note – that the work would barely have felt worth doing if it had not gone beyond description to, in some way, advance theory. Finally, we were lucky that we had no bitterness regarding publication, and we did have an explicit conversation early on in our meetings about publication norms. Nonetheless, it is a good practice for any collaborative project to have a written agreement articulating criteria for authorship and processes for approving publications.

Short of having the kind of substantial funding that we did, it is worth considering, in closing, whether there are alternative, perhaps more virtual, approaches to collaborative research. Multi-day topically focused retreats and workshops, edited volumes, conference panels, special journal issues, or even knowledge networks (Natividad et al. 2012) can create moments of comparison and intellectual explosion; our networked professional lives, combined with the relative luxury of unlimited access to peer-reviewed publications and professional meetings, without a doubt create opportunities for moments of comparison. (We note the relative luxury of developed-world bibliographic resources as well as well-developed professional organizations, in comparison to some of the challenges of advancing social scientific research in other contexts [Vasquez et al. 2013], where it has become very clear that the absence of all kinds of research infrastructure that scholars in developed-world settings take for granted hinders the advancement of all kinds of science.) From that initial dissertation write-up seminar in which Smith, Wardlow, and Hirsch first began to explore how ideas about companionate intimacy resonated through our work, through our two 1999 AAA panels on global romance that allowed us to expand our intellectual network, and then the four meetings that formed the collaborative backbone of our project, we conclude by arguing strongly that there is no intellectual substitute for being together.

In-person gatherings provide an unparalleled opportunity not only for unplanned, meandering, "during the coffee break" conversations but also for the development and solidification of actual social relationships. In future collaborations, we may not be lucky enough to adore our collaborators, but drawing on this experience, we believe it is important to like them as people and to know them. The wash of nostalgia engendered by looking back over the agendas from our first two project meetings, and even by the names of the restaurants where we gathered after very long days of intense work, is just one powerful reminder of how affective concerns lay the groundwork for effective comparative research. There are technical and logistical elements to successful collaboration, and we have enumerated earlier how shared concepts, instruments, and sampling plans, along with frequent communication and overlapping interests, were crucial for the success of our comparative research. But the collaboration that is necessary for comparative work is as much about human relations, and so we close by recalling the respect we feel for one another as scholars and the trust that we placed in each other by trading the self-reliance of single-sited research for the shared responsibility for a project much larger than any of us could ever have managed on our own.

References

Basch, Linda, Nina G. Schiller, and Christina S. Blanc. 1994. *Nations Unbound: Transnational Projects, Postcolonial Predicaments, and Deterritorialized Nation-States*. Langhorne, PA: Gordon and Breach.

Collier, Jane F. 1997. *From Duty to Desire: Remaking Families in a Spanish Village*. Princeton, NJ: Princeton University Press.

Hirsch, Jennifer. 2003. *A Courtship after Marriage: Sexuality and Love in Mexican Transnational Families*. Berkeley: University of California Press.

Hirsch, Jennifer, and Constance Nathanson. 1998. "Demografia Informal: Como Utilizar Las Redes Sociales Para Construir Una Muestra Etnografica Sistematica de Mujeres Mexicanas En Smbos Lados de La Frontera." *Estudios Demográficos y Urbanos* 12 (1/2): 177–99.

Hirsch, Jennifer S., and Holly Wardlow. 2006. *Modern Loves: The Anthropology of Romantic Courtship & Companionate Marriage*. Ann Arbor: University of Michigan Press.

Hirsch, Jennifer S., Holly Wardlow, Daniel Jordan Smith, Harriet Phinney, Shanti Parikh, and Constance A. Nathanson. 2009. *The Secret: Love, Marriage, and HIV*. Nashville, TN: Vanderbilt University Press.

Hirsch, Jennifer S., Holly Wardlow, and Harriet Phinney. 2012. "'No One Saw Us': Reputation as an Axis of Sexual Identity." In *Understanding Global Sexualities: New Frontiers*, edited by Peter Aggleton, Paul Boyce, Henrietta L. Moore, and Richard G. Parker, 91–107. London: Routledge.

Hirsch, Jennifer S., Sergio Meneses, Brenda Thompson, Mirka Negroni, Blanca Pelcastre, and Carlos del Rio. 2007. "The Inevitability of Infidelity: Sexual Reputation, Social Geographies, and Marital HIV Risk in Rural Mexico." *American Journal of Public Health* 97 (6): 986–96.

Inhorn, Marcia C. 1996. *Infertility and Patriarchy: The Cultural Politics of Gender and Family Life in Egypt*. Philadelphia: University of Pennsylvania Press.

Nathanson, Constance A. 2007. *Disease Prevention as Social Change: The State, Society, and Public Health in the United States, France, Great Britain, and Canada*. New York: Russell Sage Foundation.

National Institute of Child Health and Human Development (NICHD), and National Institute of Mental Health (NIMH). November 28, 2000. RFA-HD-01-002. The Influence of Gender on HIV Risk. https://grants.nih.gov/grants/guide/rfa-files/RFA-HD-01-002.html. Accessed December 5, 2019.

Natividad, Maria Dulce F., Kirk J. Fiereck, and Richard Parker. 2012. "Knowledge Networks for Global Public Health." *Global Public Health* 7 (supl): 73–81.

Parikh, Shanti A. 2007. "The Political Economy of Marriage and HIV: The ABC Approach, 'Safe' Infidelity, and Managing Moral Risk in Uganda." *American Journal of Public Health* 97 (7): 1198–208.

Parikh, Shanti A. 2016. *Regulating Romance: Youth Love Letters, Moral Anxiety, and Intervention in Uganda's Time of AIDS*. Nashville, TN: Vanderbilt University Press.

Phinney, Harriet M. 2008. "'Rice Is Essential but Tiresome; You Should Get Some Noodles': Doi Moi and the Political Economy of Men's Extramarital Sexual Relations and Marital HIV Risk in Hanoi, Vietnam." *American Journal of Public Health* 98 (4): 650–60.

Schneider, Jane, and Peter Schneider. 1996. *Festival of the Poor: Fertility Decline & the Ideology of Class in Sicily, 1860–1980.* Tucson: University of Arizona Press.

Smith, Daniel Jordan. 2007. "Modern Marriage, Men's Extramarital Sex, and HIV Risk in Southeastern Nigeria." *American Journal of Public Health* 97 (6): 997–1005.

Smith, Daniel Jordan. 2010. *A Culture of Corruption: Everyday Deception and Popular Discontent in Nigeria.* Princeton, NJ: Princeton University Press.

Smith, Daniel Jordan. 2014. *AIDS Doesn't Show Its Face: Inequality, Morality, and Social Change in Nigeria.* Chicago, IL: University of Chicago Press.

Smith, Daniel Jordan. 2017. *To Be a Man Is Not a One-Day Job: Masculinity, Money, and Intimacy in Nigeria.* Chicago, IL: University of Chicago Press.

Vasquez, Emily E., Jennifer S. Hirsch, Le Minh Giang, and Richard G. Parker. 2013. "Rethinking Health Research Capacity Strengthening." *Global Public Health* 8 (supl): 104–24.

Wardlow, Holly. 2006. *Wayward Women: Sexuality and Agency in a New Guinea Society.* Berkeley: University of California Press.

Wardlow, Holly. 2007. "Men's Extramarital Sexuality in Rural Papua New Guinea." *American Journal of Public Health* 97 (6): 1006–14.

Wedland, Claire L. 2008. "Research, Therapy, and Bioethical Hegemony: The Controversy over Perinatal AZT Trials in Africa." *African Studies Review* 51 (3): 1–23.

8 Research across Cultures and Disciplines

Methodological Challenges in an Interdisciplinary and Comparative Research Project on Emotion Socialization

Birgitt Röttger-Rössler

Over the past two decades, emotions have become a prominent subject of study in a number of disciplines. This increasing interest has led to the emergence of several interdisciplinary research groups and centers in which the humanities and the sciences worked together on exploring human emotionality.[1] One of the central issues within this interdisciplinary research on emotions concerns how far and in what way human emotionality is shaped by cultural and social dynamics. Social and cultural anthropology offers rich and dense empirical data illustrating the enormous intercultural variability of emotion codes. Most emotion researchers in the social sciences and cultural studies view this intersocietal and intrasocietal polymorphism of emotional forms of behavior and expression as the outcome of complex biocultural and psychosocial interaction processes, and they call for interdisciplinary collaboration in order to analyze these processes. One promising way to investigate this interplay between biocultural and psychosocial processes in the formation of feelings is to look at the ways in which emotions are socialized and how these processes vary in different cultural settings; that is, to take a comparative approach.

In this chapter, I present a bidisciplinary research project that investigated how children growing up in different social and cultural contexts learn the emotional repertoire of their specific community (see Funk forthcoming; Funk et al. 2012; Jung forthcoming; Röttger-Rössler et al. 2013, 2015; Scheidecker 2017).[2] The overall aim of this collaboration between social anthropology and developmental psychology was to gain deeper insights into the dynamic interplay between culture-specific practices of child-rearing and emotional development. Hence, the project set out to explore how culture-specific forms of emotion socialization shape and structure the ontogenetic development of emotions. By addressing this research question, the project followed the interdisciplinary research tradition of cross-cultural human development studies that became a research area in its own right in the 1980s. It is characterized by a collaboration between cross-cultural developmental psychologists and psychological anthropologists (Gielen 2004).

In the following discussion, I start with some basic theoretical considerations and sketch our main research questions and assumptions. Then I outline the research design we developed along with the methods applied, and I discuss which specific demands were imposed by the different methodological standards of the two disciplines involved. In particular, I reflect on the problems we encountered in the different field sites when trying to apply the same methods across all contexts. After a condensed "nutshell" presentation of our main findings, I conclude the chapter by discussing the "lessons learned" within this bidisciplinary comparative project, paying special attention to the target conflict between context-sensitive validity and generalizability that so strongly characterized our collaboration.

Theoretical Considerations, Leading Questions, and Assumptions

Our approach is based on two lines of research stemming from different disciplines: (1) anthropology of childhood and (2) developmental psychology. Social anthropology has a long history of studying socialization and different forms of childcare. Particularly in its early days, these studies were characterized by comparative and interdisciplinary approaches. Good examples are the large-scale comparative studies by Whiting and Whiting (*Children of Six Cultures* 1975), Munroe and Munroe (*Cross-Cultural Human Development* 1975), and Whiting and Edwards (*Children of Different Worlds* 1988).[3] However, these early works did not focus on aspects of emotion socialization. Although emotions were always covered implicitly, they only started to become an explicit focus of attention in the late 1980s and 1990s (e.g. Briggs 1998; Lutz 1988). Nonetheless, most of these more recent studies were then no longer characterized by a comparative perspective but dedicated primarily to the cultural relativity paradigm. Correspondingly, they studied forms of emotion socialization predominantly in relation to specific local contexts. Such a focus on local, culture-specific emotion models and feeling rules inevitably led to a marginalization of interest in the influence of cultural socialization styles and practices on the biopsychological constitution of humans; that is, on ontogenetic emotional development as an interlocking pattern of biophysical and social-psychological maturation processes (D'Andrade 2000; Gielen 2004, 11).

An exception is Naomi Quinn's (2005) comparative study on the "Universals of Child Rearing" published in *Anthropological Theory*.[4] In this landmark study, which served as a major inspiration for our approach, Quinn undertook a close comparative reading of ethnographic texts describing child-rearing practices in various cultures.[5] The results of her comparative analysis indicate that even in cultures with quite different social structures, behavioral standards, values, and therefore also child-rearing goals, we can find a limited and thus probably universal set of child-rearing strategies that are used to socialize children in line with the given standards of their society. One strategy used in all cultures, according to Quinn, encompasses techniques of disciplining that make the child's experience of learning certain lessons emotionally arousing: for example, by means of frightening, beating, teasing, shaming, or praising.[6] It was this aspect that directed our attention toward the emotionally arousing socialization strategies implemented by caregivers and led us to articulate the concept of socializing emotions – to which I turn later.[7]

In developmental psychology, the relation between socialization and emotional development is an established topic, although most of the corresponding empirical studies focus on so-called WEIRD (Western, educated, industrialized, rich, and democratic) people (Henrichs et al. 2010); that is, on Euro-American contexts and, within these, primarily on the middle classes (Holodynski 2004; Holodynski and Friedlmeier 2006; Shipman and Zeman 2001).[8] Irrespective of this Euro-American bias, the models formulated by developmental psychology provide important starting points for investigating the relation between cultural socialization practices and emotional development. Researchers such as Sroufe (1996), Stenberg and Campos (1990), and Fonagy et al. (2002) emphasize the crucial importance of child-caregiver interactions for the ontogenetic formation of emotions.[9] This aspect also plays a dominant role within the "internalization model of emotional development" formulated by Manfred Holodynski (2009; Holodynski and Friedlmeier 2006, 2012), the psychological cooperation partner within our project. According to his internalization model of emotional development, the initially unspecific affects of neonates are gradually molded through interactive regulatory transactions between infants and caregivers into highly specific emotions. Holodynski argues, in line with Sroufe (1996), that neonates are equipped with five "precursor" emotions that are initially triggered only by physical stimulus thresholds and are thus more reflex-like.[10] They have appeal character; that is, they are designed to prompt caregivers to satisfy the neonate's need (be it for food, warmth, body contact, etc.). According to Holodynski (2009, 148), these precursor emotions represent "the biological cradle for emotional development." It is through the culturally molded responses of the caregivers to the signals of the newborns that their "precursor emotions" turn over time into highly complex emotions. Thus, even the intrapersonal components of full-blown emotions emerge ontogenetically from interpersonal interaction patterns that are highly susceptible to social and cultural influences.[11] This model points to the microprocesses of emotional attunement in infant-caregiver interactions and views the different interaction patterns and styles between children and their caregivers as decisive modulators within the ontogenetic development of emotions.[12]

Our main research aim was to investigate how children acquire the particular emotional repertoire of their social environment. We were interested in how they transform their initially unspecific affects or "precursor emotions" into culturally specified forms of emotion. Approaches from developmental psychology, such as Holodynski's internalization model, directed our attention toward microprocesses of emotional attunement in child-caregiver interactions, whereas the work of Quinn directed our interest particularly toward the role of emotionally arousing child-rearing practices within these processes. We assumed that these practices help to form particular emotions (e.g. shame or anxiety) in such a way that they play a pivotal role in the internalization of social norms and values (including the emotion codes and "feeling rules" of a given society). We conceptualized these emotions as *socializing emotions*. We supposed further that which particular emotional qualities are elaborated as socializing emotions depends on the specific cultural context and corresponding child-rearing practices. The culture-specific formation of socializing emotions strongly affects the development of other emotions and thus contributes to the particular emotional repertoire of a given cultural setting. This last assumption is of crucial importance for theories in developmental psychology on putative universals within emotional development in childhood. This is where research cooperations between social anthropology and developmental psychology working with cultural comparisons that focus on patterns of emotional development beyond WEIRD worlds unfold their special potential.

Four concrete research questions guided our empirical investigations:

1. Which emotionally arousing child-rearing strategies (positive as well as negative ones) are used by caregivers in the given cultural contexts?
2. What are the educational values and norms as well as the ethnotheories behind these practices?
3. How do socializing emotions develop in each cultural setting in line with the strategies of disciplining applied?
4. How do socializing emotions influence the development of other emotions?

Research Design and Methods

The most challenging aspect of our research cooperation was the need to bridge the methodological gap between our disciplines; that is, the "sharp divide separating those who do small-*N*, qualitative studies from those who do large-*N*, quantitative studies" (Ragin 1998, 106). We shared the opinion of Ragin (1998), who views both types of research as complementary:

> With variable-oriented techniques, for example, it is very difficult to address actors' motives or subjectivities or to observe event sequences and causal processes.

Case-oriented methods, by contrast, excel in these areas. With case-oriented techniques, however, it is difficult to gain confidence that inferences are grounded or that findings are general in any way. These are central strengths of the variable-oriented approach. (106–07)

Although bridging this gap calls for a lot of compromises, it also encourages reflection and the development of new methodological approaches.

Right at the beginning of our collaboration, we had already decided to look only at "non-Western cultures" in order to counterbalance the predominance of data gathered in Euro-American middle-class populations in psychological studies on emotional development. Another reason for this choice was to avoid the common dichotomization of Western and non-Western contexts in cross-cultural psychology, with its tendency to underestimate the major differences between non-Western contexts. We further decided to conduct a "contrastive cultural comparison"; that is, to select cultural settings delivering the greatest possible contrast in terms of social and economic organization, religion, kinship, and the level of formal education.[13] We expected those differences in central societal structures to correspond with specific socialization trajectories. However, we aimed to compare communities with similar ecosocial conditions to avoid additional effects on emotion socialization such as those engendered by different degrees of urbanization or integration into the national market economy; hence, all communities were rural and largely subsistence based.[14] The communities we selected for comparison were from the Minangkabau in West Sumatra, Indonesia; the Bara in the south of Madagascar; and the Tao on the Taiwanese island of Lanyu (formerly known as Orchid Island). All three reveal major differences in their social structure, kinship organization, economies, religious orientation, and level of formal (school) education (see Table 8.1).

The only common denominator of all three cultural settings is that they belong to the West-Austronesian language family. This has to do with the complex historical connections in the more distant past. The ancestors of the Tao, for example, migrated approximately 800 years ago from the northern Philippines to Lanyu, and Madagascar was also settled more than 1,500 years ago by migrants from the Malay Archipelago. The choice of three cultural groups that are maximally contrastive with regard to their societal and economic structure, their religious orientation, and so forth but belong to the same language family was based on the consideration that the abundant linguistic data collected in the three field studies, particularly the extensive dataset of emotion vocabularies, would permit interesting linguistic comparisons in later analyses.

To avoid any misunderstandings, we did not set out to compare "whole cultures" – let aside the fact that cultures as homogeneous entities do not exist – but small "local worlds" (Kleinman 1992) or *Lebenswelten* that display a certain degree of coherence in the norms and values that structure the behavior of their members.

Table 8.1 *Case characteristics*

	Bara	Minangkabau	Tao
Social organization	Segmentary	Stratified	Egalitarian
Kinship system	Patrilineal	Matrilineal	Bilateral
Central social entity	Extended family; clan	Extended family	Nuclear family
Economic system	Pastoral, cattle breeding	Rice growing, plantations, trade, migration	Fishery, horticulture, wage labor, labor migration to Taiwan
Religion	Ancestor worship	Islam	Christianity; elements of pre-Christian religion
Formal education	No schools	Complex school system	School system still young

In line with this focus on local worlds, the empirical research was conducted by three ethnographers within the frame of twelve-month-long ethnographic field studies in the "classical" village studies format.[15] This decision was based on two considerations: (1) Villages of a moderate size are manageable; it is much easier for the ethnographer to integrate himself or herself into the local community, participate in everyday life, and gain access to all relevant social groupings than in large urban settings. In other words, it is easier to identify different "communities of practice" (Schnegg 2014, 60) in small local communities than in urban contexts. (2) Villages with an ethnic or culturally nearly homogeneous population might reduce the variances in lifestyle and value orientation among their inhabitants. This is not to say that a village population is a homogeneous entity, isolated from the rest of the world and cut off from globalization, but if the villagers have mostly the same sociocultural background, they might differ less in terms of central norms, values, and practices compared to people living in multiethnic or multicultural urban contexts.[16]

To take appropriate account of the specific cultural conditions, we took a relatively open and explorative methodological approach. In line with the main research questions outlined earlier, the research focused mainly on the following domains:

1. Local knowledge or "ethnotheories" about emotions (concepts and labels of emotion; evaluation of emotions as, for example, good or bad; local definitions of emotional competencies, etc.).
2. Local ideas about child development in general and emotional development in particular, including explicit parenting goals and child-rearing practices.

3. Emotional behavior displayed in everyday interactions. Our concern was to discover the patterns of emotion education of emotion-related socialization practices in everyday situations. Mainly by systematically observing the ways in which children of different ages interacted with their social partners, we tried to gain insight into the respective culture-specific pathways. Hence, we paid attention to not only the emotional facets of caregiver-child interactions but also the emotional interaction patterns of all the children's other social partners.

We tried to make the data comparable in two ways: first, by precisely defining which social field would be studied (e.g. primary social partners of children) and which dimensions should then be observed (e.g. forms of interactions with the child); second, by trying to standardize the methods as far as possible. For example, for the social field of "primary social partners of children," we systematically documented which persons (mother, father, grandparents, siblings, neighbors, etc.) interact most frequently with young children and how these configurations change as the children grow up both in terms of the persons they interact with and the type of interaction. Regarding the "forms of interaction" dimension, in all field sites, we systematically documented whether body or face-to-face contact was more predominant in infant care, which forms of body stimulation were applied, whether the modes of interaction varied depending on the caregiver, and how much they changed as the child grew older.

To gain comparable results, we put together a series of methods in advance. We assumed that, in addition to participant observation, the following methodological avenues would work in all three communities: (1) unstructured and semistructured interviews to investigate the cultural models of child development and parenting; (2) ethno-lexicographical approaches to assess the local emotion concepts; and (3) systematic observation of emotional episodes in everyday interactions. In the following discussion, I discuss these methods and their limits in more detail.

1. *Semistructured interviews* were conducted with adults, to investigate cultural models of child development and parenting, and with caregivers, to study their socializing practices. In addition, we conducted narrative interviews with children addressing their socializing experiences. Interviews were conducted in the mother tongue of the interlocutors – Malagasy in the case of the Bara, Bahasa Indonesia in the case of the Minangkabau, and Yami and Mandarin Chinese in the case of the Tao. Unstructured and semistructured interviews were possible in all three communities but with certain restraints. Whereas conducting interviews with adults was unproblematic in Minangkabau society, it was more difficult for Susanne Jung, the female ethnographer (who was accompanied by her husband and her little son), to talk with children about their experiences. The children

felt uncomfortable when she set out to involve them in a conversation and tried to escape the situation. This was mainly due to the fact that children in Minangkabau society are expected to behave shyly in the presence of adults and not to talk to them frankly. In Bara society, in contrast, it was unproblematic for Gabriel Scheidecker, the male ethnographer, to talk with children of both sexes after some time of familiarization. Although children are taught and expected to be fearful, this emotion is directed mostly toward those elders who are actually entitled to sanction the child. Leberecht Funk, the male ethnographer who worked among the Tao on Lanyu – and who was also accompanied by his family (wife and two sons) – had no problems in interviewing children but encountered serious problems in interviewing adults. The Tao did not want to make appointments for interviews and talk about their lives or thoughts, because they believe that they are being spied on constantly by malicious spirits (*Anito*) that will try to upset the plans of people once they learn what they intend. Hence, he relied, to a larger extent, on informal conversations, and it was, of course, not possible to record these. The differences in terms of responsiveness of the children are interesting, because in all three societies, relations between the younger and the elder are governed by the principle of seniority and children are expected to behave in a reserved and respectful way in front of elders. But only Minangkabau children reacted with such strong shyness and restraint that it was impossible for Susanne Jung to engage in deeper conversations with them. This is probably due to two aspects of their socialization: first to the strong emphasis that Minangkabau – like many other Indonesians societies – place on shy and shameful behavior. Shamefulness is seen as a virtue, and from early childhood on, children are trained to become shameful, to "know shame" (*tahu malu*). The second aspect is that talking about oneself is evaluated as bad and shameless behavior (Röttger-Rössler 2000). Hence, in this case, facets of local emotion socialization impact deeply on the applicability of research methods. However, the apparent failure of the method turned out to be a relevant datum itself.

Nonetheless, the different densities of data, due in part not only to culture-specific idiosyncrasies but also to the different personalities of the researchers involved, strongly limit the comparability of our field studies. This is a common problem in any comparative study working with qualitative data. However, the ethnographers in our project developed methodological approaches that were acceptable for the local population while at the same time enabling the researcher to collect relevant data within the respective (predetermined) study dimensions. Susanne Jung, for example, created a photo-elicitation study in order to talk with the Minangkabau children.[17] This was a great success. She took a set of photographs she had made of local children displaying different emotional expressions and discussed the photographs with small focus groups. The children enjoyed this game-like format, and the researcher gained a lot of valuable information and emotion stories via this method. Even though she was not able to conduct individual interviews with the children about their experiences, the photo-elicitation technique allowed her to collect children's narratives about emotional experiences that could be compared with the material from the Bara. Hence, even though these data were collected in extremely different ways in each setting and, in the second field site (Minangkabau), they were not self-referential, each of these different datasets can still be viewed as a "set of cases" (as understood by Ragin 1998, 104) that refer to one of the selected study dimensions. As a result, they can be analyzed by looking for decisive patterns of similarities and differences. Nonetheless, the different data categories resulting from the necessary adaptations to local conditions do form an obstacle for any comparative analysis. Thus, it is of utmost importance to make the research process transparent and lay open how the ethnographer achieved his or her results and how the facts being compared were produced (Schnegg 2014, 62). If cross-cultural comparative studies specify in advance which social fields should be studied with which methods, then the different possible ways of applying individual methods in studying the social settings generate important findings or data.

2. *Ethno-lexicographical approach:* To assess local emotion concepts, lists of emotion terms were compiled from written texts such as dictionaries as well as through free listing by research participants. These lists were checked and supplemented constantly in interviews as well as informal conversations. The meaning of each emotion word on the list was investigated by asking interview partners to narrate emotion stories; that is, episodes in which they or somebody else experienced the respective emotions. We collected a minimum of ten emotion stories for each word and several dozen narratives in the case of emotion concepts that appeared to be of central importance. In order to analyze the meanings of the emotion words, we coded the emotional components of each emotion narrative and included antecedents, appraisals, dimensions of (bodily) feeling, expression signs, resulting action tendencies, and emotion evaluations. In this vein, we analyzed more than 100 emotion terms in the three local settings. The ethno-lexicographical approach was applicable in all three settings (Röttger-Rössler et al. 2015).
3. *Systematic observation and documentation of emotion episodes*, occurring in everyday interactions between children of different age grades and caregivers as well as between peers, were conducted. There was a strong emphasis on applying forms of systematic observation in this project.

> To make data comparable, we took great care to specify the observation dimensions, select observation criteria in advance, and ensure that these were oriented toward the theoretical emotion model agreed upon in the project (see later). The researchers used specially prepared observation protocols to document each emotion-triggering event and the persons involved in it, with the focus always on a specific child and that child's interaction partner. Hence, observations were person centered. Interactions were observed and documented separately for the child and for that child's interaction partner according to the following criteria: (1) action (HA), (2) speech (SP), and (3) expression sign (AZ). The last was broken down into gaze behavior (BV), facial expression (M), body posture (K), gesture (G), intensity (I), behavior in space (RV), and touch (B) (see Figure 8.1).

These observation criteria are based on the underlying emotion concept in our project. We do not conceive of emotions as "internal states" but as dynamic bio-psycho-sociocultural processes. From this perspective, an emotional episode encompasses several components: the eliciting event, its appraisal, bodily and expressive reactions, feeling components, and action tendencies. The appraisal process (of an event) triggers a bodily reaction and an expressive reaction in the individual perceiving it. The expressive reaction encompasses the externally perceivable expressions, mimicry, gestures, body posture, and verbal reactions that other persons who are present can interpret as the expression of an emotion. During ontogenesis, such expressive reactions become increasingly subject to intentional control in ways that depend strongly on sociocultural factors. Culture-specific expression conventions, so-called display rules, prescribe the appropriate emotional expression behavior. They regulate which emotions are expressed or suppressed in which ways toward whom in which situations. Children learn the expression conventions of their society during social interaction.

The bodily reaction directly accompanying the expressive reaction consists of physiological changes, such as an increase in heart rate, that are not necessarily perceivable for others but may well be registered or felt by the person concerned as a somatic reaction, a "feeling." Taken together, these components lead to an action impulse that might be suppressed. An emotion (in the sense of a conscious feeling) arises only when "feedback loops" link these perceived somatic processes back to the event triggering them (Holodynski and Friedlmeier 2006, 42).[18] Working with observation protocols based on this emotion concept proved to be highly productive in all three field contexts and generated rich data material.[19]

Besides this, we originally intended to do video-based *spot observations* in each field site with a sample of thirty children of different ages (0–2, 2–4, and 4–6 years) in each case in order to gain quantitative data on who interacts

Observation Protocol _ Emotion episode

Person observed: Episode no.:

Date: Time: Reason for logging episode? Serial no.:

Location: Event Expression sign

Event of episode:

Child		Interaction partner	
HA:		**HA:**	
SP:		**SP:**	
AZ:		**AZ:**	
BV M		BV M	
K G		K G	
I		I	
RV		RV	
B		B	
HA:		**HA:**	
SP:		**SP:**	
AZ: BV		**AZ:** BV	
M		M	
K		K	
G		G	
I RV		I RV	
B		B	
HA:		**HA:**	
SP:		**SP:**	
AZ: BV		**AZ:** BV	
M K		M K	
G		G	
I RV		I RV	
B		B	

Figure 8.1 Emotion episode protocol.

in what ways with children at what times of the day and on how these patterns change as children grow older. Spot observation is a time-sampling method in which the observer takes a "mental snapshot" of the activity that is going on at the moment when he or she is entering a scene.[20] It is a form of "controlled naturalistic observation" (Munroe et al. 1984) and has long been used within social anthropology in cross-cultural comparative studies (LeVine et al. 1994; Munroe and Munroe 1971). Spot observations in which researchers specifically note the social situations in which the child in question is engaged at different times of day are also applied frequently in cross-cultural developmental psychology (e.g. Keller 2007). One significant element of this method is for researchers to write down who is interacting with the child or what the child is doing in the first moments in which they approach a scenario and before their presence starts to change it. These first seconds are documented separately in either specially prepared protocols or video recordings. However, video-based spot observations are not always possible. In our case, videotaping was unproblematic in Bara society but could not be used among the Tao, who have been exposed to the sometimes rather disrespectful behavior of Taiwanese tourists over the past three decades and have thus developed an aversion to being filmed or photographed. In accordance with ethical considerations, visual recording had to be abandoned in this context. Among the Minangkabau, videotaping was no problem in general, but it was not possible to carry out systematic video-based spot observations that required, as in our case, the researcher to take short videos (filmed "snapshots") of the interaction between child and caregiver at different times during the day. This was mainly due to the fact that Minangkabau strongly dislike being videotaped (or photographed) in everyday situations in which they perceive themselves as being not properly dressed and presentable. Hence, they were not ready to participate in this kind of study. We could apply this method only among the Bara. The material obtained was extremely rich. The greatest benefit is that the video documents allowed us to analyze micro-interactions that otherwise would have escaped normal observation such as very brief averting of gaze, raising of eyebrow, or raising of hand. Furthermore, the video material enabled us to analyze the interactions jointly as a research team, and this shaped the observational behavior in the two other field sites by guiding the researchers' attention to certain behavioral features that otherwise would have escaped their attention. Observers started to pay systematic attention to more fine-grained and short micro-interactions in child-caregiver interactions.

References of such kind were possible only because our overall research design planned for a phase of collaborative intermediate data analysis. After twelve months of fieldwork, the three ethnographers returned to Berlin for several months in order to analyze the data collected so far by the single ethnographers. This was done together in extensive meetings attended by the whole team. The aim was to identify open questions and formulate some empirically grounded hypotheses that could be explored during a second two- to three-month field trip – constituting the next project phase.

Results in a Nutshell

Our comparative study on emotionally arousing child-rearing practices and their effects on the socialization of emotions shows that the prominent *socializing emotions* differ clearly across the three communities: among the Minangkabau in Indonesia, *malu,* a highly elaborated form of shame, is the dominant socializing emotion. The related child-rearing practices consist of publicly shaming and teasing children who misbehave. The central socializing emotion among the Bara is *tahotsy*, a kind of fear of elders and ancestral spirits that is socialized mainly through different forms of corporal punishment as the dominant disciplining strategy.[21] Among the Tao, the dominant socializing emotion is *maniahey*, a ubiquitous form of diffuse anxiety that is inculcated through socialization practices that possess a deliberately irritating and ambivalent character (such as teasing and ridiculing).[22] Each of these culture-specific practices is linked to different child-rearing goals:

> The child-rearing strategies of the Minangkabau based on shaming aim to make children continuously aware of being watched over and controlled by their social environment. They are oriented toward the constant monitoring through "others' eyes." As a result, they become extremely sensitive to social expectations and social etiquette. They thereby comply with norms in order to avoid the public ridicule they would have to anticipate for any violation (Röttger-Rössler 2013).

The inculcation of fear as a socializing emotion in the Bara community enables children to strongly modulate their demeanor to match the current social context. In relation to particular authority figures such as fathers or paternal ancestral spirits, they learn to act fearfully, be extremely humble, and follow the strict norms imposed by these authority figures. In relation to others, especially unrelated peers, whom they do not have to fear as authority figures, they learn to perform in a distinctly confident and often dominant way (see Scheidecker 2017).

The Tao, in contrast, aim specifically to impart a feeling of diffuse and permanent danger and threat to their children. Tao children should become aware of the unpredictability of life; they should develop a fundamentally suspicious and cautious disposition. Such a fundamental mistrust is considered to be advantageous when dealing with a natural and social environment that is perceived to be so uncertain.

The different socializing emotions and the related socializing practices are deeply embedded in the sociocultural structures of the respective societies and lead via complex psychosocial microprocesses to differing trajectories in ontogenetic development. The dominant socializing emotions have a deep impact on the shaping and differentiation of other emotions such as anger during ontogeny. Children of the Minangkabau community learn from early on, concomitant with the formation of a pronounced shame disposition, to control their anger meticulously, regardless of the particular social context or situation they are in. Correspondingly, anger is generally evaluated negatively, ascribed to diabolic influences and subject to shame if not controlled successfully. In the community of the Bara, in contrast, children acquire a huge range of differently regulated anger emotions that are embedded in distinct social relationships: in relation to fearfully respected authority figures, they learn to completely suppress all aggressive components of anger, because this would be punished harshly. This constellation gives rise to a set of anger emotions that are characterized by certain sulking expressions and strong negative feelings located in the stomach. While these emotions are regulated through fear of elders, children also learn to inculcate fear in others, preferably younger children, by using a set of anger emotions that are characterized by terrifying expressions and a readiness to inflict corporal punishment. When interacting with unrelated peers, children are encouraged to respond vehemently to any offense. This fosters a set of retaliating anger emotions that may help to overcome fear of a strong competitor.

Our results show clearly that a universal pathway of emotional development does not exist. But this does not automatically mean that the number of developmental trajectories is infinite. The question emerging within this context is whether there is a possible correlation between sociocultural structures, child-rearing practices, and emotions. However, more comparative studies will be needed to approach this issue.

Conclusion

The central question in the project presented here is to what extent different socialization styles and practices influence the emotional development of children. This can be studied only through applying a comparative approach and through social anthropologists cooperating with developmental psychologists. Social and cultural anthropology possesses extensive empirical data on the diversity of cultural socialization styles and their close ties to specific forms of social organization as well as to economic, political, and religious structures. Developmental psychology, in contrast, offers complex models of emotional development that nonetheless draw mainly on empirical studies in Euro-American contexts. However, by taking this bidisciplinary approach, the project had to straddle two greatly differing methodological traditions (and epistemological beliefs) right from the start. This meant that it had to face the challenge of bridging the target conflict between context-sensitive validity and generalizability.

The project team decided to gather empirical data in the form of long-term, on-site, context-sensitive, ethnographic field studies and to make the data comparable by precisely defining the social fields to be studied and standardizing methods as far as possible. The project, in general, had a strong emphasis on systematic observation, which I consider to be one of the main methodological tools for comparative research. We tried to carry out a qualitative comparative analysis as proposed by Ragin (1998) and thus to strike a balance between the contrary methodological standards of the two disciplines. One central problem for the project proved to be that it was not possible to apply all the set assessment methods to an equal extent at each different field site. I sketched some of the solutions we applied earlier where I argued that even the necessary adaptations of methods to local conditions do not necessarily diminish the comparability of the data as long as the modified methods address the same domains of study or sets of cases. Moreover, I pointed out that the "failure" of methods can also be viewed as an empirical fact and should be integrated into the analysis on a higher level.

However, research projects do not end with the analysis of the collected data. They also include the dissemination of findings in the form of publications and conference papers. This poses far greater challenges to bidisciplinary projects straddling different methodological traditions. I would like to close by addressing these. One far from trivial problem is that the editors of many established journals – in which a publication can particularly promote the career of a young academic – have very clear ideas about which methods have to be used to obtain valid data – whether with context-sensitive, qualitative, or quantitative and experimental approaches. These journals function as powerful authorities that exert a strong influence on the dissemination of research findings and thereby also on research itself. Hence, this leaves only interdisciplinary journals. For our field of research, we are fortunate in having some very good ones such as *Ethos, Mind and Activity, Emotion Review*, and *Cross-Cultural Psychology*. The situation is similar for book publications. It is not easy to find publishers for books taking an interdisciplinary approach, especially when the disciplines concerned are not neighboring ones that follow a similar methodological agenda. Nonetheless, such publishers can also be found, although these are often not considered to be equally renowned in each of the individual disciplines. This, in turn, can be disadvantageous for a young academic's career. Nonetheless, in my opinion, the greatest obstacle blocking the academic careers of young scientists working in interdisciplinary fields is the lack of recognition that many disciplines give to interdisciplinary research – and this also includes social and cultural anthropology. This stands in marked contrast to the continuous calls for and support given to the idea of interdisciplinarity. Frequently, young academics gain their qualifications through interdisciplinary work in collaborative projects. However, this is by no means always to their benefit. As a member of appointment boards – for both professorships and research assistant posts – at German universities, I have frequently experienced how interdisciplinary research and corresponding publications that are not published in the standard journals of the specific discipline are considered to be of lesser value. Such candidates are frequently not nominated or are ranked second to their colleagues who are more committed to the subject-specific mainstream. Given that interdisciplinary research imposes additional challenges, this results in a marked discrepancy between achievements and their recognition. As a "senior" who has been working in interdisciplinary fields for more than twenty years, I unfortunately have to note that there has been little change here despite the marked increase in large-scale interdisciplinary research cooperations in recent years.

What can be learned from this? In my opinion, this obliges established academics and heads of interdisciplinary projects to plan publication strategies in detail, particularly with the careers of their young academics in mind. For the project presented here, we decided to place a few joint publications in interdisciplinary and international journals but to publish the majority of findings obtained in the three different cultural settings as doctoral theses in the form of classical anthropological monographs. This is currently still the best possible strategy in the interest of young academics who have to present work that will be broadly accepted within their discipline. However, it is not a good strategy for presenting and disseminating collaborative interdisciplinary research findings. Jointly authored journal articles can present these only in abbreviated form. Therefore, we spent a long time thinking about a joint book, but we dropped this plan because the work involved would have interfered with the individual dissertation projects.

Lessons learned? First, it is much easier to do research across cultures than across disciplines; second, it is much easier to do research across disciplines than to publish across disciplines. In short, much still needs to be improved.

Notes

1 For example, the Interdisciplinary Center of Excellence Languages of Emotion (2007–14) at Freie Universität Berlin, Germany; the research group Emotions as Biocultural Processes (2003–06) at the Centre of Advanced Interdisciplinary Studies, Bielefeld University, Germany; the ongoing Geneva Emotion Research Group within the Center for Affective Sciences, University of Geneva, Switzerland; or smaller research groups such as the Animal Emotionale project based at the University of Osnabrück and the Charité in Berlin.

2 The project titled Socialization and Ontogeny of Emotions in Cross-Cultural Comparison (2009–13) was funded by the Deutsche Forschungsgemeinschaft within the framework of the Research Cluster Languages of Emotion, Freie

Universität Berlin. Alongside the author, the research team consisted of developmental psychologist Manfred Holodynski and three PhD candidates in social anthropology who conducted the ethnographic fieldwork: Susanne Jung, Leberecht Funk, and Gabriel Scheidecker. I thank them all for their deep commitment, thoughtfulness, and wonderful team spirit. Working with them was always inspiring and a great pleasure.

3 Gielen (2004) offers a review of the extensive comparative studies of human development.

4 Quinn (2005, 477) starts her article with the following highly indicative remark: "This may be a singularly unpropitious time, given a climate of ethnographic particularism and anti-psychologism in American anthropology today, to propose cultural universals rooted in human psychology."

5 The ethnographies reexamined by Quinn are the works of Peggy J. Miller et al. (1996, 1997) on the Taiwanese middle class, of Heidi Fung (1999) on China, of Catherine Lutz (1988) on the Ifaluk, of Jean Briggs (1982, 1998) on the Inuit, and of Robert and Barbara LeVine (1966) on the Gusii in Kenya.

6 In interpreting her findings, Quinn refers to the work of the brain researcher LeDoux (2002), arguing that emotionally arousing child-rearing practices are especially effective in imparting to children the values they should learn, because they are tuned to learning mechanisms of the human brain. They seem to be rooted in or connected to certain neurobiological processes that embed experiences in memory and thus prevent lessons once learned from being forgotten. According to the findings of brain researchers and neurobiologists such as LeDoux, emotional arousal makes experiences especially memorable: hormones released during emotional arousal strengthen synaptic connections, and emotional arousal organizes brain activity by crowding all but the emotionally relevant experience out of consciousness (Quinn 2005, 481).

7 For a more detailed discussion of Quinn's study, see Röttger-Rössler et al. (2013, 2015).

8 See Henrich et al.'s (2010) criticism of the reductionist restriction to studying members of the Euro-American middle classes that is predominant in psychology. See also Gielen (2004, 6) and Holodynski (2009, 159).

9 The subdiscipline of cross-cultural developmental psychology offers rich empirical data on child-caregiver constellations in different societies (e.g. Cole et al. 2002; Eisenberg et al. 2001; Friedlmeier and Trommsdorff 1999; Keller 2007). However, only a few studies have concentrated explicitly on the relation between child-rearing practices and emotional development (e.g. Chang et al. 2003; Keller and Otto 2009; Lieber et al. 2006). Moreover, these studies from the field of cross-cultural developmental psychology observe – like developmental psychology in general – only single aspects of child-caregiver interactions isolated from their total context. Hence, in (cross-cultural) developmental psychology, there is a lack of studies focusing explicitly on the interdependencies between culture-specific values, emotion concepts, child-rearing concepts, child-rearing practices, and socioeconomic structures and conditions (Trommsdorff 2003).

10 Research on emotional reactions of neonates (e.g. Izard and Malatesta 1987) points to five discernible classes of triggers with five different patterns of expression that Sroufe (1996) and Holodynski and Friedlmeier (2006) conceive as "precursor emotions." These are namely distress, disgust, fright, interest, and endogenous pleasure.

11 For a short overview, see Holodynski (2013).
12 For a more detailed discussion of Holodynski's internalization model and its contribution to our theorizing, see Röttger-Rössler et al. (2013).
13 The work of Beatrice and John Whiting (1975) on socialization practices in six cultures is a prime example of this approach that is also known as "most different case study design" (see also Schnegg 2014).
14 It would assuredly also be worth comparing aspects of emotion socialization in communities with different ecosocial parameters (see, e.g. Scheidecker et al. 2019). In this case, however, it seems advisable to select communities from the same region or with a shared cultural heritage in order to retain some commonalities.
15 Susanne Jung researched in Indonesia (Minangkabau); Leberecht Funk in Lanyu, Taiwan (Tao); and Gabriel Scheidecker in Madagaskar (Bara).
16 Our project confirmed that the village societies under study acted relatively consistently regarding their respective styles and practices of socialization and thus can be identified as "communities of socialization practices" that could be explained due to the fact that "small local worlds" promote conformity.
17 See, for example, Harper (2002).
18 See also Holodynski and Friedlmeier (2012) and Shweder et al. (2008).
19 Working with standardized observation protocols has a long tradition in comparative social anthropology, especially in childhood and socialization studies (e.g. Munroe et al. 1981; Whiting et al. 1966; Whiting and Whiting 1975).
20 Well known in social anthropology are the time allocation studies by Hewlett (1991) and Johnson (1975).
21 For a comparison of socializing emotions between the Minangkabau and Bara, see Röttger-Rössler et al. (2013).
22 For a comparison between the Bara and the Tao, see Funk et al. (2012) and Röttger-Rössler et al. (2015).

References

Briggs, Jean L. 1982. "Living Dangerously: The Contradictory Foundations of Value in Canadian Inuit Society." In *Politics and History in Band Societies,* edited by Eleanor Leacock and Richard B. Lee, 109–31. Cambridge: Cambridge University Press.

Briggs, Jean L. 1998. *Inuit Morality Play. The Emotional Education of a Three-Year-Old.* New Haven, CT: Yale University Press.

Chang, Lei, David Schwartz, Kenneth Dodge, and Catherine McBride-Chang. 2003. "Harsh Parenting in Relation to Child Emotion Regulation and Aggression." *Journal of Family Psychology* 17 (4): 598–606.

Cole, Pamela M., Tracy A. Dennis, Ichiro Mizuta, and Carolyn Zahn-Waxler. 2002. "Self in Context: Autonomy and Relatedness in Japanese and U.S. Mother-Preschooler Dyads." *Child Development* 73 (6): 1803–17.

D'Andrade, Roy. 2000. "The Sad Story of Anthropology, 1950–1999." *Cross-Cultural Research* 34 (3): 219–32.

Eisenberg, Nancy, Sri Pidada, and Jeffrey Liew. 2001. "The Relations of Regulation and Negative Emotionality to Indonesian Children's Social Functioning." *Child Development* 72 (6): 1747–63.

Fonagy, Peter, György Gergely, Elliot L. Jurist, and Mary Target. 2002. *Affect Regulation, Mentalization, and the Development of the Self.* New York: Other Press.

Friedlmeier, Wolfgang, and Gisela Trommsdorff. 1999. "Emotion Regulation in Early Childhood: A Cross-Cultural Comparison between German and Japanese Toddlers." *Journal of Cross-Cultural Psychology* 30 (6): 684–711.

Fung, Heidi. 1999. "Becoming a Moral Child. The Socialization of Shame among Young Chinese Children." *Ethos, Journal of the Society for Psychological Anthropology* 27 (2): 180–209.

Funk, Leberecht. Forthcoming. *Society, Cosmology, and Socialization of Emotion among the Tao in Taiwan.*

Funk, Leberecht, Birgitt Röttger-Rössler, and Gabriel Scheidecker. 2012. "Fühlen(d) Lernen: Zur Sozialisation und Entwicklung von Emotionen im Kulturvergleich." *Zeitschrift für Erziehungswissenschaft* 15: 217–38.

Gielen, Uwe P. 2004. "The Cross-Cultural Study of Human Development: An Opinionated Historical Introduction." In *Childhood and Adolescence: Cross-Cultural Perspectives and Applications*, edited by Uwe P. Gielen and Jaipaul L. Roopnarine, 3–45. Westport, CT: Praeger.

Harper, Douglas. 2002. "Talking about Pictures: A Case for Photo Elicitation." *Visual Studies* 17 (1): 13–26.

Henrichs, Joseph, Steven J. Heine, and Ara Norenzayan. 2010. "The Weirdest People in the World?" *Behavioral and Brain Sciences* 33 (2–3): 61–135.

Hewlett, Barry S. 1991. *Intimate Fathers: The Nature and Context of Aka Pgymy Paternal Infant Care.* Ann Arbor: University of Michigan Press.

Holodynski, Manfred. 2004. "Die Entwicklung von Emotion und Ausdruck. Vom biologischen zum kulturellen Erbe." *ZiF-Mitteilungen* 6: 1–16.

Holodynski, Manfred. 2009. "Milestones and Mechanisms of Emotional Development." In *Emotions as Bio-cultural Processes,* edited by Birgitt Röttger-Rössler and Hans J.Markowitsch, 139–63. New York: Springer.

Holodynski, Manfred. 2013. "The Internalization Theory of Emotions: A Cultural Historical Approach to the Development of Emotions." *Mind, Culture, and Activity* 20 (1): 4–38.

Holodynski, Manfred, and Wolfgang Friedlmeier. 2006. *The Development of Emotions and Emotion Regulation.* New York: Springer.

Holodynski, Manfred, and Wolfgang Friedlmeier. 2012. "Affect and Culture." In *The Oxford Handbook of Culture and Psychology*, edited by Jaan Valsiner, 957–86. New York: Oxford University Press.

Izard, Carroll E., and Carol Z. Malatesta. 1987. "Perspectives on Emotional Development I: Differential Emotions Theory of Early Emotional Development." In *Handbook of Infant Development,* 2nd ed., edited by Joy D. Osofsky, 494–554. New York: Wiley.

Johnson, Allan. 1975. "Time Allocation in a Machiguenga Society." *Ethnology* 14 (3): 301–10.

Jung, Susanne. Forthcoming. *Sozialisation von Emotionen in einer indonesischen Gesellschaft (Minangkabau).*

Keller, Heidi. 2007. *Cultures of Infancy.* Mahwah, NJ: Erlbaum.

Keller, Heidi, and Hiltrud Otto. 2009. "The Cultural Socialization of Emotion Regulation during Infancy." *Journal of Cross-Cultural Psychology* 40 (6): 996–1011.

Kleinman, Arthur. 1992. "Pain and Resistance: The Delegitimation and Relegitimation of Local Worlds." In *Pain as Human Experience: An Anthropological Perspective,* edited by Mary-Jo DelVecchio Good, Paul Brodwin, Byron J.Good, and Arthur Kleinman, 169–97. Berkeley and Los Angeles: University of California Press.

LeDoux, Joseph E. 2002. *The Synaptic Self. How Our Brains Become Who We Are.* New York: Viking.

LeVine, Robert A., and Barbara B. LeVine. 1966. *Nyansongo: A Gusii Community in Kenia.* Huntington, NY: Robert E. Krieger Publishing Company.

LeVine, Robert A., Suzanne Dixon, Sarah LeVine, Amy Richman, P. Herbert Leiderman, Constanze H. Keefer, and T. Berry Brazelton. 1994. *Child Care and Culture: Lessons from Africa.* Cambridge: Cambridge University Press.

Lieber, Eli, Heidi Fung, and Patrick W. L. Leung. 2006. "Chinese Child-Rearing Beliefs: Key Dimensions and Contributions to the Development of Culture-Appropriate Assessment." *Asian Journal of Social Psychology* 9 (2): 140–47.

Lutz, Catherine. 1988. *Unnatural Emotions. Everyday Sentiment on a Micronesian Atoll and Their Challenge to Western Theory.* Chicago, IL: University of Chicago Press.

Miller, Peggy J., Angela R. Wiley, Heidi Fung, and Chung-Hui Liang. 1997. "Personal Storytelling as a Medium of Socialization in Chinese and American Families." *Child Development* 8 (3): 557–68.

Miller, Peggy J., Heidi Fung, and Judith Mintz. 1996. "Self-Construction through Narrative Practices: A Chinese and American Comparison of Early Socialization." *Ethos, Journal of the Society for Psychological Anthropology* 24 (2): 237–80.

Munroe, Robert L., and Ruth H. Munroe. 1975. *Cross-Cultural Human Development.* Monterey, CA: Brooks-Cole.

Munroe, Robert, Ruth H. Munroe, and Beatrice B. Whiting, eds. 1981. *Handbook of Cross-Cultural Human Development.* New York: Garland STPM Press.

Munroe, Ruth H., and Robert L. Munroe. 1971. "Household Density and Infant Care in an East African Society." *Journal of Social Psychology* 83 (1): 295–315.

Munroe, Ruth H., Robert L. Munroe, and Harold S.Shimming. 1984. "Children's Work in Four Cultures: Determinants and Consequences." *American Anthropologist* 86 (2): 369–79.

Quinn, Naomi. 2005. "Universals of Child Rearing." *Anthropological Theory* 5 (4): 477–516.

Ragin, Charles C. 1998. "The Logic of Qualitative Comparative Analysis." *International Review of Social History* 43 (56): 105–24.

Röttger-Rössler, Birgitt. 2000. "Selbstrepräsentation und Kultur. Malaiische und indonesische Formen autobiographischen Erzählens." In *Erzählte Identitäten*, edited by Michael Neumann, 135–52. München: Fink Verlag.

Röttger-Rössler, Birgitt. 2013. "In the Eyes of the Other: Shame and Social Conformity in the Context of Indonesian Societies." In *Shame between Punishment and Penance*, edited by Bénédicte Sére and Jörg Wettlaufer, 405–19. Paris: Micrologus.

Röttger-Rössler, Birgitt, Gabriel Scheidecker, Leberecht Funk, and Manfred Holodynski. 2015. "Learning (by) Feeling: A Cross-Cultural Comparison of the Socialization and Development of Emotions." *Ethos. Journal of the Society for Psychological Anthropology* 43 (3): 187–220.

Röttger-Rössler, Birgitt, Gabriel Scheidecker, Susanne Jung, and Manfred Holodynski. 2013. "Socializing Emotions in Childhood: A Cross-Cultural Comparison between the Bara in Madagascar and the Minangkabau in Indonesia." *Mind, Culture, and Activity. An International Journal.* Special Issue, "Psychology of Emotions and Cultural Historical Activity Theory" 20 (3): 260–87.

Scheidecker, Gabriel. 2017. *Kindheit, Kultur und moralische Emotionen. Zur Sozialisation von Furcht und Wut im ländlichen Madagaskar.* Bielefeld: Transcript.

Scheidecker, Gabriel, Ariane Gernhardt, Hartmut Rübeling, Jona Holtmannspötter, and Heidi Keller. 2019. "How Young Adolescents Draw Themselves: A Comparison across Three Ecosocial Contexts in Southern Madagascar." *Cross Cultural Research* 53 (1): 33–57.

Schnegg, Michael. 2014. "Anthropology and Comparison: Methodological Challenges and Tentative Solutions." *Zeitschrift für Ethnologie* 139: 55–71.

Shipman, Kimberly L., and Janice Zeman. 2001. "Socialization of Children's Emotion Regulation in Mother–Child Dyads: A Developmental Psychopathology Perspective." *Development and Psychopathology* 13 (2): 317–36.

Shweder, Richard A., Jonathan Haidt, Randall Horton, and Joseph Craig. 2008. "The Cultural Psychology of the Emotions. Ancient and Renewed." In *Handbook of Emotions,* 3rd ed., edited by Michael Lewis, Jeannette M. Haviland-Jones and Lisa F. Barrett, 409–27. New York: Guilford Press.

Sroufe, L. Alan. 1996. *Emotional Development: The Organization of Emotional Life in the Early Years.* New York: Cambridge University Press.

Stenberg, Craig R., and Joseph J. Campos. 1990. "The Development of Anger Expressions in Infancy." In *Psychological and Biological Approaches to Emotion*, edited by Nancy L.Stein, Bennett Leventhal and Tom R. Trabasso, 247–82. Hillsdale, NJ: Lawrence Erlbaum.

Trommsdorff, Gisela. 2003. "Kulturvergleichende Entwicklungspsychologie." In *Kulturvergleichende Psychologie: Eine Einführung*, edited by Alexander Thomas, 139–79. Göttingen: Hogrefe.

Whiting, Beatrice B., and Carolyn P. Edwards. 1988. *Children of Different Worlds: The Formation of Social Behavior.* Cambridge, MA: Harvard University Press.

Whiting, Beatrice B., and John W. M. Whiting. 1975. *Children of Six Cultures: A Psycho-cultural Analysis.* Cambridge, MA: Harvard University Press.

Whiting, John W. M., Irvin L. Child, and William W. Lambert. 1966. *Field Guide for a Study of Socialization.* New York: Wiley.

9 Global Sport Industries, Comparison, and Economies of Scales

Niko Besnier and Daniel Guinness

Comparison has a long and complicated history in anthropology. A concern for comparison was part and parcel of nineteenth-century anthropological endeavors, but in a way from which most anthropologists today would wish to distance themselves. In the course of the twentieth century, models such as Franz Boas's particularism and Clifford Geertz's call for "thick description," more bent on description than on comparative abstraction, took attention away from comparison of social and cultural systems, at least in North American anthropology. Even in British and Continental anthropology, long dominated by models like structural functionalism and structuralism that were resolutely committed to comparison, the turn away from these models has also meant a waning enthusiasm for social and cultural comparison. By the end of the twentieth century, anthropologists had largely abandoned comparison as their fundamental epistemological pursuit because of concerns about its potential to erase complexity through generalization and categorization (Gingrich 2012).

Yet, the emergence of questions of globalization in the discipline in the 1990s generated a new interest in questions of scale, particularly in the groundbreaking works of Sidney Mintz and Eric Wolf. The tension between local configurations and large-scale phenomena – that is, between the production of detailed ethnographies and the types of abstractions at analytical and theoretical levels necessary for comparison – saw many anthropologists question the decades-long commitment to understanding the particular (e.g. Abu-Lughod 1991), although this questioning was not unanimous. Investigating "global" phenomena requires approaches that can not only identify the effect of the outside on the "local" but also show that the effects operate differently in various locations. As a result, anthropologists are increasingly carrying out multisited projects or working in groups of researchers in order to draw attention to the interrelatedness of the global and the local.

The research reported in this chapter received funding from the European Research Council under Grant Agreement 295769 for the project titled Globalization, Sport, and the Precarity of Masculinity. We thank Michael Schnegg and Edward Lowe for having invited the first author to the Hamburg conference on which this volume is based.

Large-scale projects that incorporate several researchers, each engaged in the long-term ethnography of a single location, enable forms of collaboration and comparison rarely seen previously. Here, "collaboration" refers to the cooperative work between different researchers as part of a larger project rather than (but not exclusive of) the coproduction of ethnographic representation with research interlocutors advocated by the "writing culture" critique (Clifford and Marcus 1986; Marcus and Fisher 1986). This form of collaboration relies on communication at planning stages, during fieldwork, and through the writing-up process in ways that are new for most anthropologists and require a set of skills that is outside the training conventions in the discipline.

New approaches to comparison in the context of collaborative projects recast the tension between large-scale and small-scale configurations precisely to reveal the interconnectedness of the "global." In contrast with the fixed categories of investigation deployed in most twentieth-century comparative projects, contemporary comparison focuses on criteria of a general nature. Projects are not motivated by a search for the essence of a particular category, to be revealed by comparison of its various translations into different cultural contexts (Gingrich 2012). Rather, anthropologists increasingly begin with loosely defined parameters of investigation, drawing on comparison with existing work but allowing themselves significant space to delve deeply and broadly into themes, following the intricacies and contradictions of life on the ground.

Collaboration and comparison shed light on dynamics in each field site that the individual researchers may have missed had other seemingly incommensurable cases not been juxtaposed against their own ethnography. A posteriori comparison builds upon the messiness of each local context toward analytical abstraction. But a priori and a posteriori comparisons need not be of the same quality and theoretical ambition; this is where the power of ethnographic methods lies, namely, in opening new fields of comparison that no one expects in the first place. What frequently emerges is a far more complex set of interactions between geographically and socially distinct locations than would have been imaginable without explicit comparison of global and local phenomena. It is precisely this collaboration that allows teams of anthropologists to investigate questions on a scale unachievable otherwise, producing a coherence of interests during research design that facilitates the collection of empirical materials that are more productively compared.

As is often remarked upon informally but rarely elaborated upon explicitly, the course, scope, and outcomes of any research project, whether comparative or not, are shaped in significant ways by its logistics, particularly its funding. This is where we begin our discussion.

Comparison, Collaboration, and the Realities of Funding

The research on which we base our reflections on comparison in contemporary anthropology is a collaborative project titled Globalization, Sport, and the Precarity of Masculinity (acronym GLOBALSPORT), which ran between 2012 and 2017 under the first author's direction. We briefly outline some of its logistical features because these are pertinent to the role that comparison played in the project. The Principal Investigator received funding from the European Research Council (ERC), which, since its establishment in 2007 by the European Commission, has become the most important funder of research in the European Union and a number of neighboring countries with which the council has signed agreements. One can safely state that ERC funding has transformed the landscape of research in Europe in radical ways, making it considerably more globally competitive than it has ever been.

But there are drawbacks. In typical European Union fashion, ERC values uniformity, assuming that research across all disciplines is organized in the same way, namely, according to a STEM-discipline model primarily designed for laboratory work, in which a theory-driven umbrella project directed by one senior scholar can be broken down into a number of subprojects conducted by junior researchers (PhD students and postdoctoral fellows) and later resynthesized into the umbrella project. It thus assumes that research is always the product of collaborative work.

Niko Besnier had not explicitly sought to conduct collaborative research and ethnographic comparison in the first instance; he was forced to engage to meet the conditions of the application for funding. The ERC model of project organization has reintroduced collaboration and comparison into sociocultural anthropology in interesting ways, namely, as what Andre Gingrich (2012, 214) called an a priori program of how the research is to be conducted. It is in fact difficult to imagine how an ERC proposal in sociocultural anthropology could be successful without a priori comparison involving various researchers figuring prominently in the research design; comparative works in anthropology by a single researcher (which are few and far between in the first place) are invariably the product of work conducted over an entire lifetime, such as Clifford Geertz's comparative study of Islam in several locations, and very few scholars achieve this. In an era when "projects" are events that are defined by funding bodies as clearly bounded in time, such long-term endeavors are increasingly difficult to conceptualize other than under the most privileged conditions (such were Geertz's). Yet, to many observers' surprise, sociocultural anthropology, a stereotypically (and ironically) "individualistic" discipline despite its long-term epistemological commitment to implicit comparison, has been remarkably successful in obtaining ERC funding.

A priori collaborative and comparative research projects in social and cultural anthropology on both sides of the Atlantic (and probably beyond) are, of course, not new. Notable in the annals of the discipline are such milestones as the 1898 Cambridge Anthropological Expedition to Torres Straits (Herle and Rouse 1998), which was primarily collaborative rather than comparative and was an endeavor that took place in an age when the discipline was asking different kinds of questions and searching for different kinds of answers. In the post–World War II years, members of the Coordinated Investigation of Micronesian Anthropology (CIMA) worked closely with the US military administration of the US Trust Territory of the Pacific Islands to strengthen US domination over the islands (which made possible, among other things, devastating nuclear testing in the Marshall Islands). In the spirit of Boasian anthropology, CIMA anthropologists and linguists conducted "salvage" ethnography on what they saw as rapidly changing lifeways, pushing aside along the way all evidence of the previous Japanese presence in the region, including scholarship. The careers of influential North American anthropologists such as David Schneider, Douglas Oliver, and Alexander Spoehr owed a considerable debt to their early participation in this project (Kiste and Marshall 1998). Equally memorable in the history of North American anthropology are Julian Steward's comparative Puerto Rico Project (1947–56), which launched the distinguished careers of Stanley Diamond, Robert Manners, Sidney Mintz, and Eric Wolf (Silverman 2011), and the Harvard Chiapas Project led by Evon Vogt, which began in 1957 and lasted thirty-five years, generating numerous PhD dissertations and publications and launching the careers of a substantial cadre of anthropologists in the United States (Vogt 1994).

GLOBALSPORT was designed and conducted in quite different circumstances from these venerable antecedents, although it shared with them a focus on both comparison and collaboration. It aimed to understand how hopes for employment and success in the global sport industries operate in the context of the fundamental geopolitical inequalities between the Global South and the Global North, which have become a major motivation for young people, mostly young men, from the Global South to seek to migrate to wealthy countries. We explored these questions in the context of three sports, namely, rugby, soccer, and cricket, to which we added a fourth world sport, marathon running, and a local sport, Senegalese wrestling. These sports involve migration along different geographical trajectories, such as the Pacific Islands to New Zealand and Europe in rugby, West Africa to Europe in soccer, East Africa to Japan in running, and rural Senegal to urban Senegal in wrestling (the latter being a contrasting case). The hope that young men in poor countries of the Global South harbor to launch a successful sport career in the

Global North has configured masculinity, work, and ideas about the future (Besnier et al. 2018b).

From the second year of the funding, the project involved, besides the principal investigator, two postdoctoral fellows (including the second author of this chapter), four fully funded post-MA PhD students, and one self-funded PhD student. Some reshuffling was necessary in the third, fourth, and fifth years, with three PhD students dropping out at various times and for various reasons and having to be replaced. In the last fifteen months of the project, two postdoctoral fellows were added to the team.[1]

The common, a priori comparison for the research was determined in the original grant proposal as the funders required. Each subproject has focused on (or at least taken into consideration) themes relevant to the sport industries, the athletic body, transnational mobility, masculinity and gender, global inequalities, precarity, and nationalism while attending to the specificities of the field site in which the subproject was based, which foregrounded some themes while backgrounding others. In the second year of funding, we strengthened our comparative approach in a series of workshops, to which guest speakers were invited and that focused on relevant general themes, including masculinity, precarity, mobility, body culture, care, and ethics. These workshops had a pedagogical function, particularly for the PhD students, in a European context in which PhD training involves little or no formal coursework. The result was not a uniform set of techniques nor even a homogeneously held set of research foci but rather a solid awareness on the part of each participant of what other researchers were thinking and planning on doing. This proved to be an important bellwether when daily life in the field failed to provide inspiration.

As originally proposed, the project sought to shed light on a number of broad theoretical problems in the contemporary world: how masculinity articulates with the body, consumption, and the global condition; how it operates as a guide for social action in contexts in which poverty and marginality have seriously undermined the ability to hope; and how nationalism, citizenship, and belonging operate in a field in which global dynamics have seriously disrupted their taken-for-granted nature, while they simultaneously remain at the forefront of public debates.

The research relied heavily on comparison, both as a way of understanding how the sport industries operate in various locations and as a method to investigate the present state and future of masculinity in the context of economic and social crises. It explored the changing fate of men's bodies as they circulated in search for employment in three sports: rugby, soccer, and cricket – to which two more, marathon running and wrestling, were added later.

Comparison, Locality, and Scale

The project had two characteristics that each generated their own comparative questions and agendas. One is the fact that the researchers conducted fieldwork in locations that exhibited both commonalities – particularly the fact that sport occupied an important place in people's lives – and differences in such features as geographical location, population size, social diversity, social stratification, relative economic wealth, historical trajectory, and religious landscape. This diversity made for what Sian Lazar (2012) called "disjunctive comparison" or what Richard Handler (2009) termed "incommensurate comparison" – the ethnographic comparison of local configurations that are radically different from one another. However, all subprojects referred to a single umbrella social fact, namely, sport.

The other characteristic that centralizes comparison as a method and object of inquiry is the fact that the research was informed by the now-classic rethinking of ethnography in late capitalism, namely, the turn to "multisited" research (Marcus 1995), i.e. ethnography that is no longer centered on a community anchored in one location and that assumes the naturalness of this anchoring but instead interrogates the constitution of the local, in light of the fact that most people around the world today are mobile in one fashion or another – if not physically, then at least in terms of the frame of reference in which they organize their economic, social, cultural, and political activities. Thus, the researchers focused on the movements of people (whether actual or imagined), ideas (e.g. of success, social mobility, belonging), images (e.g. of celebrity, bodies, consumption), wealth, and redistribution (e.g. in the form of remittances), all of which necessarily place comparison at the center of the research.

At the same time, the researchers recognized the enduring importance of locality in people's lives and avoided being seduced by the illusion that the local no longer matters because people happen to be mobile or aspire to be: problems of belonging, alienation, and "in-betweenness" are all too real for migrants, be they athletes or not, in both their places of origin and adoptive homes. So the fieldworkers did privilege one geographical and social site in the trajectory of athletic migrants, which in most cases was the athletes' country of origin, conducting the classic one-year fieldwork in this location, thus avoiding the potential pitfall inherent to multisited ethnography that consists in a passing acquaintance with many contexts devoid of an in-depth understanding of any one context.

Cutting across these two dimensions is a problem of scale: what takes place at the level of the global, the regional, the nation-state, or any other context that encompasses significant chunks of territory, significant amounts of material resources, or large numbers of people affects what takes place in the nitty-gritty of people's daily lives and vice versa. The notion of scale came to anthropology from Marxist-inspired social geography (e.g. Lefebvre 1974; Harvey 1968), where it has long been used as a metaphorical extension of the cartographic meaning of the term (i.e. the measure of how much a map's representation compresses the terrain). Anthropologists attend to scale in their efforts to capture the frame of reference in terms of which people, including analysts, make sense of particular phenomena and, in the same process, construct it (Tsing 2005; West 2006; and many others). Thus, a large-scale event (e.g. transnational migration, the global economy, or global warming) requires that we understand it in all its manifestations and ramifications for different regions of the world, in different configurations, and over a significant period of time, and it concurrently constructs the global. A small-scale event, in contrast, is confined to local sites, a few people, and a limited number of aspects of social life, with a limited temporality, and it contributes to what the local consists of.

What is particularly important is the relationship between different scales, which involves its own kind of comparison. Global warming, for example, is a large-scale event because it is caused by industrial and domestic emissions everywhere in the world and because emissions are not stopped by, say, national boundaries, and it will radically threaten the organization and even existence of many megacities and entire states. But it is also experienced in very specific ways by people in their everyday lives; for example, when the first author conducted fieldwork on an atoll of Tuvalu in the Central Pacific in 1980–82, before "global warming" was even a term, the 350 inhabitants of the atoll had reorganized the village's division of labor so that all able-bodied young men spent their working days building seawalls from coral rocks to try to protect the pit gardens from seawater seepage, a very tedious task that turned out to be largely ineffective. This created intergenerational tensions, as the young men felt that they were being underpaid and under-appreciated; it contributed to the reduction of the importance of nonmonetary exchange; and it hastened the commoditization of labor, which, in turn, increased people's already-present desires to migrate to industrial countries (Besnier 2009). This is an example of an event of global scale affecting and, in turn, being affected by events on a very small scale, in a cycle of mutually constituted effects.

As we see presently, this cycle is deeply pertinent to the way in which the global sport industries and the everyday lives of ordinary people in many parts of the world are mutually affected. Of course, the lives of all inhabitants of the planet are affected by events on different scales, but some lives, such as those of people whose control over their destiny is particularly curtailed by poverty, marginality, or lack of political agency, are more likely than others to be affected by large-scale events (e.g. economic downturn, climatic change, and geopolitical upheaval). For example, people in the Global South whose livelihood depends on being able to sell agricultural products that are the object of financial speculation in the futures markets of the world are considerably more vulnerable to these global dynamics than people who lead middle-class lives in the Global North. At an abstract level, this is one idea that the GLOBALSPORT project was interested in understanding.

The Global Sport Industries at Different Scales

The common thread among all GLOBALSPORT subprojects was the looming presence of the global sport industries over people's lived experiences. Sport had long been important to many people's lives, and professional athletes had been circulating from country to country since sports as we know them were invented in nineteenth-century Great Britain and North America. Their circulation was in fact instrumental in spreading the very idea of sport to all four corners of the globe, piggybacking on colonial expansion, missionary efforts, and other forms of global hegemony (Guttmann 1994). In the early twentieth century, sports teams often hired nonlocal players but based their decisions on "safe" criteria, defined in terms of "cultural similarities" between nations, or on the basis of personal relations among club managers, players, and potential recruits (McGovern 2002; Taylor 2006). But at the end of the century, these patterns underwent major transformations as the sport industries in all countries went through major reconfigurations through corporatization, mediatization, and commercialization. These dynamics have promoted sport to a position of much greater importance in the lives of a much larger number of people around the world. They have also brought about a radical reconfiguration of how clubs and teams compete with one another. This competition is now no longer a simple matter of athletic performance but, even more importantly, a competition for human labor and material resources (e.g. Andrews and Silk 2012; Miller et al. 1999; Scherer and Jackson 2010).

As a result, the stakes of hiring became higher, players were transformed into professional workers, the cost of the most successful among them rose dramatically, and recruiters went further afield into more "risky" territory to search for talent, which has led to a dramatic increase in athletes' transnational mobility (Besnier et al. 2018a). But these changes took place as many local economies were experiencing dramatic economic downturns and a shrinkage of livelihood possibilities, particularly as a result of the growing importance of neoliberal economic policies across the world, such as the austerity measures that the International Monetary Fund and the World Bank impose on national economies as a condition for financial rescue packages. These policies, combined with other factors such as unpredictable commodity prices and the abolition of tariffs, have had devastating effects on local labor markets, particularly for the young, and on the economic safety measures that people in many parts of the world could previously count on (Besnier et al. 2018b).[2]

Paradoxically, in marginal regions of the world, the young are simultaneously embedded in global dynamics of consumption, hope, and self-expression. Whether they partake in hip-hop culture, Pentecostal or Islamic revival, or political mobilization, youth seek to claim a sense of belonging in global forms of community. These efforts are not devoid of problems, as their legitimacy is often contested and the promise of revolution (or just self-esteem) thwarted by poverty and immobility.

These historical junctures have led to sport careers acquiring, in the late 1980s and early 1990s, a presence they had never had previously in the range of life projects imagined by young men in the Global South and to a remarkable increase in the number of foreign-born or ethnically marked athletes employed in athletic workplaces in the industrial world, particularly those emerging from countries of the Global South. This mobility and the industries that create and sustain it have restructured individual lives, social relations, and cultural expectations as preconditions for success, affecting not only the way people move and catch balls but also the way they think, act, speak, interact, and conceptualize the future.

At a local scale, for young men in many impoverished countries, professional sport represents at once hope for survival, a spectacular form of participation in the production of global images of male success, and the resolution of the contradiction between local exclusion and global inclusion. Marketed as men's culture and as a hypermasculine spectacle for global consumption, the sport industries epitomize masculinity (Burstyn 1999). Women also partake in the sport industries, but men's enduring numerical and structural dominance in team sports limits the participation of women, who logically tend to seek their fortunes elsewhere.

Unlike the circulation of underclass workers, sports migrations evoke millenarian images of sudden success and unimagined prosperity, affording young men the fantasy of redistributing untold wealth, often in preference to keeping it for themselves, and thus reclaiming male productive citizenship. The resulting enchantment is illustrative of a "casino capitalism," the magical emergence of wealth from nothing, which many see as a signature feature of the turn of the millennium (Comaroff and Comaroff 2000). While in reality only the lucky few from the Global South gain widespread recognition, the possibility of success in professional sports in the Global North informs the actions and haunts the dreams of countless others. These dreams are given concrete substance, for example, in the "football farms" that European clubs have established in West Africa: training camps attended by boys (often at the expense of regular schooling), in which clubs seek to recruit the most talented at the cheapest moment of their sporting careers (Darby et al. 2007; Esson 2013, 2015). These dynamics often expose young hopefuls to exploitation, some forms of which evoke tropes of human trafficking (e.g. clandestine border crossing, procurement of faked documents, and deceitful promises of employment).

In certain parts of the world, entire nations are investing in the production of sporting bodies for export (e.g. Tonga for rugby and Kenya for athletics), and the remittances from internationally based athletes figure prominently in their economies. These efforts are reminiscent of other forms of society-wide socioeconomic dependence on highly specialized, gendered, and impermanent skills that are vulnerable to the caprices of global agents and trends, such as the export of domestic workers, caregivers to the elderly, and sex workers (e.g. Gamburd 2000; Rodriguez 2010). The protracted worldwide economic crisis that began in 2008 is making the precarious nature of these national policies all too apparent, given the extreme dependence of contemporary professional sports on corporate interests. The migration of athletes operates in the context of complex networks of people, institutions, and emotions. On a global scale, it is fueled by radical changes in the structure of global capital; on a local scale, it results from hopes for a better life where poverty and precarity dominate.

Like the circulation of underclass workers, sports migrations are precarious, unpredictable, and often disappointing (Besnier and Brownell 2012). At the very least, the mobility of athletes operates within a dialectic of flow and closure, hampered by serious constraints (e.g. increased constraints on work visas) as easily as they are enabled by emergent possibilities (e.g. the loosening of citizenship restrictions by sport-regulating authorities). The brevity of youthful masculine vigor, the specter of injury, the capricious nature of corporate interests, the precariousness of adoptive forms of belonging, and the unforgiving responses of publics all bestow on athletic careers a profoundly fragile quality. Many end abruptly because of poor health, substance abuse, scandal, or simply rapidly declining performance. While these problems characterize all careers in this industry, for athletes from the Global South, the fall is often particularly dramatic, given the investment of so many others and their heightened vulnerability to exploitation by teams, agents, and other stakeholders.

The sports that the project investigated were not chosen at random. Soccer, rugby, and cricket originated in Britain in the nineteenth century and were exported to the rest of the world alongside colonial and related projects. Their distribution covers a substantial area of the globe, and they mobilize the interest of a large proportion of the world's population, although their geographical distribution and sociocultural associations in various locations differ considerably. The two sports that were added later, namely, marathon running and Senegalese wrestling, provide particularly interesting contrasting features, in that one is an individual sport and another is a local sport that by and large does not offer the possibility of transnational migration, although migration plays an important role in that most wrestlers in Senegal belong to families that migrated from impoverished rural areas to try to make a living in Dakar, with the successive Sahel droughts playing an important role in these migrations. These variations, as well as the different geographical and social routes that migrants follow, provided the research team with a range of cases on which useful comparisons can be based.

The GLOBALSPORT Project

Four researchers in the project focused on rugby union (hereafter "rugby"), collaborating in fieldwork and analysis. Rugby is the national sport of Fiji and Tonga, insular nations in the Southwest Pacific, as well as New Zealand. For the past twenty years, it has also offered young men from the islands the possibility of a career, both in New Zealand and in the professional leagues of Europe, Japan, and Australia. Niko Besnier's previous research on Tongan rugby players in Japan was the foundation stone of the GLOBALSPORT project (Besnier 2012). Daniel Guinness had also previously worked for his PhD dissertation with Fijians as they aspire to move through various locations in the global sport and conducted additional fieldwork in collaboration with Niko Besnier (Guinness and Besnier 2016). Postdoctoral fellow Domenica Calabrò's work focused on indigenous Māori rugby players in New Zealand, as well as those contracted to professional clubs in France, Italy, and the Netherlands. The three Pacific Island nations, Fiji, Tonga, and New Zealand, have reconfigured themselves in response to the possibilities of professional sport. In contrast, the Argentine rugby establishment, on which both Daniel Guinness and postdoctoral fellow Sebastián Fuentes conducted fieldwork, has resisted integration into the global professional industry. There, rugby remains deeply implicated in the social and moral formation of national elites, who view professional rugby and the migrations it enables as morally tainting.

Some of the most visible migrant athletes move through the elaborate scouting networks of soccer, which three subprojects explored in African contexts. One, carried out by then - PhD student Uroš Kovač (2018), was based in Cameroon, where soccer has become a central activity in the lives of almost all young men. Soccer academies have proliferated in the country, offering young men the hope of an international career in a context where few young men are able to secure meaningful employment. Kovač's fieldwork in Cameroon was supplemented by briefer periods of fieldwork with Cameroonian footballers in Europe, which dovetailed neatly into the subproject of then - PhD student Paweł Banaś, who carried out fieldwork into the lives of African footballers playing in lower division clubs in Poland, on the margin of European soccer, which migrants hope will be a step toward a contract in the major competitions of Western Europe.

Senegal was the focus of another subproject conducted by then - PhD student Mark Hann (2018). There, many young men play soccer, but overall the sport is eclipsed by another sport, Senegalese wrestling, a spectacular form of one-to-one combat with roots in rural society, which has gained enormous importance on a national scale in the past few decades. There is a sharp contrast between soccer and wrestling: while the former does generate hopes of migrating to contracts overseas, the latter remains grounded in the local scene, and instead fuels hopes of national celebrity, but without much material reward. The Senegalese context thus provided a configuration of ethnographic materials that did not compare with any of the other settings in a straightforward way: while sports compete for national attention in other ethnographic contexts (e.g. soccer and rugby in Argentina), the tensions that these patterns engender are not associated with the presence and absence of life possibilities in such a stark manner. Yet, as we will see, the comparison of the two sports, and of sport in Senegal with sport in other locations, does yield important insights into the structure of configurations.

Cricket presents different global dynamics from the other world sports, as became clear in the work of postdoctoral fellow Adnan Hossain in the Caribbean and South Asia. In these two contexts, athletic mobilities are considerably less obviously associated with global inequalities. In fact, India is the temporary migratory destination of athletes from wealthy countries (e.g. Australia), who move to South Asia for the duration of a season to play in the Indian Premier League (IPL), thus reversing patterns with which we are familiar in other settings. In the Caribbean, while many young men aspire to play in the wealthy IPL, the majority remain in regional competitions or move to the professional tournament in Trinidad, the wealthiest country in the region.

The final migratory pattern a GLOBALSPORT researcher, PhD student Michael Peters, investigated is that of Kenyan marathon runners moving to Japan, largely on a temporary basis. In Japan, runners are employed by companies or local authorities or are the beneficiaries of high school or university scholarships. Migrants from Kenya acquire the highest profile in the sport, but their otherness keeps them in a marginal position in Japan, where they are tolerated as long as they perform. Nevertheless, Japan offers possibilities to earn salaries or stipends that are vastly superior to what most people earn in Kenya, which enables the migrant runners to send valuable remittances back home.

Configuration and Scale

Because all the contexts in which the participants in the GLOBALSPORT project have conducted fieldwork have presented complex and diverse configurations of categories and processes, many kinds of comparisons have emerged a posteriori, some of which were anticipated a priori, while others were not. Most fundamentally, the project showcased comparison in two different ways: within each subproject, geographical mobility necessarily highlighted the similarities and differences among different sites, an exercise that our informants themselves constantly engaged in, as they compared, for instance, the economic and social opportunities available to them in different countries, while across the subprojects, differences emerged among the material, cultural, and historical configurations of the various ethnographic contexts.

But there are other ways in which comparison was dictated by the ethnographic realities of each field site, in that comparison was central to people's theories about themselves and their society. So comparison is integral to the very act of conducting ethnography because the people whose lives we documented themselves spend considerable time comparing and are doing so through the lens of sport. But these comparisons take on various configurations in different contexts.[3]

For example, in Senegal, the two most popular sports index divergent paths in life, different conceptualizations of the present and future, and distinctive positions in society. On the one hand, wrestling is deeply embedded in a magico-religious system, whereby wrestlers rely heavily on the esoteric services of marabouts, which are based on a mixture of Islam and magical practices seen to emanate from rural contexts, viewed by many as essential to wrestling success. On the other hand, footballers and their coaches explicitly distance themselves from magical practices as antiquated "superstition" ill-designed for a world sport and relate ambiguously to Islam's proscriptions and interdictions, such as fasting, which they view as morally important but antithetical to sporting success. The two sports diverge in other ways, such as the kinds of bodies they generate: The wrestler's body is far more imposing than that of the footballer and has been increasing in size over the years. The wrestlers seek fame in the local context, building a fan base in a neighborhood and seeking the patronage of wealthy and politically important men, while the footballers dream of success overseas. In short, comparing the two sports revealed tensions between bifurcated life trajectories for young men within the same society.

Trinidad and Tobago present another example of a contrast that demands comparison. The society is divided along ethnic lines between Indo-Trinidadians, descendants of indentured laborers brought by British colonial authorities, and Afro-Trinidadians, descendants of African slaves, and comparisons between the two groups are central to daily life. The two groups have roughly the same population, and political power oscillates between them. The divisions between the two groups are enacted through cricket, the national sport, with both groups vying for control of and visibility in the sport. The two groups view each other and themselves as having different bodies, characters, and sporting aptitudes. For example, Indo-Trinidadians are regarded as superior spin bowlers (analogous to pitchers in baseball), who produce a slower-paced bowl that deceives the batsman, while Afro-Trinidadians are seen as aggressive fast bowlers, who beat batsmen with speed and power. These qualities are supposed to iconize the "character" of each group: Indo-Trinidadians as "cunning" and Afro-Trinidadians as "powerful." In addition, Indo-Trinidadians pride themselves on their organizational skills and thus see themselves as better managers of the sport, while Afro-Trinidadians view their powerful physical masculinity as particularly suited to winning games. Both Indo-Caribbeans and Afro-Caribbeans use cricket as a site around which to assert intraethnic solidarity and demonstrate their ethnic superiority over the other.

In Fiji, sport also showcases divisions in the society although in different ways. Rugby is the national sport, but it is played almost exclusively by indigenous (*i-Taukei*) men. Indigenous women and members of the significant Indo-Fijian ethnic minority are largely excluded from practicing the sport despite their active support of a game that has come to define the nation, a process to which fans the world over unwittingly contribute through their adulation of indigenous migrant athletes and ignorance of the country's ethnic diversity. Comparison of the life trajectories of *i-Taukei* men with those of other Fijians reveals deeply held tensions that have underlain political unrest in the country since 1987, but that superficially have nothing to do with sport. Rugby, a game that a significant number of *i-Taukei* men play to world-elite level, has become an important nexus of ethno-nationalist politics, supposedly demonstrating not only *i-Taukei* men's physical superiority over Indo-Fijians but also the superiority and universality they attribute to their Christian faith, which most Indo-Fijians do not share. The global success of the men's national team, which is made up entirely of *i-Taukei*, and the personal success of individual players recruited in overseas teams showcase a particular version of Fiji – masculine, indigenous, and Christian. Here, sport becomes a microcosm of national and ethnic politics rather than merely being subject to these external dynamics.

In addition to the ethnographic necessity of focusing on comparison, ethnography in collaborative projects enables comparisons between the field sites in ways that highlight the operation of scale. In different situations, the vastly different reactions to common global structures, in this case the global sports industry system, showcase how global dynamics interact with local ones. For instance, despite the vast differences between Fiji and Argentina, the comparison of ethno-nationalist politics at play in rugby in Fiji with the class politics associated with rugby in Argentina highlights the specificities of each situation, as well as the peculiar power of sport to encapsulate broader political dynamics. In Argentina, rugby is a sport played by the upper-middle classes in exclusive social clubs, which produce men with local business and social networks as much as they produce athletes. Most Argentine rugby players' life plans consist in a locally grounded education, business and professional ventures, and personal family projects in preference to pursuing a rugby career in Europe (the very best players being the exception). Most regularly decline potentially lucrative long-term career opportunities overseas when they are offered to them, considering these morally tainting and thus placing the men in danger of being marginalized on their home turf. Because these class-based dynamics are naturalized by the people themselves, they could easily have escaped ethnographic scrutiny, but they became all too apparent through comparison with the aspirations of Fijian rugby players, which are resolutely oriented toward migrating and thus showing to the world Fijians' moral worth. In turn, the comparison of the two cases sheds light on what underlies these transnational aspirations. Argentines and Fijians occupy different positions in the globalized world, although material considerations do not explain the differences in their totality, and the comparison interrogates simplistic models of the global.

The comparison across the various sports and geographical locations has showcased certain themes that had not been foreseen in the original formulation of the project but that ended up playing a central role in the ethnography. A salient one is the role of religion in sport and its relationship to the social world that surrounds sport. For instance, Māori rugby players in New Zealand and overseas see their sporting success as an instantiation of their indigenous mana or supernatural power (Tomlinson and Tengan 2016). The category harks back to the precolonial cosmology, in which mana was channeled by great warriors, the oft-cited ancestral figures of rugby players, and has figured prominently in the indigenous renaissance since the 1960s, thus entangling rugby with contemporary indigenous politics and the construction of the past. In Cameroon, soccer is entwined with Pentecostal Christianity: individuals and teams pray for success and consult Pentecostal preachers and prophets to expel female spirits that they believe bring sexual and other kinds of temptations that distract them from their migratory athletic projects. Pentecostalism plays a comparable role in Fiji, as Islam does in Senegal. In contrast, religious practices in Argentina are notably absent from the task of preparing young men for rugby despite most players being devout Catholics. Here, the social elites who play rugby use both the sport and Catholicism to build a self-referential community. Without doubt, the differing roles of sport and religion, as well as their connection, are partly a product of the socioeconomic precarity experienced by one group but not the other. However, what comparison helps to reveal is the reason why religion permeates people's life projects in different ways and to different extents in the various field sites.

Theory from Comparison

Comparison between multiple field sites can be theoretically productive beyond the insights one can gain about a field site or sport by comparing it (disjunctively or relationally) with others. This is particularly the case with scalar comparison, which seeks not only to delineate different configurations of a particular social feature in various locations but also to analyze how the various locations relate to different scales. This kind of comparison was at the heart of the design of the original project, which highlighted the linkages between local masculinities and the neoliberal sports industries. In the last year of the project, a subgroup of the GLOBALSPORT team brought together the different sporting masculinities associated with Cameroonian soccer, Fijian rugby, and Senegalese wrestling, not only in terms of their specific local contexts but also under a different light, specifically the different ways they are shaped by neoliberalism (Besnier et al. 2018b).

As we explained earlier, sport around the world became a business in the 1990s. One consequence of this transformation was that athletes themselves had to change. In team sports, for example, clubs no longer treated athletes as lifelong members, as was often the case previously, but as employees, the best of whom were paid extravagantly, but all of whom were readily disposable. Athletes thus had to become adaptable, self-controlled, and ready to sell themselves again at short notice. Their training, performance, and private lives gradually became both the object of intense and constant analysis by coaches and other managerial staff and the object of self-scrutiny by the athletes themselves. The boundary between work and private life gradually disappeared. What emerged is a sporting version of the neoliberal self (Gershon 2011; Gershon and Alexy 2011; McGuigan 2014; Rose and Miller 2008).

What is particularly interesting is that these dynamics also diffused back to societies that are not at the core of the capitalist world but that produce athletes for the sport industries. In Fiji, for example, the notion that hard work, self-control, and individual determination are important to prospective migrant rugby careers. God's role in rugby has changed: many players have moved from the communitarian Methodist and Catholic churches to Pentecostal denominations, where their interaction with God is a more direct one and where God is more directly involved in shaping individual life trajectories. The meaning of indigeneity also changed. It is still a way for *i-Taukei* as an ethnic group to claim ownership of the country, but it is also an asset marketable in the global world of rugby, where spectators in Europe and elsewhere relish the exoticism of Fijians' pregame "war dances" (*bole*), their tattoos, large bodies, kava-drinking rituals, and impressive church choir singing (but where coaches also dread their car crashes, lack of punctuality, and relapses into alcohol consumption). The rugby career as a neoliberal individual enterprise has trickled back to Fiji but has been given a particular religious twist.

Similarly, in Cameroon, soccer has become a pivotal site for the emergence of a new Pentecostal masculinity that is God-fearing, humble, and obedient yet particularly successful in migratory soccer projects because these qualities correspond to what team managers and coaches (whether Pentecostal or not) seek in a new recruit. These recruiters know what kind of players are sought in the North, but they also choose the young men who are most likely to do well and thus generate money for the recruiters. Young Pentecostal footballers contrast their masculinity with other forms, including that of the womanizing braggart with nightclub notoriety, who is quickly branded as a "useless man" because he does nothing to support his kindred, and that of the old-style rural big man who has many wives and sires many children but is mired in a now-undesirable "tradition" that includes witchcraft. Pentecostal masculinity is not only constructed in the local context but also shaped by gatekeepers who mediate between the global and the local (as well as look after their own interests). Again, new forms of acting and being, particularly of being a man, emerge at the convergence of the neoliberalization of the global sport industries and the reinterpretation of its requirements in the local context, in which Pentecostalism, itself the product of an ongoing global explosion (Coleman 2007; and many others), plays a pivotal role.

Perhaps most surprising is the fact that similar dynamics are at play in Senegalese wrestling, an individual sport practiced in a predominantly Muslim society. While it is often described as being profoundly rooted in a timeless traditional past ("the Senegambian peoples have always wrestled and always will"), Senegalese wrestling is in fact the product of a very contemporary modernity. Since the 1990s, the influx of sponsorship money, the increasing importance of television, and new regimes of masculine body culture have reconfigured wrestlers into entrepreneurs of the self, who draw on both techniques of global neoliberalized sport and local practices constructed as traditional and devout. In a context of scarce economic opportunities, young men who pursue masculinity through wrestling not only perform an imagined ancestral past but also present themselves as entrepreneurial, self-reliant, and purposeful – images that strongly resemble characteristics of the neoliberal self. Here again, a good wrestler is deemed to be not only devoutly religious and respectful of tradition but also conscientious and self-motivated in training and in the care of the body.

We compared the three case studies in terms of how masculinity is embedded in socioeconomic contexts and temporally situated; relational, for being constructed at the interstices of people and projects; and scalar, in that it is informed by the global, the local, and their complex intersections. What is particularly striking is the fact that, in these very different societies, the triangular relationship among neoliberalism, sport, and masculinity operates on multiple scales and on multiple fronts. Scalar comparison revealed that in each context, the types of gendered subjectivities that are emerging draw upon the local cultural material that most closely resembles neoliberal subjectivity, such as Pentecostalism and maraboutism. Through the conduit of sport, the masculine self has been transformed into a neoliberal subject in locations where this is least expected.

In all three contexts, the hope for success in sport increasingly fills the gap left by the evacuation of other life possibilities, and, at least for young men whose lives are not buoyed by the advantages of birth, masculinity is not about reproducing old values but about the possibility of participating in a global system of mobility, work, and glory that will resurrect one's ability to provide for others. Yet, the probability of this taking place is, for most, very slim. Despite this paradox, young men struggle to become the kinds of neoliberal subjects that the global sport industries require: hardworking despite the uncertainty about the results of hard work; self-improving even though improvement guarantees nothing; and being responsible for one's destiny, including both successes and failures.

We witnessed masculinities that were directly related to different relationships to the global sports industries, in ways that diverged from understandings of masculinity presented in the very influential work of Raewyn W. Connell (1995), whose model of "hegemonic masculinity" rests on the recognition of "the combination of the plurality of masculinities and the hierarchy of masculinities" (Connell and Messerschmidt 2005, 846). We agree with the uncontroversial claim that masculinity is diverse; where we part company with Connell is in the claim that masculinities are organized in clearly identifiable hierarchies, with a "hegemonic" masculinity dominating "subordinate" masculinities and "marginalizing" others. What our scalar comparison revealed is that forms of masculinity that appear to be dominant in certain ways are in fact precarious in other ways, and what emerged was a new approach to masculinity that eschews explanations based on the simple recognition of diverse and hierarchically organized masculinities and instead locates gender in general and masculinity in particular in a political economic framework (echoing developments in feminist anthropology since the 1990s, e.g. di Leonardo 1990) that is attuned to the mutual constitution of seemingly unrelated events taking place at different scales.

Conclusion

Comparison and collaboration are of course two different ways of conducting research in anthropology, in that comparison can be the product of a single researcher, while collaboration does not necessarily entail comparison. However, funding policies that are currently dominant in the expanded European Union have encouraged collaborative work over a bounded period of time, which is by default comparative. This model is somewhat new in anthropology, and it has opened the door for new ways of thinking about anthropological research, which the project we have documented here illustrates.

There is no doubt that the collaborative nature of the GLOBALSPORT project has enabled comparisons that would never have been considered had the subprojects been conducted independently of one another. Collaboration encourages communication at planning stages, during fieldwork, and through the writing-up process. Collaboration and comparison have also shone light on dynamics in each field site that the individual researchers may have missed had other seemingly incommensurable cases not been juxtaposed with their own ethnography. A case in point is the taken-for-granted role of Catholicism among upper-middle-class Argentine rugby players and the emergence of the neoliberal self among Senegalese wrestlers despite their insistence on the traditional grounding of their sport.

What emerged as particularly interesting is the interaction of effects of scale with the incommensurable configuration of field sites, which are so dense and multiplex that comparison seemed unlikely or unwise at first glance. Scale is concretized most visibly in sport, a field in which homogeneity and uniformity play a defining role, particularly in world sports such as soccer, rugby, and cricket, since theoretically anyone anywhere in the world can take part in a sport and is then expected to follow the same rules codified by a supragovernmental body somewhere in the world (which nevertheless invariably happens to be located in the Global North). Approaching the processes that we have been interested in, including the formation of gendered selves, the strategizing of life courses under conditions of economic precarity, the role played by religious cosmologies, and decision-making about whether to migrate, through the lens of the global phenomenon that sport represents, transforms incommensurable ethnographic situations into systematically comparable cases, out of which emerge patterns of great theoretical potential, as illustrated by the comparison of neoliberal athletic masculinity in three societies.

Notes

1 This brief timeline evokes one aspect of collaborative anthropological projects that we are not touching on here but that are nevertheless determinative of the course of the research and the kind of comparison it makes possible, namely, the unpredictability of such factors as lack of performance, illness, personal insecurity, and other trajectory-altering events.

2 There are of course exceptions to these broad generalizations, such as the new redistributive policies that some economies have implemented (e.g. Brazil under Lula), but these are not without problems (Ferguson 2015).

3 While the examples we provide presently are all of binary comparisons, at least they avoid the problems associated with tacit comparisons between "them" and "us" that invariably background all anthropological projects, in which "us" is assumed to be an unspecified collectivity in the Global North.

References

Abu-Lughod, Lila. 1991. "Writing against Culture." In *Recapturing Anthropology: Working in the Present*, edited by Richard Fox, 137–62. Santa Fe, NM: School of American Research.

Andrews, David L., and Michael L. Silk, eds. 2012. *Sport and Neoliberalism: Politics, Consumption, and Culture*. Philadelphia, PA: Temple University Press.

Besnier, Niko. 2009. *Gossip and the Everyday Production of Politics*. Honolulu: University of Hawai'i Press.

Besnier, Niko. 2012. "The Athlete's Body and the Global Condition: Tongan Rugby Players in Japan." *American Ethnologist* 39 (3): 491–510.

Besnier, Niko, and Susan Brownell. 2012. "Sport, Modernity, and the Body." *Annual Review of Anthropology* 41: 443–59.

Besnier, Niko, Susan Brownell, and Thomas F. Carter. 2018a. *The Anthropology of Sport: Bodies, Borders, Biopolitics*. Oakland: University of California Press.

Besnier, Niko, Daniel Guinness, Mark Hann, and Uroš Kovač. 2018b. "Rethinking Masculinity in the Neoliberal Age: Cameroonian Footballers, Fijian Rugby Players, and Senegalese Wrestlers." *Comparative Studies in Society and History* 60 (4): 839–72.

Burstyn, Varda. 1999. *The Rites of Men: Manhood, Politics, and the Culture of Sport*. Toronto: University of Toronto Press.

Clifford, James, and George E. Marcus, eds. 1986. *Writing Culture: The Poetics and Politics of Ethnography*. Berkeley: University of California Press.

Coleman, Simon, 2007. *The Globalisation of Charismatic Christianity*. Cambridge: Cambridge University Press.

Comaroff, Jean, and John L. Comaroff. 2000. "Millennial Capitalism: First Thoughts on a Second Coming." *Public Culture* 12 (2): 291–43.

Connell, Raewyn W. 1995. *Masculinities*. Berkeley: University of California Press.

Connell, Raewyn W., and James W. Messerschmidt. 2005. "Hegemonic Masculinity: Rethinking the Concept." *Gender & Society* 19 (6): 829–59.

Darby, Paul, Gerard Akindes, and Matthew Kirwin. 2007. "Football Academies and the Migration of African Football Labour to Europe." *Journal of Sport and Social Issues* 31 (2): 143–61.

di Leonardo, Micaela, ed. 1990. *Gender at the Crossroads of Knowledge: Feminist Anthropology in the Postmodern Era*. Berkeley: University of California Press.

Esson, James. 2013. "A Body and a Dream at a Vital Conjuncture: Ghanaian Youth, Uncertainty and the Allure of Football." *Geoforum* 47 (June): 84–89.

Esson, James. 2015. "You Have to Try your Luck: Male Ghanaian Youth and the Uncertainty of Football Migration." *Environment and Planning A* 47 (6): 1383–97.

Ferguson, James. 2015. *Give a Man a Fish: Reflections on the New Politics of Distribution*. Durham, NC: Duke University Press.

Gamburd, Michele R. 2000. *The Kitchen Spoon's Handle: Transnationalism and Sri Lanka's Migrant Housemaids.* Ithaca, NY: Cornell University Press.

Gershon, Ilana. 2011. "Neoliberal Agency." *Current Anthropology* 52 (4): 537–55.

Gershon, Ilana, and Allison Alexy. 2011. "The Ethics of Disconnection in a Neoliberal Age." *Anthropological Quarterly* 84 (4): 799–808.

Gingrich, Andre. 2012. "Comparative Methods in Socio-Cultural Anthropology Today." In *The SAGE Handbook of Social Anthropology,* edited by Richard Fardon, Oliva Harris, Trevor H. J. Marchand, Mark Nuttall, Cris Shore, Veronica Strang, and Richard A. Wilson, 211–22. Los Angeles, CA: Sage.

Guinness, Daniel, and Niko Besnier. 2016. "Nation, Nationalism, and Sport: Fijian Rugby in the Local–Global Nexus." *Anthropological Quarterly* 89 (4): 1107–40.

Guttmann, Allen. 1994. *Games and Empires: Modern Sports and Cultural Imperialism.* New York: Columbia University Press.

Handler, Richard. 2009. "The Uses of Incommensurability in Anthropology." *New Literary History* 40 (3): 627–47.

Hann, Mark. 2018. "Sporting Aspirations: Football, Wrestling, and Neoliberal Subjectivity in Urban Senegal." PhD thesis, Amsterdam Institute for Social Science Research, University of Amsterdam.

Harvey, David W. 1968. "Pattern, Process, and the Scale Problem in Geographical Research." *Transactions of the Institute of British Geographers* 45 (September): 71–78.

Herle, Anita, and Sandra Rouse, eds. 1998. *Cambridge and the Torres Strait: Centenary Essays on the 1898 Anthropological Expedition.* Cambridge: Cambridge University Press.

Kiste, Robert C., and Mac Marshall, eds. 1998. *American Anthropology in Micronesia: An Assessment.* Honolulu: University of Hawai'i Press.

Kovač, Uroš. 2018. "The Precarity of Masculinity: Football, Pentecostalism, and Transnational Aspirations in Cameroon." PhD thesis, Amsterdam Institute for Social Science Research, University of Amsterdam.

Lazar, Sian. 2012. "Disjunctive Comparison: Citizenship and Trade Unionism in Bolivia and Argentina." *Journal of the Royal Anthropological Institute (n.s.)* 18 (2): 349–68.

Lefebvre, Henri. 1974. "La production de l'espace." *L'homme et la société* 31 (1): 15–32.

Marcus, George E. 1995. "Ethnography in/of the World System: The Emergence of Multi-Sited Ethnography." *Annual Review of Anthropology* 24: 95–117.

Marcus, George E., and Michael M. J. Fisher, eds. 1986. *Anthropology as Cultural Critique: An Experimental Moment in the Human Sciences.* Chicago, IL: University of Chicago Press.

McGovern, Patrick. 2002. "Globalization or Internationalization? Foreign Footballers in the English League, 1946–95." *Sociology* 36 (1): 23–42.

McGuigan, Jim. 2014. "The Neoliberal Self." *Culture Unbound* 6: 223–40.

Miller, Toby, Geoffrey Lawrence, Jim McKay, and David Rowe. 1999. "Modifying the Sign: Sport and Globalization." *Social Text* 17: 15–33.

Rodriguez, Robyn M. 2010. *Migrants for Export: How the Philippine State Brokers Labor to the World.* Minneapolis: University of Minnesota Press.

Rose, Nikolas, and Peter Miller. 2008. *Governing the Present: Administering Economic, Social and Personal Life.* Cambridge: Polity.

Scherer, Jay, and Steve Jackson. 2010. *Globalization, Sport and Corporate Nationalism: The New Cultural Economy of the New Zealand All Blacks*. Oxford: Peter Lang.

Silverman, Sydel. 2011. "The Puerto Rico Project: Reflections Sixty Years Later." *Identities* 18 (3): 179–84.

Taylor, Matthew. 2006. "Global Players? Football, Migration and Globalization, c1930–2000." *Historical Social Research* 31 (1): 7–30.

Tomlinson, Matt, and Ty P. Kāwika Tengan, eds. 2016. *New Mana: Transformations of a Classic Concept in Pacific Languages and Cultures*. Canberra: ANU ePress.

Tsing, Anna Lowenhaupt. 2005. *Friction: An Ethnography of Global Connection*. Princeton, NJ: Princeton University Press.

Vogt, Evon Z. 1994. *Fieldwork among the Maya: Reflections on the Harvard Chiapas Project*. Albuquerque: University of New Mexico Press.

West, Paige. 2006. *Conservation Is Our Government Now: The Politics of Ecology in Papua New Guinea*. Durham, NC: Duke University Press.

Index